# SUPER HOROSCOPE
# AQUARIUS

# 2009

## JANUARY 20 – FEBRUARY 18

BERKLEY BOOKS, NEW YORK

**THE BERKLEY PUBLISHING GROUP**
**Published by the Penguin Group**
**Penguin Group (USA) Inc.**
**375 Hudson Street, New York, New York 10014, USA**
Penguin Group (Canada), 90 Eglinton Avenue East, Suite 700, Toronto, Ontario M4P 2Y3, Canada
(a division of Pearson Penguin Canada Inc.)
Penguin Books Ltd., 80 Strand, London WC2R 0RL, England
Penguin Group Ireland, 25 St. Stephen's Green, Dublin 2, Ireland (a division of Penguin Books Ltd.)
Penguin Group (Australia), 250 Camberwell Road, Camberwell, Victoria 3124, Australia
(a division of Pearson Australia Group Pty. Ltd.)
Penguin Books India Pvt. Ltd., 11 Community Centre, Panchsheel Park, New Delhi—110 017, India
Penguin Group (NZ), 67 Apollo Drive,  Rosedale, North Shore 0632, New Zealand
(a division of Pearson New Zealand Ltd.)
Penguin Books (South Africa) (Pty.) Ltd., 24 Sturdee Avenue, Rosebank, Johannesburg 2196,
South Africa

Penguin Books Ltd., Registered Offices: 80 Strand, London WC2R 0RL, England

2009 SUPER HOROSCOPE AQUARIUS

The publishers regret that they cannot answer individual letters requesting personal horoscope information.

PRINTING HISTORY
Berkley trade paperback edition / July 2008

Berkley trade paperback ISBN: 978-0-425-22007-8

Library of Congress Cataloging-in-Publication Data

ISSN: 1535-8925

PRINTED IN THE UNITED STATES OF AMERICA

10  9  8  7  6  5  4  3  2  1

# CONTENTS

# THE CUSP-BORN AQUARIUS

Are you *really* an Aquarius? If your birthday falls during the fourth week of January, at the beginning of Aquarius, will you still retain the traits of Capricorn, the sign of the Zodiac before Aquarius? And what if you were born late in February—are you more Pisces than Aquarius? Many people born at the edge, or cusp, of a sign have difficulty determining exactly what sign they are. If you are one of these people, here's how you can figure it out, once and for all.

Consult the cusp table on the facing page, then locate the year of your birth. The table will tell you the precise days on which the Sun entered and left your sign for the year of your birth. In that way you can determine if you are a true Aquarius—or whether you are a Capricorn or Pisces—according to the variations in cusp dates from year to year (see also page 17).

If you were born at the beginning or end of Aquarius, yours is a lifetime reflecting a process of subtle transformation. Your life on Earth will symbolize a significant change in consciousness, because you are either about to enter a whole new way of living or are leaving one behind.

If you were born around the last two weeks of January, you want to be free. You're committed somewhere because you want to be, not because some heavy figure stands behind you pulling the strings. You may want to read the horoscope book for Capricorn as well as Aquarius, for Capricorn holds the keys to many of your hidden uncertainties, secret guilts, subtle motivations, and all your cosmic unfoldment from an occult point of view.

You are a person who will always break free from limitations or obstacles or break your leg trying.

When it comes to discipline, you are ambiguous and complex. You need discipline to survive and succeed, but you openly reject it. Inwardly you find it hard to escape from the old problems of total freedom vs. strict routine and structure.

You have a grain of the conservative in you, a bit of the authority figure, and a thirst for power you can't seem to shake. Yet peace is your mission and friendliness your purpose.

If you were born the third week of February, you are either a mad genius or are just avoiding jail by the skin of your teeth. You may want to read the horoscope book for Pisces as well as Aquarius, for through Pisces you tap your talents and convert your assets into profit for others as well as yourself.

Your great love is ad-libbing, for there is no thrill like pulling something off at the last minute and succeeding. Your great successes come from last-minute reversals, unexpected turns of fate, and the famous cavalry coming charging over the hill. You have the touch of the prophet—utopia with a touch of doomsday thrown in. When you are at your best you are being a friend.

## THE CUSPS OF AQUARIUS

### DATES SUN ENTERS AQUARIUS (LEAVES CAPRICORN)

January 20 every year from 1900 to 2010, except for the following:

| January 19 | | | January 21 | | |
|---|---|---|---|---|---|
| 1977 | 1989 | 2001 | 1903 | 1920 | 1932 |
| 81 | 93 | 2005 | 04 | 24 | 36 |
| 85 | 97 | 2009 | 08 | 28 | 44 |
| | | | 12 | | |

### DATES SUN LEAVES AQUARIUS (ENTERS PISCES)

February 19 every year from 1900 to 2010, except for the following:

| February 18 | | | | | February 20 |
|---|---|---|---|---|---|
| 1900 | 1954 | 1973 | 1989 | 2001 | 1917 |
| 21 | 57 | 74 | 90 | 2002 | |
| 25 | 58 | 77 | 91 | 2003 | |
| 29 | 61 | 78 | 93 | 2005 | |
| 33 | 62 | 81 | 94 | 2006 | |
| 37 | 65 | 82 | 95 | 2007 | |
| 41 | 66 | 85 | 97 | 2009 | |
| 45 | 69 | 86 | 98 | 2010 | |
| 49 | 70 | 87 | 99 | | |
| 53 | | | | | |

# THE ASCENDANT: AQUARIUS RISING

Could you be a "double" Aquarius? That is, could you have Aquarius as your Rising sign as well as your Sun sign? The tables on pages 8–9 will tell you Aquarius what your Rising sign happens to be. Just find the hour of your birth, then find the day of your birth, and you will see which sign of the Zodiac is your Ascendant, as the Rising sign is called. The Ascendant is called that because it is the sign rising on the eastern horizon at the time of your birth. For a more detailed discussion of the Rising sign and the twelve houses of the Zodiac, see pages 17–20.

The Ascendant, or Rising sign, is placed on the 1st house in a horoscope, of which there are twelve houses. The 1st house represents your response to the environment—your unique response. Call it identity, personality, ego, self-image, facade, come-on, body-mind-spirit—whatever term best conveys to you the meaning of the you that acts and reacts in the world. It is a you that is always changing, discovering a new you. Your identity started with birth and early environment, over which you had little conscious control, and continues to experience, to adjust, to express itself. The 1st house also represents how others see you. Has anyone ever guessed your sign to be your Rising sign? People may respond to that personality, that facade, that body type governed by your Rising sign.

Your Ascendant, or Rising sign, modifies your basic Sun sign personality, and it affects the way you act out the daily predictions for your Sun sign. If your Rising sign is indeed Aquarius, what follows is a description of its effects on your horoscope. If your Rising sign is not Aquarius, but some other sign of the Zodiac, you may wish to read the horoscope book for that sign as well.

With Aquarius Rising, that is, in the 1st house, your two planetary rulers—Uranus and Saturn—are in the 1st house, making a study in opposites, contrasts, and complementary qualities. Uranus gives that impulsive, individualistic streak to the personality; Saturn confers a shy yet determined manner. Uranus accents the radical, eccentric tendencies of mind; Saturn roots you in the traditional, sober values of group consensus. Both planets reinforce an independent, stubborn nature.

Where Uranus promotes a restless search for adventure and sur-prise, Saturn dampens with caution and the realities of life. The intuition necessary to transform practical ideas into inspirational ones comes from Uranus. And the discipline needed to correct your often erratic ways and to tune in to your subconscious comes from Saturn.

You with Aquarius Rising may often live your life as a reformer. If you're not actually dedicated to a group or a cause whose goal is revamping societal or intellectual ideals, then you're reforming your children, your own lifestyle, your work methods, your social standards, your wayward friends; if you don't have any of the latter, you'll pick up plenty en route in your zeal. In practical terms, that makes you an excellent organizer because you can streamline any mode of thought or action. And you're absolutely determined to do so, no matter how long it takes or how much opposition you meet along the way.

As a matter of fact, an adversary position suits you nicely because you have equal mixtures of determination and shyness. The impersonality of public debate, ideological struggle hides a wavering, almost blushing, sense of personal self. Some people accuse you of being casual and indifferent, but they should only know how painful it is for you to assert yourself in the area of feel-ings, emotions, idle longings. Sometimes the personal crunch makes the difference whether you will stay in a project, a relationship, or leave it. Often it is your oversensitivity to people, rather than a search for new intellectual challenge, that is the conflict you cannot bear.

You could win both the most valuable member award and the most popular person award, such is your array of talents and native genius. You're good at almost every subject—mechanical, artistic, logical, verbal. And you have a breezy, open friendliness, shorn of sentimentality or heavy emotion, that makes people like you on instinct. You don't trust or give of yourself too freely, but prefer to circulate with a lot of people where you will not be limited by the short-range demands of friendship or by the deeper needs of one-to-one communion in which intense sexuality and love are expected. Being easily and painfully disappointed, you sometimes opt for humaneness over humanness.

Freedom and friendship are two key words associated with Aquarius Rising. Apply them in efforts to expand your lifestyle, deepen and strengthen your commitments, rather than letting them keep you an aloof, solitary figure.

## RISING SIGNS FOR AQUARIUS

| Hour of Birth* | Day of Birth | | |
|---|---|---|---|
| | January 19–23 | January 24–28 | January 29–31 |
| Midnight | Libra | Libra | Scorpio |
| 1 AM | Scorpio | Scorpio | Scorpio |
| 2 AM | Scorpio | Scorpio | Scorpio |
| 3 AM | Scorpio; Sagittarius 1/21 | Sagittarius | Sagittarius |
| 4 AM | Sagittarius | Sagittarius | Sagittarius |
| 5 AM | Sagittarius | Sagittarius; Capricorn 1/26 | Capricorn |
| 6 AM | Capricorn | Capricorn | Capricorn |
| 7 AM | Capricorn | Aquarius | Aquarius |
| 8 AM | Aquarius | Aquarius | Aquarius |
| 9 AM | Pisces | Pisces | Pisces |
| 10 AM | Pisces; Aries 1/21 | Aries | Aries |
| 11 AM | Aries | Taurus | Taurus |
| Noon | Taurus | Taurus | Taurus |
| 1 PM | Gemini | Gemini | Gemini |
| 2 PM | Gemini | Gemini | Gemini; Cancer 1/31 |
| 3 PM | Cancer | Cancer | Cancer |
| 4 PM | Cancer | Cancer | Cancer |
| 5 PM | Cancer; Leo 1/21 | Leo | Leo |
| 6 PM | Leo | Leo | Leo |
| 7 PM | Leo | Leo | Virgo |
| 8 PM | Virgo | Virgo | Virgo |
| 9 PM | Virgo | Virgo | Virgo |
| 10 PM | Virgo; Libra 1/21 | Libra | Libra |
| 11 PM | Libra | Libra | Libra |

*Hour of birth given here is for Standard Time in any time zone. If your hour of birth was recorded in Daylight Saving Time, subtract one hour from it and consult that hour in the table above. For example, if you were born at 7 AM. D.S.T., see 6 AM above.

| Hour of Birth* | Day of Birth | | |
|---|---|---|---|
| | February 1–6 | February 7–12 | February 13–19 |
| Midnight | Scorpio | Scorpio | Scorpio |
| 1 AM | Scorpio | Scorpio | Scorpio |
| 2 AM | Scorpio; Sagittarius 2/5 | Sagittarius | Sagittarius |
| 3 AM | Sagittarius | Sagittarius | Sagittarius |
| 4 AM | Sagittarius | Sagittarius; Capricorn 2/10 | Capricorn |
| 5 AM | Capricorn | Capricorn | Capricorn |
| 6 AM | Capricorn | Capricorn; Aquarius 2/10 | Capricorn |
| 7 AM | Aquarius | Aquarius | Aquarius; Pisces 2/17 |
| 8 AM | Pisces | Pisces | Pisces |
| 9 AM | Pisces; Aries 2/5 | Aries | Aries |
| 10 AM | Aries | Taurus | Taurus |
| 11 AM | Taurus | Taurus | Taurus; Gemini 2/16 |
| Noon | Gemini | Gemini | Gemini |
| 1 PM | Gemini | Gemini | Cancer |
| 2 PM | Cancer | Cancer | Cancer |
| 3 PM | Cancer | Cancer | Cancer |
| 4 PM | Cancer | Leo | Leo |
| 5 PM | Leo | Leo | Leo |
| 6 PM | Leo | Leo | Virgo |
| 7 PM | Virgo | Virgo | Virgo |
| 8 PM | Virgo | Virgo | Virgo |
| 9 PM | Virgo; Libra 2/5 | Libra | Libra |
| 10 PM | Libra | Libra | Libra |
| 11 PM | Libra | Libra | Scorpio |

*See note on facing page.

# THE PLACE OF ASTROLOGY IN TODAY'S WORLD

Does astrology have a place in the fast-moving, ultra-scientific world we live in today? Can it be justified in a sophisticated society whose outriders are already preparing to step off the moon into the deep space of the planets themselves? Or is it just a hangover of ancient superstition, a psychological dummy for neurotics and dreamers of every historical age?

These are the kind of questions that any inquiring person can be expected to ask when they approach a subject like astrology which goes beyond, but never excludes, the materialistic side of life.

The simple, single answer is that astrology works. It works for many millions of people in the western world alone. In the United States there are 10 million followers and in Europe, an estimated 25 million. America has more than 4000 practicing astrologers, Europe nearly three times as many. Even down-under Australia has its hundreds of thousands of adherents. In the eastern countries, astrology has enormous followings, again, because it has been proved to work. In India, for example, brides and grooms for centuries have been chosen on the basis of their astrological compatibility.

Astrology today is more vital than ever before, more practicable because all over the world the media devotes much space and time to it, more valid because science itself is confirming the precepts of astrological knowledge with every new exciting step. The ordinary person who daily applies astrology intelligently does not have to wonder whether it is true nor believe in it blindly. He can see it working for himself. And, if he can use it—and this book is designed to help the reader to do just that—he can make living a far richer experience, and become a more developed personality and a better person.

## Astrology and Relationships

Astrology is the science of relationships. It is not just a study of planetary influences on man and his environment. It is the study of man himself.

We are at the center of our personal universe, of all our relationships. And our happiness or sadness depends on how we act, how we relate to the people and things that surround us. The emotions that we generate have a distinct effect—for better or worse—on the world around us. Our friends and our enemies will confirm this. Just look in the mirror the next time you are angry. In other words, each of us is a kind of sun or planet or star radiating our feelings on the environment around us. Our influence on our personal universe, whether loving, helpful, or destructive, varies with our changing moods, expressed through our individual character.

Our personal "radiations" are potent in the way they affect our moods and our ability to control them. But we usually are able to throw off our emotion in some sort of action—we have a good cry, walk it off, or tell someone our troubles—before it can build up too far and make us physically ill. Astrology helps us to understand the universal forces working on us, and through this understanding, we can become more properly adjusted to our surroundings so that we find ourselves coping where others may flounder.

# The Challenge of Love

The challenge of love lies in recognizing the difference between infatuation, emotion, sex, and, sometimes, the intentional deceit of the other person. Mankind, with its record of broken marriages, despair, and disillusionment, is obviously not very good at making these distinctions.

Can astrology help?

Yes. In the same way that advance knowledge can usually help in any human situation. And there is probably no situation as human, as poignant, as pathetic and universal, as the failure of man's love.

Love, of course, is not just between man and woman. It involves love of children, parents, home, and friends. But the big problems usually involve the choice of partner.

Astrology has established degrees of compatibility that exist between people born under the various signs of the Zodiac. Because people are individuals, there are numerous variations and modifications. So the astrologer, when approached on mate and marriage matters, makes allowances for them. But the fact remains that some groups of people are suited for each other and some are not, and astrology has expressed this in terms of characteristics we all can study and use as a personal guide.

No matter how much enjoyment and pleasure we find in the different aspects of each other's character, if it is not an overall compatibility, the chances of our finding fulfillment or enduring happiness in each other are pretty hopeless. And astrology can help us to find someone compatible.

# Astrology and Science

Closely related to our emotions is the "other side" of our personal universe, our physical welfare. Our body, of course, is largely influenced by things around us over which we have very little control. The phone rings, we hear it. The train runs late. We snag our stocking or cut our face shaving. Our body is under a constant bombardment of events that influence our daily lives to varying degrees.

The question that arises from all this is, what makes each of us act so that we have to involve other people and keep the ball of activity and evolution rolling? This is the question that both science and astrology are involved with. The scientists have attacked it from different angles: anthropology, the study of human evolution as body, mind and response to environment; anatomy, the study of bodily structure; psychology, the science of the human mind; and so on. These studies have produced very impressive classifications and valuable information, but because the approach to the problem is fragmented, so is the result. They remain "branches" of science. Science generally studies effects. It keeps turning up wonderful answers but no lasting solutions. Astrology, on the other hand, approaches the question from the broader viewpoint. Astrology began its inquiry with the totality of human experience and saw it as an effect. It then looked to find the cause, or at least the prime movers, and during thousands of years of observation of man and his *universal* environment came up with the extraordinary principle of planetary influence—or astrology, which, from the Greek, means the science of the stars.

Modern science, as we shall see, has confirmed much of astrology's foundations—most of it unintentionally, some of it reluctantly, but still, indisputably.

It is not difficult to imagine that there must be a connection between outer space and Earth. Even today, scientists are not too sure how our Earth was created, but it is generally agreed that it is only a tiny part of the universe. And as a part of the universe, people on Earth see and feel the influence of heavenly bodies in almost every aspect of our existence. There is no doubt that the Sun has the greatest influence on life on this planet. Without it there would be no life, for without it there would be no warmth, no division into day and night, no cycles of time or season at all. This is clear and easy to see. The influence of the Moon, on the other hand, is more subtle, though no less definite.

There are many ways in which the influence of the Moon manifests itself here on Earth, both on human and animal life. It is a well-known fact, for instance, that the large movements of water on our planet—that is the ebb and flow of the tides—are caused by the Moon's gravitational pull. Since this is so, it follows that these water movements do not occur only in the oceans, but that all bodies of water are affected, even down to the tiniest puddle.

The human body, too, which consists of about 70 percent water, falls within the scope of this lunar influence. For example the menstrual cycle of most women corresponds to the 28-day lunar month; the period of pregnancy in humans is 273 days, or equal to nine lunar months. Similarly, many illnesses reach a crisis at the change of the Moon, and statistics in many countries have shown that the crime rate is highest at the time of the Full Moon. Even human sexual desire has been associated with the phases of the Moon. But it is in the movement of the tides that we get the clearest demonstration of planetary influence, which leads to the irresistible correspondence between the so-called metaphysical and the physical.

Tide tables are prepared years in advance by calculating the future positions of the Moon. Science has known for a long time that the Moon is the main cause of tidal action. But only in the last few years has it begun to realize the possible extent of this influence on mankind. To begin with, the ocean tides do not rise and fall as we might imagine from our personal observations of them. The Moon as it orbits around Earth sets up a circular wave of attraction which pulls the oceans of the world after it, broadly in an east to west direction. This influence is like a phantom wave crest, a loop of power stretching from pole to pole which passes over and around the Earth like an invisible shadow. It travels with equal effect across the land masses and, as scientists were recently amazed to observe, caused oysters placed in the dark in the middle of the United States where there is no sea to open their shells to receive the nonexistent tide. If the land-locked oysters react to this invisible signal, what effect does it have on us who not so long ago in evolutionary time came out of the sea and still have its salt in our blood and sweat?

Less well known is the fact that the Moon is also the primary force behind the circulation of blood in human beings and animals, and the movement of sap in trees and plants. Agriculturists have established that the Moon has a distinct influence on crops, which explains why for centuries people have planted according to Moon cycles. The habits of many animals, too, are directed by the movement of the Moon. Migratory birds, for instance, depart only at or near the time of the Full Moon. And certain sea creatures, eels in particular, move only in accordance with certain phases of the Moon.

# Know Thyself—Why?

In today's fast-changing world, everyone still longs to know what the future holds. It is the one thing that everyone has in common: rich and poor, famous and infamous, all are deeply concerned about tomorrow.

But the key to the future, as every historian knows, lies in the past. This is as true of individual people as it is of nations. You cannot understand your future without first understanding your past, which is simply another way of saying that you must first of all know yourself.

The motto "know thyself" seems obvious enough nowadays, but it was originally put forward as the foundation of wisdom by the ancient Greek philosophers. It was then adopted by the "mystery religions" of the ancient Middle East, Greece, Rome, and is still used in all genuine schools of mind training or mystical discipline, both in those of the East, based on yoga, and those of the West. So it is universally accepted now, and has been through the ages.

But how do you go about discovering what sort of person you are? The first step is usually classification into some sort of system of types. Astrology did this long before the birth of Christ. Psychology has also done it. So has modern medicine, in its way.

One system classifies people according to the source of the impulses they respond to most readily: the muscles, leading to direct bodily action; the digestive organs, resulting in emotion; or the brain and nerves, giving rise to thinking. Another such system says that character is determined by the endocrine glands, and gives us such labels as "pituitary," "thyroid," and "hyperthyroid" types. These different systems are neither contradictory nor mutually exclusive. In fact, they are very often different ways of saying the same thing.

Very popular, useful classifications were devised by Carl Jung, the eminent disciple of Freud. Jung observed among the different faculties of the mind, four which have a predominant influence on character. These four faculties exist in all of us without exception, but not in perfect balance. So when we say, for instance, that someone is a "thinking type," it means that in any situation he or she tries to be rational. Emotion, which may be the opposite of thinking, will be his or her weakest function. This thinking type can be sensible and reasonable, or calculating and unsympathetic. The emotional type, on the other hand, can often be recognized by exaggerated language—everything is either marvelous or terrible—and in extreme cases they even invent dramas and quarrels out of nothing just to make life more interesting.

The other two faculties are intuition and physical sensation. The sensation type does not only care for food and drink, nice clothes and furniture; he or she is also interested in all forms of physical experience. Many scientists are sensation types as are athletes and nature-lovers. Like sensation, intuition is a form of perception and we all possess it. But it works through that part of the mind which is not under conscious control—consequently it sees meanings and connections which are not obvious to thought or emotion. Inventors and original thinkers are always intuitive, but so, too, are superstitious people who see meanings where none exist.

Thus, sensation tells us what is going on in the world, feeling (that is, emotion) tells us how important it is to ourselves, thinking enables us to interpret it and work out what we should do about it, and intuition tells us what it means to ourselves and others. All four faculties are essential, and all are present in every one of us. But some people are guided chiefly by one, others by another. In addition, Jung also observed a division of the human personality into the extrovert and the introvert, which cuts across these four types.

A disadvantage of all these systems of classification is that one cannot tell very easily where to place oneself. Some people are reluctant to admit that they act to please their emotions. So they deceive themselves for years by trying to belong to whichever type they think is the "best." Of course, there is no best; each has its faults and each has its good points.

The advantage of the signs of the Zodiac is that they simplify classification. Not only that, but your date of birth is personal—

it is unarguably yours. What better way to know yourself than by going back as far as possible to the very moment of your birth? And this is precisely what your horoscope is all about, as we shall see in the next section.

# WHAT IS A HOROSCOPE?

If you had been able to take a picture of the skies at the moment of your birth, that photograph would be your horoscope. Lacking such a snapshot, it is still possible to recreate the picture—and this is at the basis of the astrologer's art. In other words, your horoscope is a representation of the skies with the planets in the exact positions they occupied at the time you were born.

The year of birth tells an astrologer the positions of the distant, slow-moving planets Jupiter, Saturn, Uranus, Neptune, and Pluto. The month of birth indicates the Sun sign, or birth sign as it is commonly called, as well as indicating the positions of the rapidly moving planets Venus, Mercury, and Mars. The day and time of birth will locate the position of our Moon. And the moment—the exact hour and minute—of birth determines the houses through what is called the Ascendant, or Rising sign.

With this information the astrologer consults various tables to calculate the specific positions of the Sun, Moon, and other planets relative to your birthplace at the moment you were born. Then he or she locates them by means of the Zodiac.

## The Zodiac

The Zodiac is a band of stars (constellations) in the skies, centered on the Sun's apparent path around the Earth, and is divided into twelve equal segments, or signs. What we are actually dividing up is the Earth's path around the Sun. But from our point of view here on Earth, it seems as if the Sun is making a great circle around our planet in the sky, so we say it is the Sun's apparent path. This twelvefold division, the Zodiac, is a reference system for the astrologer. At any given moment the planets—and in astrology both the Sun and Moon are considered to be planets—can all be located at a specific point along this path.

Now where in all this are you, the subject of the horoscope? Your character is largely determined by the sign the Sun is in. So that is where the astrologer looks first in your horoscope, at your Sun sign.

# The Sun Sign and the Cusp

There are twelve signs in the Zodiac, and the Sun spends approximately one month in each sign. But because of the motion of the Earth around the Sun—the Sun's apparent motion—the dates when the Sun enters and leaves each sign may change from year to year. Some people born near the cusp, or edge, of a sign have difficulty determining which is their Sun sign. But in this book a Table of Cusps is provided for the years 1900 to 2010 (page 5) so you can find out what your true Sun sign is.

Here are the twelve signs of the Zodiac, their ancient zodiacal symbol, and the dates when the Sun enters and leaves each sign for the year 2009. Remember, these dates may change from year to year.

| | | |
|---|---|---|
| ARIES | Ram | March 20–April 19 |
| TAURUS | Bull | April 19–May 20 |
| GEMINI | Twins | May 20–June 21 |
| CANCER | Crab | June 21–July 22 |
| LEO | Lion | July 22–August 22 |
| VIRGO | Virgin | August 22–September 22 |
| LIBRA | Scales | September 22–October 23 |
| SCORPIO | Scorpion | October 23–November 22 |
| SAGITTARIUS | Archer | November 22–December 21 |
| CAPRICORN | Sea Goat | December 21–January 19 |
| AQUARIUS | Water Bearer | January 19–February 18 |
| PISCES | Fish | February 18–March 20 |

It is possible to draw significant conclusions and make meaningful predictions based simply on the Sun sign of a person. There are many people who have been amazed at the accuracy of the description of their own character based only on the Sun sign. But an astrologer needs more information than just your Sun sign to interpret the photograph that is your horoscope.

# The Rising Sign and the Zodiacal Houses

An astrologer needs the exact time and place of your birth in order to construct and interpret your horoscope. The illustration on the next page shows the flat chart, or natural wheel, an astrologer uses. Note the inner circle of the wheel labeled 1 through 12. These 12 divisions are known as the houses of the Zodiac.

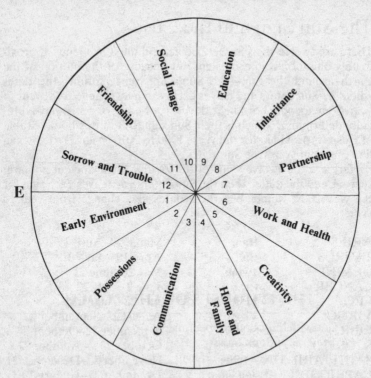

The 1st house always starts from the position marked E, which corresponds to the eastern horizon. The rest of the houses 2 through 12 follow around in a "counterclockwise" direction. The point where each house starts is known as a cusp, or edge.

The cusp, or edge, of the 1st house (point E) is where an astrologer would place your Rising sign, the Ascendant. And, as already noted, the exact time of your birth determines your Rising sign. Let's see how this works.

As the Earth rotates on its axis once every 24 hours, each one of the twelve signs of the Zodiac appears to be "rising" on the horizon, with a new one appearing about every 2 hours. Actually it is the turning of the Earth that exposes each sign to view, but in our astrological work we are discussing apparent motion. This Rising sign marks the Ascendant, and it colors the whole orientation of a horoscope. It indicates the sign governing the 1st house of the chart, and will thus determine which signs will govern all the other houses.

To visualize this idea, imagine two color wheels with twelve divisions superimposed upon each other. For just as the Zodiac is divided into twelve constellations that we identify as the signs, another twelvefold division is used to denote the houses. Now imagine one wheel (the signs) moving slowly while the other wheel (the houses) remains still. This analogy may help you see how the signs keep shifting the "color" of the houses as the Rising sign continues to change every two hours. To simplify things, a Table of Rising Signs has been provided (pages 8–9) for your specific Sun sign.

Once your Rising sign has been placed on the cusp of the 1st house, the signs that govern the rest of the 11 houses can be placed on the chart. In any individual's horoscope the signs do not necessarily correspond with the houses. For example, it could be that a sign covers part of two adjacent houses. It is the interpretation of such variations in an individual's horoscope that marks the professional astrologer.

But to gain a workable understanding of astrology, it is not necessary to go into great detail. In fact, we just need a description of the houses and their meanings, as is shown in the illustration above and in the table below.

## THE 12 HOUSES OF THE ZODIAC

| | | |
|---|---|---|
| 1st | Individuality, body appearance, general outlook on life | Personality house |
| 2nd | Finance, possessions, ethical principles, gain or loss | Money house |
| 3rd | Relatives, communication, short journeys, writing, education | Relatives house |
| 4th | Family and home, parental ties, land and property, security | Home house |
| 5th | Pleasure, children, creativity, entertainment, risk | Pleasure house |
| 6th | Health, harvest, hygiene, work and service, employees | Health house |
| 7th | Marriage and divorce, the law, partnerships and alliances | Marriage house |
| 8th | Inheritance, secret deals, sex, death, regeneration | Inheritance house |
| 9th | Travel, sports, study, philosophy and religion | Travel house |
| 10th | Career, social standing, success and honor | Business house |
| 11th | Friendship, social life, hopes and wishes | Friends house |
| 12th | Troubles, illness, secret enemies, hidden agendas | Trouble house |

# The Planets in the Houses

An astrologer, knowing the exact time and place of your birth, will use tables of planetary motion in order to locate the planets in your horoscope chart. He or she will determine which planet or planets are in which sign and in which house. It is not uncommon, in an individual's horoscope, for there to be two or more planets in the same sign and in the same house.

The characteristics of the planets modify the influence of the Sun according to their natures and strengths.

**Sun:** Source of life. Basic temperament according to the Sun sign. The conscious will. Human potential.
**Moon:** Emotions. Moods. Customs. Habits. Changeable. Adaptive. Nurturing.
**Mercury:** Communication. Intellect. Reasoning power. Curiosity. Short travels.
**Venus:** Love. Delight. Charm. Harmony. Balance. Art. Beautiful possessions.
**Mars:** Energy. Initiative. War. Anger. Adventure. Courage. Daring. Impulse.
**Jupiter:** Luck. Optimism. Generous. Expansive. Opportunities. Protection.
**Saturn:** Pessimism. Privation. Obstacles. Delay. Hard work. Research. Lasting rewards after long struggle.
**Uranus:** Fashion. Electricity. Revolution. Independence. Freedom. Sudden changes. Modern science.
**Neptune:** Sensationalism. Theater. Dreams. Inspiration. Illusion. Deception.
**Pluto:** Creation and destruction. Total transformation. Lust for power. Strong obsessions.

Superimpose the characteristics of the planets on the functions of the house in which they appear. Express the result through the character of the Sun sign, and you will get the basic idea.

Of course, many other considerations have been taken into account in producing the carefully worked out predictions in this book: the aspects of the planets to each other; their strength according to position and sign; whether they are in a house of exaltation or decline; whether they are natural enemies or not; whether a planet occupies its own sign; the position of a planet in relation to its own house or sign; whether the sign is male or female; whether the sign is a fire, earth, water, or air sign. These are only a few of the colors on the astrologer's pallet which he or she must mix with the inspiration of the artist and the accuracy of the mathematician.

## How To Use These Predictions

A person reading the predictions in this book should understand that they are produced from the daily position of the planets for a group of people and are not, of course, individually specialized. To get the full benefit of them our readers should relate the predictions to their own character and circumstances, coordinate them, and draw their own conclusions from them.

If you are a serious observer of your own life, you should find a definite pattern emerging that will be a helpful and reliable guide.

The point is that we always retain our free will. The stars indicate certain directional tendencies but we are not compelled to follow. We can do or not do, and wisdom must make the choice.

We all have our good and bad days. Sometimes they extend into cycles of weeks. It is therefore advisable to study daily predictions in a span ranging from the day before to several days ahead.

Daily predictions should be taken very generally. The word "difficult" does not necessarily indicate a whole day of obstruction or inconvenience. It is a warning to you to be cautious. Your caution will often see you around the difficulty before you are involved. This is the correct use of astrology.

In another section (pages 78–84), detailed information is given about the influence of the Moon as it passes through each of the twelve signs of the Zodiac. There are instructions on how to use the Moon Tables (pages 85–92), which provide Moon Sign Dates throughout the year as well as the Moon's role in health and daily affairs. This information should be used in conjunction with the daily forecasts to give a fuller picture of the astrological trends.

# HISTORY OF ASTROLOGY

The origins of astrology have been lost far back in history, but we do know that reference is made to it as far back as the first written records of the human race. It is not hard to see why. Even in primitive times, people must have looked for an explanation for the various happenings in their lives. They must have wanted to know why people were different from one another. And in their search they turned to the regular movements of the Sun, Moon, and stars to see if they could provide an answer.

It is interesting to note that as soon as man learned to use his tools in any type of design, or his mind in any kind of calculation, he turned his attention to the heavens. Ancient cave dwellings reveal dim crescents and circles representative of the Sun and Moon, rulers of day and night. Mesopotamia and the civilization of Chaldea, in itself the foundation of those of Babylonia and Assyria, show a complete picture of astronomical observation and well-developed astrological interpretation.

Humanity has a natural instinct for order. The study of anthropology reveals that primitive people—even as far back as prehistoric times—were striving to achieve a certain order in their lives. They tried to organize the apparent chaos of the universe. They had the desire to attach meaning to things. This demand for order has persisted throughout the history of man. So that observing the regularity of the heavenly bodies made it logical that primitive peoples should turn heavenward in their search for an understanding of the world in which they found themselves so random and alone.

And they did find a significance in the movements of the stars. Shepherds tending their flocks, for instance, observed that when the cluster of stars now known as the constellation Aries was in sight, it was the time of fertility and they associated it with the Ram. And they noticed that the growth of plants and plant life corresponded with different phases of the Moon, so that certain times were favorable for the planting of crops, and other times were not. In this way, there grew up a tradition of seasons and causes connected with the passage of the Sun through the twelve signs of the Zodiac.

Astrology was valued so highly that the king was kept informed of the daily and monthly changes in the heavenly bodies, and the results of astrological studies regarding events of the future. Head astrologers were clearly men of great rank and position, and the office was said to be a hereditary one.

Omens were taken, not only from eclipses and conjunctions of the Moon or Sun with one of the planets, but also from storms and earthquakes. In the eastern civilizations, particularly, the reverence inspired by astrology appears to have remained unbroken since the very earliest days. In ancient China, astrology, astronomy, and religion went hand in hand. The astrologer, who was also an astronomer, was part of the official government service and had his own corner in the Imperial Palace. The duties of the Imperial astrologer, whose office was one of the most important in the land, were clearly defined, as this extract from early records shows:

This exalted gentleman must concern himself with the stars in the heavens, keeping a record of the changes and movements of the Planets, the Sun and the Moon, in order to examine the movements of the terrestrial world with the object of prognosticating good and bad fortune. He divides the territories of the nine regions of the empire in accordance with their dependence on particular celestial bodies. All the fiefs and principalities are connected with the stars and from this their prosperity or misfortune should be ascertained. He makes prognostications according to the twelve years of the Jupiter cycle of good and evil of the terrestrial world. From the colors of the five kinds of clouds, he determines the coming of floods or droughts, abundance or famine. From the twelve winds, he draws conclusions about the state of harmony of heaven and earth, and takes note of good and bad signs that result from their accord or disaccord. In general, he concerns himself with five kinds of phenomena so as to warn the Emperor to come to the aid of the government and to allow for variations in the ceremonies according to their circumstances.

The Chinese were also keen observers of the fixed stars, giving them such unusual names as Ghost Vehicle, Sun of Imperial Concubine, Imperial Prince, Pivot of Heaven, Twinkling Brilliance, Weaving Girl. But, great astrologers though they may have been, the Chinese lacked one aspect of mathematics that the Greeks applied to astrology—deductive geometry. Deductive geometry was the basis of much classical astrology in and after the time of the Greeks, and this explains the different methods of prognostication used in the East and West.

Down through the ages the astrologer's art has depended, not so much on the uncovering of new facts, though this is important, as on the interpretation of the facts already known. This is the essence of the astrologer's skill.

But why should the signs of the Zodiac have any effect at all on the formation of human character? It is easy to see why people thought they did, and even now we constantly use astrological expressions in our everyday speech. The thoughts of "lucky star," "ill-fated," "star-crossed," "mooning around," are interwoven into the very structure of our language.

Wherever the concept of the Zodiac is understood and used, it could well appear to have an influence on the human character. Does this mean, then, that the human race, in whose civilization the idea of the twelve signs of the Zodiac has long been embedded, is divided into only twelve types? Can we honestly believe that it is really as simple as that? If so, there must be pretty wide ranges of variation within each type. And if, to explain the variation, we call in heredity and environment, experiences in early childhood, the thyroid and other glands, and also the four functions of the mind together with extroversion and introversion, then one begins to wonder if the original classification was worth making at all. No sensible person believes that his favorite system explains everything. But even so, he will not find the system much use at all if it does not even save him the trouble of bothering with the others.

In the same way, if we were to put every person under only one sign of the Zodiac, the system becomes too rigid and unlike life. Besides, it was never intended to be used like that. It may be convenient to have only twelve types, but we know that in practice there is every possible gradation between aggressiveness and timidity, or between conscientiousness and laziness. How, then, do we account for this?

A person born under any given Sun sign can be mainly influenced by one or two of the other signs that appear in their individual horoscope. For instance, famous persons born under the sign of Gemini include Henry VIII, whom nothing and no one could have induced to abdicate, and Edward VIII, who did just that. Obviously, then, the sign Gemini does not fully explain the complete character of either of them.

Again, under the opposite sign, Sagittarius, were both Stalin, who was totally consumed with the notion of power, and Charles V, who freely gave up an empire because he preferred to go into a monastery. And we find under Scorpio many uncompromising characters such as Luther, de Gaulle, Indira Gandhi, and Montgomery, but also Petain, a successful commander whose name later became synonymous with collaboration.

A single sign is therefore obviously inadequate to explain the differences between people; it can only explain resemblances, such as the combativeness of the Scorpio group, or the far-reaching devotion of Charles V and Stalin to their respective ideals—the Christian heaven and the Communist utopia.

But very few people have only one sign in their horoscope chart.

In addition to the month of birth, the day and, even more, the hour to the nearest minute if possible, ought to be considered. Without this, it is impossible to have an actual horoscope, for the word horoscope literally means "a consideration of the hour."

The month of birth tells you only which sign of the Zodiac was occupied by the Sun. The day and hour tell you what sign was occupied by the Moon. And the minute tells you which sign was rising on the eastern horizon. This is called the Ascendant, and, as some astrologers believe, it is supposed to be the most important thing in the whole horoscope.

The Sun is said to signify one's heart, that is to say, one's deepest desires and inmost nature. This is quite different from the Moon, which signifies one's superficial way of behaving. When the ancient Romans referred to the Emperor Augustus as a Capricorn, they meant that he had the Moon in Capricorn. Or, to take another example, a modern astrologer would call Disraeli a Scorpion because he had Scorpio Rising, but most people would call him Sagittarius because he had the Sun there. The Romans would have called him Leo because his Moon was in Leo.

So if one does not seem to fit one's birth month, it is always worthwhile reading the other signs, for one may have been born at a time when any of them were rising or occupied by the Moon. It also seems to be the case that the influence of the Sun develops as life goes on, so that the month of birth is easier to guess in people over the age of forty. The young are supposed to be influenced mainly by their Ascendant, the Rising sign, which characterizes the body and physical personality as a whole.

It is nonsense to assume that all people born at a certain time will exhibit the same characteristics, or that they will even behave in the same manner. It is quite obvious that, from the very moment of its birth, a child is subject to the effects of its environment, and that this in turn will influence its character and heritage to a decisive extent. Also to be taken into account are education and economic conditions, which play a very important part in the formation of one's character as well.

People have, in general, certain character traits and qualities which, according to their environment, develop in either a positive or a negative manner. Therefore, selfishness (inherent selfishness, that is) might emerge as unselfishness; kindness and consideration as cruelty and lack of consideration toward others. In the same way, a naturally constructive person may, through frustration, become destructive, and so on. The latent characteristics with which people are born can, therefore, through environment and good or bad training, become something that would appear to be its opposite, and so give the lie to the astrologer's description of their character.

But this is not the case. The true character is still there, but it is buried deep beneath these external superficialities.

Careful study of the character traits of various signs of the Zodiac are of immeasurable help, and can render beneficial service to the intelligent person. Undoubtedly, the reader will already have discovered that, while he is able to get on very well with some people, he just "cannot stand" others. The causes sometimes seem inexplicable. At times there is intense dislike, at other times immediate sympathy. And there is, too, the phenomenon of love at first sight, which is also apparently inexplicable. People appear to be either sympathetic or unsympathetic toward each other for no apparent reason.

Now if we look at this in the light of the Zodiac, we find that people born under different signs are either compatible or incompatible with each other. In other words, there are good and bad interrelating factors among the various signs. This does not, of course, mean that humanity can be divided into groups of hostile camps. It would be quite wrong to be hostile or indifferent toward people who happen to be born under an incompatible sign. There is no reason why everybody should not, or cannot, learn to control and adjust their feelings and actions, especially after they are aware of the positive qualities of other people by studying their character analyses, among other things.

Every person born under a certain sign has both positive and negative qualities, which are developed more or less according to our free will. Nobody is entirely good or entirely bad, and it is up to each of us to learn to control ourselves on the one hand and at the same time to endeavor to learn about ourselves and others.

It cannot be emphasized often enough that it is free will that determines whether we will make really good use of our talents and abilities. Using our free will, we can either overcome our failings or allow them to rule us. Our free will enables us to exert sufficient willpower to control our failings so that they do not harm ourselves or others.

Astrology can reveal our inclinations and tendencies. Astrology can tell us about ourselves so that we are able to use our free will to overcome our shortcomings. In this way astrology helps us do our best to become needed and valuable members of society as well as helpmates to our family and our friends. Astrology also can save us a great deal of unhappiness and remorse.

Yet it may seem absurd that an ancient philosophy could be a prop to modern men and women. But below the materialistic surface of modern life, there are hidden streams of feeling and thought. Symbology is reappearing as a study worthy of the scholar; the psychosomatic factor in illness has passed from the writings of the crank to those of the specialist; spiritual healing in all its forms is no longer a pious hope but an accepted phenomenon. And it is into this context that we consider astrology, in the sense that it is an analysis of human types.

Astrology and medicine had a long journey together, and only parted company a couple of centuries ago. There still remain in medical language such astrological terms as "saturnine," "choleric," and "mercurial," used in the diagnosis of physical tendencies. The herbalist, for long the handyman of the medical profession, has been dominated by astrology since the days of the Greeks. Certain herbs traditionally respond to certain planetary influences, and diseases must therefore be treated to ensure harmony between the medicine and the disease.

But the stars are expected to foretell and not only to diagnose.

Astrological forecasting has been remarkably accurate, but often it is wide of the mark. The brave person who cares to predict world events takes dangerous chances. Individual forecasting is less clear cut; it can be a help or a disillusionment. Then we come to the nagging question: if it is possible to foreknow, is it right to foretell? This is a point of ethics on which it is hard to pronounce judgment. The doctor faces the same dilemma if he finds that symptoms of a mortal disease are present in his patient and that he can only prognosticate a steady decline. How much to tell an individual in a crisis is a problem that has perplexed many distinguished scholars. Honest and conscientious astrologers in this modern world, where so many people are seeking guidance, face the same problem.

Five hundred years ago it was customary to call in a learned man who was an astrologer who was probably also a doctor and a philosopher. By his knowledge of astrology, his study of planetary influences, he felt himself qualified to guide those in distress. The world has moved forward at a fantastic rate since then, and yet people are still uncertain of themselves. At first sight it seems fantastic in the light of modern thinking that they turn to the most ancient of all studies, and get someone to calculate a horoscope for them. But is it really so fantastic if you take a second look? For astrology is concerned with tomorrow, with survival. And in a world such as ours, tomorrow and survival are the keywords for the twenty-first century.

# ASTROLOGICAL BRIDGE TO THE 21st CENTURY

Themes connecting past, present, and future are in play as the first decade reveals hidden paths and personal hints for achieving your potential. Make the most of the messages from the planets.

With the dawning of the twenty-first century look first to Jupiter, the planet of good fortune. Each new yearly Jupiter cycle follows the natural progression of the Zodiac. First is Jupiter in Aries and in Taurus through spring 2000, next Jupiter is in Gemini to summer 2001, then in Cancer to midsummer 2002, in Leo to late summer 2003, in Virgo to early autumn 2004, in Libra to midautumn 2005, and so on through Jupiter in Pisces through June 2010. The beneficent planet Jupiter promotes your professional and educational goals while urging informed choice and deliberation, providing a rich medium for creativity. Planet Jupiter's influence is protective, the generous helper that comes to the rescue just in the nick of time. And while safeguarding good luck, Jupiter can turn unusual risks into achievable aims.

In order to take advantage of luck and opportunity, to gain wisdom from experience, to persevere against adversity, look to beautiful planet Saturn. Saturn, planet of reason and responsibility, began a new cycle in earthy Taurus at the turn of the century. Saturn in Taurus until spring 2001 inspires industry and affection, blends practicality and imagination, all the while inviting caution and care. Saturn in Taurus lends beauty, order, and structure to your life. Then Saturn is in Gemini, the sign of mind and communication, until June 2003. Saturn in Gemini gives a lively intellectual capacity, so the limits of creativity can be stretched and boundaries broken. Saturn in Gemini holds the promise of fruitful endeavor through sustained study, learning, and application. Saturn in Cancer from early June 2003 to mid-July 2005 poses issues of long-term security versus immediate gratification. Rely on deliberation and choice to make sense out of diversity and change. Saturn in Cancer can be a revealing cycle, leading to the desired outcomes of growth and maturity. Saturn in Leo from mid-July 2005 to early September 2007 can be a test of boldness versus caution. Here every challenge must be met with benevolent authority, matched by a caring and generous outlook. Saturn in Virgo early September 2007 into October 2009 sharpens and deepens the mind. Saturn in Virgo presents chances to excel, to gain prominence through good words and good works. Saturn in Libra end of October 2009 into November 2012 promotes artistry, balance, goodwill, and peace.

Uranus, planet of innovation and surprise, started an important new cycle in January of 1996. At that time Uranus entered its natural home in airy Aquarius. Uranus in Aquarius into the year 2003 has a profound effect on your personality and the lens through which you see the world. A basic change in the way you project yourself is just one impact of Uranus in Aquarius. More significantly, a whole new consciousness is evolving. Winds of change blowing your way emphasize movement and freedom. Uranus in Aquarius poses involvement in the larger community beyond self, family, friends, lovers, associates. Radical ideas and progressive thought signal a journey of liberation. As the new century begins, follow Uranus on the path of humanitarianism. A new Uranus cycle begins March 2003 when Uranus visits Pisces, briefly revisits Aquarius, then returns late in 2003 to Pisces where it will stay into May 2010. Uranus in Pisces, a strongly intuitive force, urges work and service for the good of humankind to make the world a better place for all people.

Neptune, planet of vision and mystery, is enjoying a long cycle that excites creativity and imaginative thinking. Neptune is in airy Aquarius from November 1998 to February of 2012. Neptune in Aquarius, the sign of the Water Bearer, represents two sides of the coin of wisdom: inspiration and reason. Here Neptune stirs powerful currents bearing a rich and varied harvest, the fertile breeding ground for idealistic aims and practical considerations. Neptune's fine intuition tunes in to your dreams, your imagination, your spirituality. You can never turn your back on the mysteries of life. Uranus and Neptune, the planets of enlightenment and idealism, give you glimpses into the future, letting you peek through secret doorways into the twenty-first century.

Pluto, dwarf planet of beginnings and endings, started a new cycle of transformative power in the year 2008. Pluto entered the earthy sign of Capricorn and journeys there for sixteen years until 2024. Pluto in Capricorn over the course of this extensive journey has the capacity to change the landscape as well as the humanscape. The transforming energy of Pluto combines with the persevering power of Capricorn to give depth and character to potential change. Pluto in Capricorn can bring focus and cohesion to disparate, diverse creativities. As new forms arise and take root, Pluto in Capricorn organizes the rebuilding process. Freedom versus limitation, freedom versus authority is part of the picture. Reasonableness struggles with recklessness to solve divisive issues. Pluto in Capricorn can teach important lessons about adversity, and the lessons will be learned.

# THE SIGNS OF THE ZODIAC

## Dominant Characteristics

### Aries: March 21–April 20

## The Positive Side of Aries

The Aries has many positive points to his character. People born under this first sign of the Zodiac are often quite strong and enthusiastic. On the whole, they are forward-looking people who are not easily discouraged by temporary setbacks. They know what they want out of life and they go out after it. Their personalities are strong. Others are usually quite impressed by the Ram's way of doing things. Quite often they are sources of inspiration for others traveling the same route. Aries men and women have a special zest for life that can be contagious; for others, they are a fine example of how life should be lived.

The Aries person usually has a quick and active mind. He is imaginative and inventive. He enjoys keeping busy and active. He generally gets along well with all kinds of people. He is interested in mankind, as a whole. He likes to be challenged. Some would say he thrives on opposition, for it is when he is set against that he often does his best. Getting over or around obstacles is a challenge he generally enjoys. All in all, Aries is quite positive and young-thinking. He likes to keep abreast of new things that are happening in the world. Aries are often fond of speed. They like things to be done quickly, and this sometimes aggravates their slower colleagues and associates.

The Aries man or woman always seems to remain young. Their whole approach to life is youthful and optimistic. They never say die, no matter what the odds. They may have an occasional setback, but it is not long before they are back on their feet again.

# The Negative Side of Aries

Everybody has his less positive qualities—and Aries is no exception. Sometimes the Aries man or woman is not very tactful in communicating with others; in his hurry to get things done he is apt to be a little callous or inconsiderate. Sensitive people are likely to find him somewhat sharp-tongued in some situations. Often in his eagerness to get the show on the road, he misses the mark altogether and cannot achieve his aims.

At times Aries can be too impulsive. He can occasionally be stubborn and refuse to listen to reason. If things do not move quickly enough to suit the Aries man or woman, he or she is apt to become rather nervous or irritable. The uncultivated Aries is not unfamiliar with moments of doubt and fear. He is capable of being destructive if he does not get his way. He can overcome some of his emotional problems by steadily trying to express himself as he really is, but this requires effort.

# Taurus: April 21–May 20

## The Positive Side of Taurus

The Taurus person is known for his ability to concentrate and for his tenacity. These are perhaps his strongest qualities. The Taurus man or woman generally has very little trouble in getting along with others; it's his nature to be helpful toward people in need. He can always be depended on by his friends, especially those in trouble.

Taurus generally achieves what he wants through his ability to persevere. He never leaves anything unfinished but works on something until it has been completed. People can usually take him at his word; he is honest and forthright in most of his dealings. The Taurus person has a good chance to make a success of his life because of his many positive qualities. The Taurus who aims high seldom falls short of his mark. He learns well by experience. He is thorough and does not believe in shortcuts of any kind. The Bull's thoroughness pays off in the end, for through his deliberateness he learns how to rely on himself and what he has learned. The Taurus person tries to get along with others, as a rule. He is not overly critical and likes people to be themselves. He is a tolerant person and enjoys peace and harmony—especially in his home life.

Taurus is usually cautious in all that he does. He is not a person

who believes in taking unnecessary risks. Before adopting any one line of action, he will weigh all of the pros and cons. The Taurus person is steadfast. Once his mind is made up it seldom changes. The person born under this sign usually is a good family person—reliable and loving.

## The Negative Side of Taurus

Sometimes the Taurus man or woman is a bit too stubborn. He won't listen to other points of view if his mind is set on something. To others, this can be quite annoying. Taurus also does not like to be told what to do. He becomes rather angry if others think him not too bright. He does not like to be told he is wrong, even when he is. He dislikes being contradicted.

Some people who are born under this sign are very suspicious of others—even of those persons close to them. They find it difficult to trust people fully. They are often afraid of being deceived or taken advantage of. The Bull often finds it difficult to forget or forgive. His love of material things sometimes makes him rather avaricious and petty.

## Gemini: May 21–June 20

## The Positive Side of Gemini

The person born under this sign of the Heavenly Twins is usually quite bright and quick-witted. Some of them are capable of doing many different things. The Gemini person very often has many different interests. He keeps an open mind and is always anxious to learn new things.

Gemini is often an analytical person. He is a person who enjoys making use of his intellect. He is governed more by his mind than by his emotions. He is a person who is not confined to one view; he can often understand both sides to a problem or question. He knows how to reason, how to make rapid decisions if need be.

He is an adaptable person and can make himself at home almost anywhere. There are all kinds of situations he can adapt to. He is a person who seldom doubts himself; he is sure of his talents and his ability to think and reason. Gemini is generally most satisfied when he is in a situation where he can make use of his intellect. Never

short of imagination, he often has strong talents for invention. He is rather a modern person when it comes to life; Gemini almost always moves along with the times—perhaps that is why he remains so youthful throughout most of his life.

Literature and art appeal to the person born under this sign. Creativity in almost any form will interest and intrigue the Gemini man or woman.

The Gemini is often quite charming. A good talker, he often is the center of attraction at any gathering. People find it easy to like a person born under this sign because he can appear easygoing and usually has a good sense of humor.

## The Negative Side of Gemini

Sometimes the Gemini person tries to do too many things at one time—and as a result, winds up finishing nothing. Some Twins are easily distracted and find it rather difficult to concentrate on one thing for too long a time. Sometimes they give in to trifling fancies and find it rather boring to become too serious about any one thing. Some of them are never dependable, no matter what they promise.

Although the Gemini man or woman often appears to be well-versed on many subjects, this is sometimes just a veneer. His knowledge may be only superficial, but because he speaks so well he gives people the impression of erudition. Some Geminis are sharp-tongued and inconsiderate; they think only of themselves and their own pleasure.

## Cancer: June 21–July 20

## The Positive Side of Cancer

The Moon Child's most positive point is his understanding nature. On the whole, he is a loving and sympathetic person. He would never go out of his way to hurt anyone. The Cancer man or woman is often very kind and tender; they give what they can to others. They hate to see others suffering and will do what they can to help someone in less fortunate circumstances than themselves. They are often very concerned about the world. Their interest in people generally goes beyond that of just their own families and close friends; they have a deep sense of community and respect humanitarian values. The Moon Child means what he says, as a rule; he is honest about his feelings.

The Cancer man or woman is a person who knows the art of patience. When something seems difficult, he is willing to wait until the situation becomes manageable again. He is a person who knows how to bide his time. Cancer knows how to concentrate on one thing at a time. When he has made his mind up he generally sticks with what he does, seeing it through to the end.

Cancer is a person who loves his home. He enjoys being surrounded by familiar things and the people he loves. Of all the signs, Cancer is the most maternal. Even the men born under this sign often have a motherly or protective quality about them. They like to take care of people in their family—to see that they are well loved and well provided for. They are usually loyal and faithful. Family ties mean a lot to the Cancer man or woman. Parents and in-laws are respected and loved. Young Cancer responds very well to adults who show faith in him. The Moon Child has a strong sense of tradition. He is very sensitive to the moods of others.

## The Negative Side of Cancer

Sometimes Cancer finds it rather hard to face life. It becomes too much for him. He can be a little timid and retiring, when things don't go too well. When unfortunate things happen, he is apt to just shrug and say, "Whatever will be will be." He can be fatalistic to a fault. The uncultivated Cancer is a bit lazy. He doesn't have very much ambition. Anything that seems a bit difficult he'll gladly leave to others. He may be lacking in initiative. Too sensitive, when he feels he's been injured, he'll crawl back into his shell and nurse his imaginary wounds. The immature Moon Child often is given to crying when the smallest thing goes wrong.

Some Cancers find it difficult to enjoy themselves in environments outside their homes. They make heavy demands on others, and need to be constantly reassured that they are loved. Lacking such reassurance, they may resort to sulking in silence.

# Leo: July 21–August 21

## The Positive Side of Leo

Often Leos make good leaders. They seem to be good organizers and administrators. Usually they are quite popular with others. Whatever group it is that they belong to, the Leo man or woman is almost sure to be or become the leader. Loyalty, one of the Lion's noblest traits, enables him or her to maintain this leadership position.

Leo is generous most of the time. It is his best characteristic. He or she likes to give gifts and presents. In making others happy, the Leo person becomes happy himself. He likes to splurge when spending money on others. In some instances it may seem that the Lion's generosity knows no boundaries. A hospitable person, the Leo man or woman is very fond of welcoming people to his house and entertaining them. He is never short of company.

Leo has plenty of energy and drive. He enjoys working toward some specific goal. When he applies himself correctly, he gets what he wants most often. The Leo person is almost never unsure of himself. He has plenty of confidence and aplomb. He is a person who is direct in almost everything he does. He has a quick mind and can make a decision in a very short time.

He usually sets a good example for others because of his ambitious manner and positive ways. He knows how to stick to something once he's started. Although Leo may be good at making a joke, he is not superficial or glib. He is a loving person, kind and thoughtful.

There is generally nothing small or petty about the Leo man or woman. He does what he can for those who are deserving. He is a person others can rely upon at all times. He means what he says. An honest person, generally speaking, he is a friend who is valued and sought out.

## The Negative Side of Leo

Leo, however, does have his faults. At times, he can be just a bit too arrogant. He thinks that no one deserves a leadership position except him. Only he is capable of doing things well. His opinion of himself is often much too high. Because of his conceit, he is

sometimes rather unpopular with a good many people. Some Leos are too materialistic; they can only think in terms of money and profit.

Some Leos enjoy lording it over others—at home or at their place of business. What is more, they feel they have the right to. Egocentric to an impossible degree, this sort of Leo cares little about how others think or feel. He can be rude and cutting.

# Virgo: August 22–September 22

## The Positive Side of Virgo

The person born under the sign of Virgo is generally a busy person. He knows how to arrange and organize things. He is a good planner. Above all, he is practical and is not afraid of hard work.

Often called the sign of the Harvester, Virgo knows how to attain what he desires. He sticks with something until it is finished. He never shirks his duties, and can always be depended upon. The Virgo person can be thoroughly trusted at all times.

The man or woman born under this sign tries to do everything to perfection. He doesn't believe in doing anything halfway. He always aims for the top. He is the sort of a person who is always learning and constantly striving to better himself—not because he wants more money or glory, but because it gives him a feeling of accomplishment.

The Virgo man or woman is a very observant person. He is sensitive to how others feel, and can see things below the surface of a situation. He usually puts this talent to constructive use.

It is not difficult for the Virgo to be open and earnest. He believes in putting his cards on the table. He is never secretive or underhanded. He's as good as his word. The Virgo person is generally plainspoken and down to earth. He has no trouble in expressing himself.

The Virgo person likes to keep up to date on new developments in his particular field. Well-informed, generally, he sometimes has a keen interest in the arts or literature. What he knows, he knows well. His ability to use his critical faculties is well-developed and sometimes startles others because of its accuracy.

Virgos adhere to a moderate way of life; they avoid excesses. Virgo is a responsible person and enjoys being of service.

# The Negative Side of Virgo

Sometimes a Virgo person is too critical. He thinks that only he can do something the way it should be done. Whatever anyone else does is inferior. He can be rather annoying in the way he quibbles over insignificant details. In telling others how things should be done, he can be rather tactless and mean.

Some Virgos seem rather emotionless and cool. They feel emotional involvement is beneath them. They are sometimes too tidy, too neat. With money they can be rather miserly. Some Virgos try to force their opinions and ideas on others.

# Libra: September 23–October 22

# The Positive Side of Libra

Libras love harmony. It is one of their most outstanding character traits. They are interested in achieving balance; they admire beauty and grace in things as well as in people. Generally speaking, they are kind and considerate people. Libras are usually very sympathetic. They go out of their way not to hurt another person's feelings. They are outgoing and do what they can to help those in need.

People born under the sign of Libra almost always make good friends. They are loyal and amiable. They enjoy the company of others. Many of them are rather moderate in their views; they believe in keeping an open mind, however, and weighing both sides of an issue fairly before making a decision.

Alert and intelligent, Libra, often known as the Lawgiver, is always fair-minded and tries to put himself in the position of the other person. They are against injustice; quite often they take up for the underdog. In most of their social dealings, they try to be tactful and kind. They dislike discord and bickering, and most Libras strive for peace and harmony in all their relationships.

The Libra man or woman has a keen sense of beauty. They appreciate handsome furnishings and clothes. Many of them are artistically inclined. Their taste is usually impeccable. They know how to use color. Their homes are almost always attractively arranged and inviting. They enjoy entertaining people and see to it that their guests always feel at home and welcome.

Libra gets along with almost everyone. He is well-liked and socially much in demand.

## The Negative Side of Libra

Some people born under this sign tend to be rather insincere. So eager are they to achieve harmony in all relationships that they will even go so far as to lie. Many of them are escapists. They find facing the truth an ordeal and prefer living in a world of make-believe.

In a serious argument, some Libras give in rather easily even when they know they are right. Arguing, even about something they believe in, is too unsettling for some of them.

Libras sometimes care too much for material things. They enjoy possessions and luxuries. Some are vain and tend to be jealous.

# Scorpio: October 23–November 22

## The Positive Side of Scorpio

The Scorpio man or woman generally knows what he or she wants out of life. He is a determined person. He sees something through to the end. Scorpio is quite sincere, and seldom says anything he doesn't mean. When he sets a goal for himself he tries to go about achieving it in a very direct way.

The Scorpion is brave and courageous. They are not afraid of hard work. Obstacles do not frighten them. They forge ahead until they achieve what they set out for. The Scorpio man or woman has a strong will.

Although Scorpio may seem rather fixed and determined, inside he is often quite tender and loving. He can care very much for others. He believes in sincerity in all relationships. His feelings about someone tend to last; they are profound and not superficial.

The Scorpio person is someone who adheres to his principles no matter what happens. He will not be deterred from a path he believes to be right.

Because of his many positive strengths, the Scorpion can often achieve happiness for himself and for those that he loves.

He is a constructive person by nature. He often has a deep understanding of people and of life, in general. He is perceptive and unafraid. Obstacles often seem to spur him on. He is a positive person who enjoys winning. He has many strengths and resources; challenge of any sort often brings out the best in him.

# The Negative Side of Scorpio

The Scorpio person is sometimes hypersensitive. Often he imagines injury when there is none. He feels that others do not bother to recognize him for his true worth. Sometimes he is given to excessive boasting in order to compensate for what he feels is neglect.

Scorpio can be proud, arrogant, and competitive. They can be sly when they put their minds to it and they enjoy outwitting persons or institutions noted for their cleverness.

Their tactics for getting what they want are sometimes devious and ruthless. They don't care too much about what others may think. If they feel others have done them an injustice, they will do their best to seek revenge. The Scorpion often has a sudden, violent temper; and this person's interest in sex is sometimes quite unbalanced or excessive.

# Sagittarius: November 23–December 20

## The Positive Side of Sagittarius

People born under this sign are honest and forthright. Their approach to life is earnest and open. Sagittarius is often quite adult in his way of seeing things. They are broad-minded and tolerant people. When dealing with others the person born under the sign of the Archer is almost always open and forthright. He doesn't believe in deceit or pretension. His standards are high. People who associate with Sagittarius generally admire and respect his tolerant viewpoint.

The Archer trusts others easily and expects them to trust him. He is never suspicious or envious and almost always thinks well of others. People always enjoy his company because he is so friendly and easygoing. The Sagittarius man or woman is often good-humored. He can always be depended upon by his friends, family, and co-workers.

The person born under this sign of the Zodiac likes a good joke every now and then. Sagittarius is eager for fun and laughs, which makes him very popular with others.

A lively person, he enjoys sports and outdoor life. The Archer is fond of animals. Intelligent and interesting, he can begin an ani-

mated conversation with ease. He likes exchanging ideas and discussing various views.

He is not selfish or proud. If someone proposes an idea or plan that is better than his, he will immediately adopt it. Imaginative yet practical, he knows how to put ideas into practice.

The Archer enjoys sport and games, and it doesn't matter if he wins or loses. He is a forgiving person, and never sulks over something that has not worked out in his favor.

He is seldom critical, and is almost always generous.

## The Negative Side of Sagittarius

Some Sagittarius are restless. They take foolish risks and seldom learn from the mistakes they make. They don't have heads for money and are often mismanaging their finances. Some of them devote much of their time to gambling.

Some are too outspoken and tactless, always putting their feet in their mouths. They hurt others carelessly by being honest at the wrong time. Sometimes they make promises which they don't keep. They don't stick close enough to their plans and go from one failure to another. They are undisciplined and waste a lot of energy.

# Capricorn: December 21–January 19

## The Positive Side of Capricorn

The person born under the sign of Capricorn, known variously as the Mountain Goat or Sea Goat, is usually very stable and patient. He sticks to whatever tasks he has and sees them through. He can always be relied upon and he is not averse to work.

An honest person, Capricorn is generally serious about whatever he does. He does not take his duties lightly. He is a practical person and believes in keeping his feet on the ground.

Quite often the person born under this sign is ambitious and knows how to get what he wants out of life. The Goat forges ahead and never gives up his goal. When he is determined about something, he almost always wins. He is a good worker—a hard worker. Although things may not come easy to him, he will not complain, but continue working until his chores are finished.

He is usually good at business matters and knows the value of money. He is not a spendthrift and knows how to put something away for a rainy day; he dislikes waste and unnecessary loss.

Capricorn knows how to make use of his self-control. He can apply himself to almost anything once he puts his mind to it. His ability to concentrate sometimes astounds others. He is diligent and does well when involved in detail work.

The Capricorn man or woman is charitable, generally speaking, and will do what is possible to help others less fortunate. As a friend, he is loyal and trustworthy. He never shirks his duties or responsibilities. He is self-reliant and never expects too much of the other fellow. He does what he can on his own. If someone does him a good turn, then he will do his best to return the favor.

## The Negative Side of Capricorn

Like everyone, Capricorn, too, has faults. At times, the Goat can be overcritical of others. He expects others to live up to his own high standards. He thinks highly of himself and tends to look down on others.

His interest in material things may be exaggerated. The Capricorn man or woman thinks too much about getting on in the world and having something to show for it. He may even be a little greedy.

He sometimes thinks he knows what's best for everyone. He is too bossy. He is always trying to organize and correct others. He may be a little narrow in his thinking.

# Aquarius: January 20–February 18

## The Positive Side of Aquarius

The Aquarius man or woman is usually very honest and forthright. These are his two greatest qualities. His standards for himself are generally very high. He can always be relied upon by others. His word is his bond.

Aquarius is perhaps the most tolerant of all the Zodiac personalities. He respects other people's beliefs and feels that everyone is entitled to his own approach to life.

He would never do anything to injure another's feelings. He is never unkind or cruel. Always considerate of others, the Water

Bearer is always willing to help a person in need. He feels a very strong tie between himself and all the other members of mankind.

The person born under this sign, called the Water Bearer, is almost always an individualist. He does not believe in teaming up with the masses, but prefers going his own way. His ideas about life and mankind are often quite advanced. There is a saying to the effect that the average Aquarius is fifty years ahead of his time.

Aquarius is community-minded. The problems of the world concern him greatly. He is interested in helping others no matter what part of the globe they live in. He is truly a humanitarian sort. He likes to be of service to others.

Giving, considerate, and without prejudice, Aquarius have no trouble getting along with others.

## The Negative Side of Aquarius

Aquarius may be too much of a dreamer. He makes plans but seldom carries them out. He is rather unrealistic. His imagination has a tendency to run away with him. Because many of his plans are impractical, he is always in some sort of a dither.

Others may not approve of him at all times because of his unconventional behavior. He may be a bit eccentric. Sometimes he is so busy with his own thoughts that he loses touch with the realities of existence.

Some Aquarius feel they are more clever and intelligent than others. They seldom admit to their own faults, even when they are quite apparent. Some become rather fanatic in their views. Their criticism of others is sometimes destructive and negative.

# Pisces: February 19–March 20

## The Positive Side of Pisces

Known as the sign of the Fishes, Pisces has a sympathetic nature. Kindly, he is often dedicated in the way he goes about helping others. The sick and the troubled often turn to him for advice and assistance. Possessing keen intuition, Pisces can easily understand people's deepest problems.

He is very broad-minded and does not criticize others for their faults. He knows how to accept people for what they are. On the whole, he is a trustworthy and earnest person. He is loyal to his friends and will do what he can to help them in time of need. Generous and good-natured, he is a lover of peace; he is often willing to help others solve their differences. People who have taken a wrong turn in life often interest him and he will do what he can to persuade them to rehabilitate themselves.

He has a strong intuitive sense and most of the time he knows how to make it work for him. Pisces is unusually perceptive and often knows what is bothering someone before that person, himself, is aware of it. The Pisces man or woman is an idealistic person, basically, and is interested in making the world a better place in which to live. Pisces believes that everyone should help each other. He is willing to do more than his share in order to achieve cooperation with others.

The person born under this sign often is talented in music or art. He is a receptive person; he is able to take the ups and downs of life with philosophic calm.

## The Negative Side of Pisces

Some Pisces are often depressed; their outlook on life is rather glum. They may feel that they have been given a bad deal in life and that others are always taking unfair advantage of them. Pisces sometimes feel that the world is a cold and cruel place. The Fishes can be easily discouraged. The Pisces man or woman may even withdraw from the harshness of reality into a secret shell of his own where he dreams and idles away a good deal of his time.

Pisces can be lazy. He lets things happen without giving the least bit of resistance. He drifts along, whether on the high road or on the low. He can be lacking in willpower.

Some Pisces people seek escape through drugs or alcohol. When temptation comes along they find it hard to resist. In matters of sex, they can be rather permissive.

# Sun Sign Personalities

**ARIES:** Hans Christian Andersen, Pearl Bailey, Marlon Brando, Wernher Von Braun, Charlie Chaplin, Joan Crawford, Da Vinci, Bette Davis, Doris Day, W. C. Fields, Alec Guinness, Adolf Hitler, William Holden, Thomas Jefferson, Nikita Khrushchev, Elton John, Arturo Toscanini, J. P. Morgan, Paul Robeson, Gloria Steinem, Sarah Vaughn, Vincent van Gogh, Tennessee Williams

**TAURUS:** Fred Astaire, Charlotte Brontë, Carol Burnett, Irving Berlin, Bing Crosby, Salvador Dali, Tchaikovsky, Queen Elizabeth II, Duke Ellington, Ella Fitzgerald, Henry Fonda, Sigmund Freud, Orson Welles, Joe Louis, Lenin, Karl Marx, Golda Meir, Eva Peron, Bertrand Russell, Shakespeare, Kate Smith, Benjamin Spock, Barbra Streisand, Shirley Temple, Harry Truman

**GEMINI:** Ruth Benedict, Josephine Baker, Rachel Carson, Carlos Chavez, Walt Whitman, Bob Dylan, Ralph Waldo Emerson, Judy Garland, Paul Gauguin, Allen Ginsberg, Benny Goodman, Bob Hope, Burl Ives, John F. Kennedy, Peggy Lee, Marilyn Monroe, Joe Namath, Cole Porter, Laurence Olivier, Harriet Beecher Stowe, Queen Victoria, John Wayne, Frank Lloyd Wright

**CANCER:** "Dear Abby," Lizzie Borden, David Brinkley, Yul Brynner, Pearl Buck, Marc Chagall, Princess Diana, Babe Didrikson, Mary Baker Eddy, Henry VIII, John Glenn, Ernest Hemingway, Lena Horne, Oscar Hammerstein, Helen Keller, Ann Landers, George Orwell, Nancy Reagan, Rembrandt, Richard Rodgers, Ginger Rogers, Rubens, Jean-Paul Sartre, O. J. Simpson

**LEO:** Neil Armstrong, James Baldwin, Lucille Ball, Emily Brontë, Wilt Chamberlain, Julia Child, William J. Clinton, Cecil B. De Mille, Ogden Nash, Amelia Earhart, Edna Ferber, Arthur Goldberg, Alfred Hitchcock, Mick Jagger, George Meany, Annie Oakley, George Bernard Shaw, Napoleon, Jacqueline Onassis, Henry Ford, Francis Scott Key, Andy Warhol, Mae West, Orville Wright

**VIRGO:** Ingrid Bergman, Warren Burger, Maurice Chevalier, Agatha Christie, Sean Connery, Lafayette, Peter Falk, Greta Garbo, Althea Gibson, Arthur Godfrey, Goethe, Buddy Hackett, Michael Jackson, Lyndon Johnson, D. H. Lawrence, Sophia Loren, Grandma Moses, Arnold Palmer, Queen Elizabeth I, Walter Reuther, Peter Sellers, Lily Tomlin, George Wallace

**LIBRA:** Brigitte Bardot, Art Buchwald, Truman Capote, Dwight D. Eisenhower, William Faulkner, F. Scott Fitzgerald, Gandhi, George Gershwin, Micky Mantle, Helen Hayes, Vladimir Horowitz, Doris Lessing, Martina Navratalova, Eugene O'Neill, Luciano Pavarotti, Emily Post, Eleanor Roosevelt, Bruce Springsteen, Margaret Thatcher, Gore Vidal, Barbara Walters, Oscar Wilde

**SCORPIO:** Vivien Leigh, Richard Burton, Art Carney, Johnny Carson, Billy Graham, Grace Kelly, Walter Cronkite, Marie Curie, Charles de Gaulle, Linda Evans, Indira Gandhi, Theodore Roosevelt, Rock Hudson, Katherine Hepburn, Robert F. Kennedy, Billie Jean King, Martin Luther, Georgia O'Keeffe, Pablo Picasso, Jonas Salk, Alan Shepard, Robert Louis Stevenson

**SAGITTARIUS:** Jane Austen, Louisa May Alcott, Woody Allen, Beethoven, Willy Brandt, Mary Martin, William F. Buckley, Maria Callas, Winston Churchill, Noel Coward, Emily Dickinson, Walt Disney, Benjamin Disraeli, James Doolittle, Kirk Douglas, Chet Huntley, Jane Fonda, Chris Evert Lloyd, Margaret Mead, Charles Schulz, John Milton, Frank Sinatra, Steven Spielberg

**CAPRICORN:** Muhammad Ali, Isaac Asimov, Pablo Casals, Dizzy Dean, Marlene Dietrich, James Farmer, Ava Gardner, Barry Goldwater, Cary Grant, J. Edgar Hoover, Howard Hughes, Joan of Arc, Gypsy Rose Lee, Martin Luther King, Jr., Rudyard Kipling, Mao Tse-tung, Richard Nixon, Gamal Nasser, Louis Pasteur, Albert Schweitzer, Stalin, Benjamin Franklin, Elvis Presley

**AQUARIUS:** Marian Anderson, Susan B. Anthony, Jack Benny, John Barrymore, Mikhail Baryshnikov, Charles Darwin, Charles Dickens, Thomas Edison, Clark Gable, Jascha Heifetz, Abraham Lincoln, Yehudi Menuhin, Mozart, Jack Nicklaus, Ronald Reagan, Jackie Robinson, Norman Rockwell, Franklin D. Roosevelt, Gertrude Stein, Charles Lindbergh, Margaret Truman

**PISCES:** Edward Albee, Harry Belafonte, Alexander Graham Bell, Chopin, Adelle Davis, Albert Einstein, Golda Meir, Jackie Gleason, Winslow Homer, Edward M. Kennedy, Victor Hugo, Mike Mansfield, Michelangelo, Edna St. Vincent Millay, Liza Minelli, John Steinbeck, Linus Pauling, Ravel, Renoir, Diana Ross, William Shirer, Elizabeth Taylor, George Washington

# The Signs and Their Key Words

|  |  | POSITIVE | NEGATIVE |
|---|---|---|---|
| ARIES | self | courage, initiative, pioneer instinct | brash rudeness, selfish impetuosity |
| TAURUS | money | endurance, loyalty, wealth | obstinacy, gluttony |
| GEMINI | mind | versatility | capriciousness, unreliability |
| CANCER | family | sympathy, homing instinct | clannishness, childishness |
| LEO | children | love, authority, integrity | egotism, force |
| VIRGO | work | purity, industry, analysis | faultfinding, cynicism |
| LIBRA | marriage | harmony, justice | vacillation, superficiality |
| SCORPIO | sex | survival, regeneration | vengeance, discord |
| SAGITTARIUS | travel | optimism, higher learning | lawlessness |
| CAPRICORN | career | depth | narrowness, gloom |
| AQUARIUS | friends | human fellowship, genius | perverse unpredictability |
| PISCES | confinement | spiritual love, universality | diffusion, escapism |

# The Elements and Qualities of The Signs

Every sign has both an *element* and a *quality* associated with it. The element indicates the basic makeup of the sign, and the quality describes the kind of activity associated with each.

| Element | Sign | Quality | Sign |
|---|---|---|---|
| FIRE | ARIES | CARDINAL | ARIES |
|  | LEO |  | LIBRA |
|  | SAGITTARIUS |  | CANCER |
|  |  |  | CAPRICORN |
| EARTH | TAURUS |  |  |
|  | VIRGO |  |  |
|  | CAPRICORN | FIXED | TAURUS |
|  |  |  | LEO |
|  |  |  | SCORPIO |
| AIR | GEMINI |  | AQUARIUS |
|  | LIBRA |  |  |
|  | AQUARIUS |  |  |
|  |  | MUTABLE | GEMINI |
| WATER | CANCER |  | VIRGO |
|  | SCORPIO |  | SAGITTARIUS |
|  | PISCES |  | PISCES |

Signs can be grouped together according to their element and quality. Signs of the same element share many basic traits in common. They tend to form stable configurations and ultimately harmonious relationships. Signs of the same quality are often less harmonious, but they share many dynamic potentials for growth as well as profound fulfillment.

Further discussion of each of these sign groupings is provided on the following pages.

# The Fire Signs

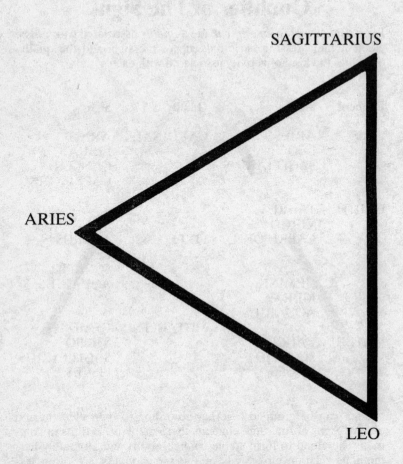

SAGITTARIUS

ARIES

LEO

This is the fire group. On the whole these are emotional, volatile types, quick to anger, quick to forgive. They are adventurous, powerful people and act as a source of inspiration for everyone. They spark into action with immediate exuberant impulses. They are intelligent, self-involved, creative, and idealistic. They all share a certain vibrancy and glow that outwardly reflects an inner flame and passion for living.

# The Earth Signs

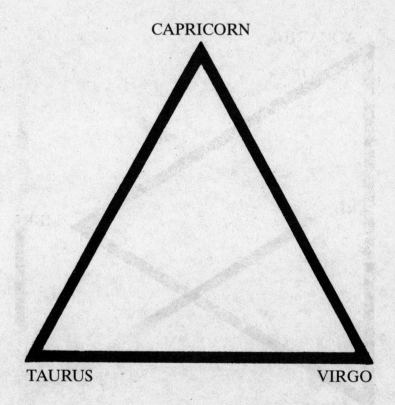

CAPRICORN

TAURUS                    VIRGO

This is the earth group. They are in constant touch with the material world and tend to be conservative. Although they are all capable of spartan self-discipline, they are earthy, sensual people who are stimulated by the tangible, elegant, and luxurious. The thread of their lives is always practical, but they do fantasize and are often attracted to dark, mysterious, emotional people. They are like great cliffs overhanging the sea, forever married to the ocean but always resisting erosion from the dark, emotional forces that thunder at their feet.

# The Air Signs

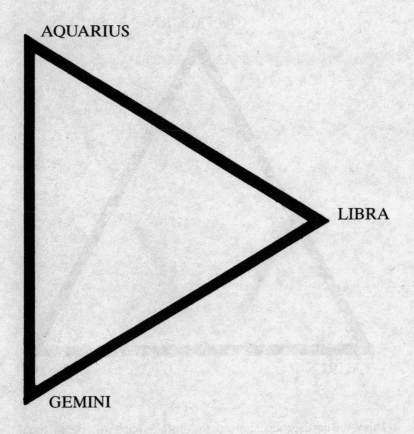

This is the air group. They are light, mental creatures desirous of contact, communication, and relationship. They are involved with people and the forming of ties on many levels. Original thinkers, they are the bearers of human news. Their language is their sense of word, color, style, and beauty. They provide an atmosphere suitable and pleasant for living. They add change and versatility to the scene, and it is through them that we can explore new territory of human intelligence and experience.

# The Water Signs

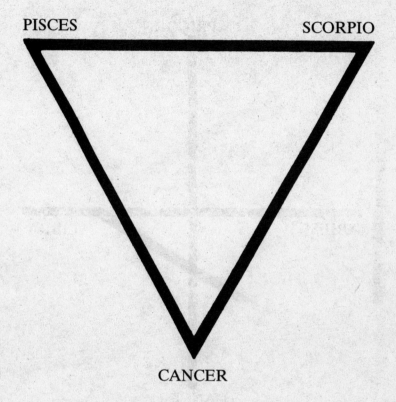

PISCES

SCORPIO

CANCER

This is the water group. Through the water people, we are all joined together on emotional, nonverbal levels. They are silent, mysterious types whose magic hypnotizes even the most determined realist. They have uncanny perceptions about people and are as rich as the oceans when it comes to feeling, emotion, or imagination. They are sensitive, mystical creatures with memories that go back beyond time. Through water, life is sustained. These people have the potential for the depths of darkness or the heights of mysticism and art.

# The Cardinal Signs

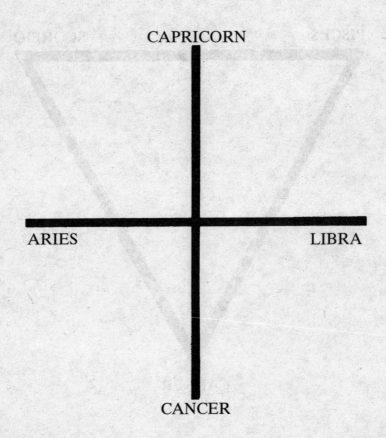

Put together, this is a clear-cut picture of dynamism, activity, tremendous stress, and remarkable achievement. These people know the meaning of great change since their lives are often characterized by significant crises and major successes. This combination is like a simultaneous storm of summer, fall, winter, and spring. The danger is chaotic diffusion of energy; the potential is irrepressible growth and victory.

# The Fixed Signs

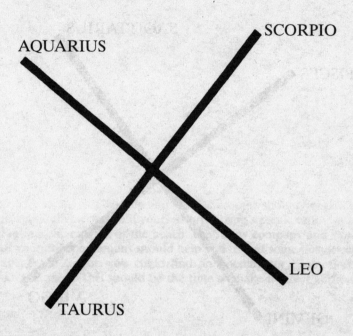

Fixed signs are always establishing themselves in a given place or area of experience. Like explorers who arrive and plant a flag, these people claim a position from which they do not enjoy being deposed. They are staunch, stalwart, upright, trusty, honorable people, although their obstinacy is well-known. Their contribution is fixity, and they are the angels who support our visible world.

# The Mutable Signs

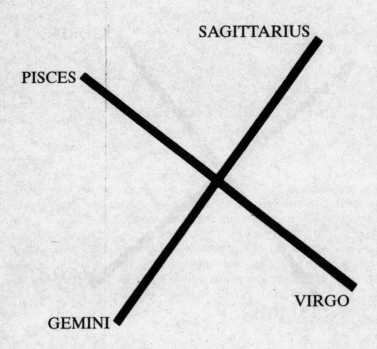

Mutable people are versatile, sensitive, intelligent, nervous, and deeply curious about life. They are the translators of all energy. They often carry out or complete tasks initiated by others. Combinations of these signs have highly developed minds; they are imaginative and jumpy and think and talk a lot. At worst their lives are a Tower of Babel. At best they are adaptable and ready creatures who can assimilate one kind of experience and enjoy it while anticipating coming changes.

# THE PLANETS
# OF THE SOLAR SYSTEM

This section describes the planets of the solar system. In astrology, both the Sun and the Moon are considered to be planets. Because of the Moon's influence in our day-to-day lives, the Moon is described in a separate section following this one.

## The Planets and the Signs
## They Rule

The signs of the Zodiac are linked to the planets in the following way. Each sign is governed or ruled by one or more planets. No matter where the planets are located in the sky at any given moment, they still rule their respective signs, and when they travel through the signs they rule, they have special dignity and their effects are stronger.

Following is a list of the planets and the signs they rule. After looking at the list, read the definitions of the planets and see if you can determine how the planet ruling *your* Sun sign has affected your life.

| SIGNS | RULING PLANETS |
|---|---|
| Aries | Mars, Pluto |
| Taurus | Venus |
| Gemini | Mercury |
| Cancer | Moon |
| Leo | Sun |
| Virgo | Mercury |
| Libra | Venus |
| Scorpio | Mars, Pluto |
| Sagittarius | Jupiter |
| Capricorn | Saturn |
| Aquarius | Saturn, Uranus |
| Pisces | Jupiter, Neptune |

# Characteristics of the Planets

The following pages give the meaning and characteristics of the planets of the solar system. They all travel around the Sun at different speeds and different distances. Taken with the Sun, they all distribute individual intelligence and ability throughout the entire chart.

The planets modify the influence of the Sun in a chart according to their own particular natures, strengths, and positions. Their positions must be calculated for each year and day, and their function and expression in a horoscope will change as they move from one area of the Zodiac to another.

We start with a description of the sun.

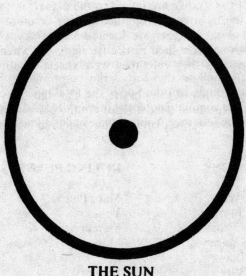

**THE SUN**

# SUN

This is the center of existence. Around this flaming sphere all the planets revolve in endless orbits. Our star is constantly sending out its beams of light and energy without which no life on Earth would be possible. In astrology it symbolizes everything we are trying to become, the center around which all of our activity in life will always revolve. It is the symbol of our basic nature and describes the natural and constant thread that runs through everything that we do from birth to death on this planet.

To early astrologers, the Sun seemed to be another planet because it crossed the heavens every day, just like the rest of the bodies in the sky.

It is the only star near enough to be seen well—it is, in fact, a dwarf star. Approximately 860,000 miles in diameter, it is about ten times as wide as the giant planet Jupiter. The next nearest star is nearly 300,000 times as far away, and if the Sun were located as far away as most of the bright stars, it would be too faint to be seen without a telescope.

Everything in the horoscope ultimately revolves around this singular body. Although other forces may be prominent in the charts of some individuals, still the Sun is the total nucleus of being and symbolizes the complete potential of every human being alive. It is vitality and the life force. Your whole essence comes from the position of the Sun.

You are always trying to express the Sun according to its position by house and sign. Possibility for all development is found in the Sun, and it marks the fundamental character of your personal radiations all around you.

It is the symbol of strength, vigor, wisdom, dignity, ardor, and generosity, and the ability for a person to function as a mature individual. It is also a creative force in society. It is consciousness of the gift of life.

The underdeveloped solar nature is arrogant, pushy, undependable, and proud, and is constantly using force.

## MERCURY

Mercury is the planet closest to the Sun. It races around our star, gathering information and translating it to the rest of the system. Mercury represents your capacity to understand the desires of your own will and to translate those desires into action.

In other words it is the planet of mind and the power of communication. Through Mercury we develop an ability to think, write, speak, and observe—to become aware of the world around us. It colors our attitudes and vision of the world, as well as our capacity to communicate our inner responses to the outside world. Some people who have serious disabilities in their power of verbal communication have often wrongly been described as people lacking intelligence.

Although this planet (and its position in the horoscope) indicates your power to communicate your thoughts and perceptions to the world, intelligence is something deeper. Intelligence is distributed throughout all the planets. It is the relationship of the planets to each other that truly describes what we call intelligence. Mercury rules speaking, language, mathematics, draft and design, students, messengers, young people, offices, teachers, and any pursuits where the mind of man has wings.

## VENUS

Venus is beauty. It symbolizes the harmony and radiance of a rare and elusive quality: beauty itself. It is refinement and delicacy, softness and charm. In astrology it indicates grace, balance, and the aesthetic sense. Where Venus is we see beauty, a gentle drawing in of energy and the need for satisfaction and completion. It is a special touch that finishes off rough edges. It is sensitivity, and affection, and it is always the place for that other elusive phenomenon: love. Venus describes our sense of what is beautiful and loving. Poorly developed, it is vulgar, tasteless, and self-indulgent. But its ideal is the flame of spiritual love—Aphrodite, goddess of love, and the sweetness and power of personal beauty.

## MARS

Mars is raw, crude energy. The planet next to Earth but outward from the Sun is a fiery red sphere that charges through the horoscope with force and fury. It represents the way you reach out for new adventure and new experience. It is energy and drive, initiative, courage, and daring. It is the power to start something and see it through. It can be thoughtless, cruel and wild, angry and hostile, causing cuts, burns, scalds, and wounds. It can stab its way through a chart, or it can be the symbol of healthy spirited adventure, well-channeled constructive power to begin and keep up the drive. If you have trouble starting things, if you lack the get-up-and-go to start the ball rolling, if you lack aggressiveness and self-confidence, chances are there's another planet influencing your Mars. Mars rules soldiers, butchers, surgeons, salesmen—any field that requires daring, bold skill, operational technique, or self-promotion.

## JUPITER

This is the largest planet of the solar system. Scientists have recently learned that Jupiter reflects more light than it receives from the Sun. In a sense it is like a star itself. In astrology it rules good luck and good cheer, health, wealth, optimism, happiness, success, and joy. It is the symbol of opportunity and always opens the way for new possibilities in your life. It rules exuberance, enthusiasm, wisdom, knowledge, generosity, and all forms of expansion in general. It rules actors, statesmen, clerics, professional people, religion, publishing, and the distribution of many people over large areas.

Sometimes Jupiter makes you think you deserve everything, and you become sloppy, wasteful, careless and rude, prodigal and lawless, in the illusion that nothing can ever go wrong. Then there is the danger of overconfidence, exaggeration, undependability, and overindulgence.

Jupiter is the minimization of limitation and the emphasis on spirituality and potential. It is the thirst for knowledge and higher learning.

## SATURN

Saturn circles our system in dark splendor with its mysterious rings, forcing us to be awakened to whatever we have neglected in the past. It will present real puzzles and problems to be solved, causing delays, obstacles, and hindrances. By doing so, Saturn stirs our own sensitivity to those areas where we are laziest.

Here we must patiently develop *method*, and only through painstaking effort can our ends be achieved. It brings order to a horoscope and imposes reason just where we are feeling least reasonable. By creating limitations and boundary, Saturn shows the consequences of being human and demands that we accept the changing cycles inevitable in human life. Saturn rules time, old age, and sobriety. It can bring depression, gloom, jealousy, and greed, or serious acceptance of responsibilities out of which success will develop. With Saturn there is nothing to do but face facts. It rules laborers, stones, granite, rocks, and crystals of all kinds.

## THE OUTER PLANETS:
## URANUS, NEPTUNE, PLUTO

Uranus, Neptune, Pluto are the outer planets. They liberate human beings from cultural conditioning, and in that sense are the law-breakers. In early times it was thought that Saturn was the last planet of the system—the outer limit beyond which we could never go. The discovery of the next three planets ushered in new phases of human history, revolution, and technology.

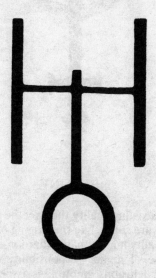

### URANUS

Uranus rules unexpected change, upheaval, revolution. It is the symbol of total independence and asserts the freedom of an individual from all restriction and restraint. It is a breakthrough planet and indicates talent, originality, and genius in a horoscope. It usually causes last-minute reversals and changes of plan, unwanted separations, accidents, catastrophes, and eccentric behavior. It can add irrational rebelliousness and perverse bohemianism to a personality or a streak of unaffected brilliance in science and art. It rules technology, aviation, and all forms of electrical and electronic advancement. It governs great leaps forward and topsy-turvy situations, and *always* turns things around at the last minute. Its effects are difficult to predict, since it rules sudden last-minute decisions and events that come like lightning out of the blue.

## NEPTUNE

Neptune dissolves existing reality the way the sea erodes the cliffs beside it. Its effects are subtle like the ringing of a buoy's bell in the fog. It suggests a reality higher than definition can usually describe. It awakens a sense of higher responsibility often causing guilt, worry, anxieties, or delusions. Neptune is associated with all forms of escape and can make things seem a certain way so convincingly that you are absolutely sure of something that eventually turns out to be quite different.

It is the planet of illusion and therefore governs the invisible realms that lie beyond our ordinary minds, beyond our simple factual ability to prove what is "real." Treachery, deceit, disillusionment, and disappointment are linked to Neptune. It describes a vague reality that promises eternity and the divine, yet in a manner so complex that we cannot really fathom it at all. At its worst Neptune is a cheap intoxicant; at its best it is the poetry, music, and inspiration of the higher planes of spiritual love. It has dominion over movies, photographs, and much of the arts.

## PLUTO

Pluto lies at the outpost of our system and therefore rules finality in a horoscope—the final closing of chapters in your life, the passing of major milestones and points of development from which there is no return. It is a final wipeout, a closeout, an evacuation. It is a distant, subtle but powerful catalyst in all transformations that occur. It creates, destroys, then recreates. Sometimes Pluto starts its influence with a minor event or insignificant incident that might even go unnoticed. Slowly but surely, little by little, everything changes, until at last there has been a total transformation in the area of your life where Pluto has been operating. It rules mass thinking and the trends that society first rejects, then adopts, and finally outgrows.

Pluto rules the dead and the underworld—all the powerful forces of creation and destruction that go on all the time beneath, around, and above us. It can bring a lust for power with strong obsessions.

It is the planet that rules the metamorphosis of the caterpillar into a butterfly, for it symbolizes the capacity to change totally and forever a person's lifestyle, way of thought, and behavior.

# THE MOON IN EACH SIGN

The Moon is the nearest planet to the Earth. It exerts more observable influence on us from day to day than any other planet. The effect is very personal, very intimate, and if we are not aware of how it works it can make us quite unstable in our ideas. And the annoying thing is that at these times we often see our own instability but can do nothing about it. A knowledge of what can be expected may help considerably. We can then be prepared to stand strong against the Moon's negative influences and use its positive ones to help us to get ahead. Who has not heard of going with the tide?

The Moon reflects, has no light of its own. It reflects the Sun—the life giver—in the form of vital movement. The Moon controls the tides, the blood rhythm, the movement of sap in trees and plants. Its nature is inconstancy and change so it signifies our moods, our superficial behavior—walking, talking, and especially thinking. Being a true reflector of other forces, the Moon is cold, watery like the surface of a still lake, brilliant and scintillating at times, but easily ruffled and disturbed by the winds of change.

The Moon takes about 27⅓ days to make a complete transit of the Zodiac. It spends just over 2¼ days in each sign. During that time it reflects the qualities, energies, and characteristics of the sign and, to a degree, the planet which rules the sign. When the Moon in its transit occupies a sign incompatible with our own birth sign, we can expect to feel a vague uneasiness, perhaps a touch of irritableness. We should not be discouraged nor let the feeling get us down, or, worse still, allow ourselves to take the discomfort out on others. Try to remember that the Moon has to change signs within 55 hours and, provided you are not physically ill, your mood will probably change with it. It is amazing how frequently depression lifts with the shift in the Moon's position. And, of course, when the Moon is transiting a sign compatible or sympathetic to yours, you will probably feel some sort of stimulation or just be plain happy to be alive.

In the horoscope, the Moon is such a powerful indicator that competent astrologers often use the sign it occupied at birth as the birth sign of the person. This is done particularly when the Sun is on the cusp, or edge, of two signs. Most experienced astrologers, however, coordinate both Sun and Moon signs by reading and confirming from one to the other and secure a far more accurate and personalized analysis.

For these reasons, the Moon tables which follow this section (see pages 86–92) are of great importance to the individual. They show the days and the exact times the Moon will enter each sign of the Zodiac for the year. Remember, you have to adjust the indicated times to local time. The corrections, already calculated for most of the main cities, are at the beginning of the tables. What follows now is a guide to the influences that will be reflected to the Earth by the Moon while it transits each of the twelve signs. The influence is at its peak about 26 hours after the Moon enters a sign. As you read the daily forecast, check the Moon sign for any given day and glance back at this guide.

## MOON IN ARIES
This is a time for action, for reaching out beyond the usual self-imposed limitations and faint-hearted cautions. If you have plans in your head or on your desk, put them into practice. New ventures, applications, new jobs, new starts of any kind—all have a good chance of success. This is the period when original and dynamic impulses are being reflected onto Earth. Such energies are extremely vital and favor the pursuit of pleasure and adventure in practically every form. Sick people should feel an improvement. Those who are well will probably find themselves exuding confidence and optimism. People fond of physical exercise should find their bodies growing with tone and well-being. Boldness, strength, determination should characterize most of your activities with a readiness to face up to old challenges. Yesterday's problems may seem petty and exaggerated—so deal with them. Strike out alone. Self-reliance will attract others to you. This is a good time for making friends. Business and marriage partners are more likely to be impressed with the man and woman of action. Opposition will be overcome or thrown aside with much less effort than usual. CAUTION: Be dominant but not domineering.

## MOON IN TAURUS
The spontaneous, action-packed person of yesterday gives way to the cautious, diligent, hardworking "thinker." In this period ideas will probably be concentrated on ways of improving finances. A great deal of time may be spent figuring out and going over

schemes and plans. It is the right time to be careful with detail. People will find themselves working longer than usual at their desks. Or devoting more time to serious thought about the future. A strong desire to put order into business and financial arrangements may cause extra work. Loved ones may complain of being neglected and may fail to appreciate that your efforts are for their ultimate benefit. Your desire for system may extend to criticism of arrangements in the home and lead to minor upsets. Health may be affected through overwork. Try to secure a reasonable amount of rest and relaxation, although the tendency will be to "keep going" despite good advice. Work done conscientiously in this period should result in a solid contribution to your future security. CAUTION: Try not to be as serious with people as the work you are engaged in.

## MOON IN GEMINI

The humdrum of routine and too much work should suddenly end. You are likely to find yourself in an expansive, quicksilver world of change and self-expression. Urges to write, to paint, to experience the freedom of some sort of artistic outpouring, may be very strong. Take full advantage of them. You may find yourself finishing something you began and put aside long ago. Or embarking on something new which could easily be prompted by a chance meeting, a new acquaintance, or even an advertisement. There may be a yearning for a change of scenery, the feeling to visit another country (not too far away), or at least to get away for a few days. This may result in short, quick journeys. Or, if you are planning a single visit, there may be some unexpected changes or detours on the way. Familiar activities will seem to give little satisfaction unless they contain a fresh element of excitement or expectation. The inclination will be toward untried pursuits, particularly those that allow you to express your inner nature. The accent is on new faces, new places. CAUTION: Do not be too quick to commit yourself emotionally.

## MOON IN CANCER

Feelings of uncertainty and vague insecurity are likely to cause problems while the Moon is in Cancer. Thoughts may turn frequently to the warmth of the home and the comfort of loved ones. Nostalgic impulses could cause you to bring out old photographs and letters and reflect on the days when your life seemed to be much more rewarding and less demanding. The love and understanding of parents and family may be important, and, if it is not forthcoming, you may have to fight against bouts of self-pity. The cordiality of friends and the thought of good times with them that are sure to be repeated will help to restore you to a happier frame of mind. The desire to be alone may follow minor setbacks or rebuffs at this time, but solitude is unlikely to help. Better to get on the telephone or visit someone. This period often causes peculiar dreams and upsurges of imaginative thinking which can be helpful to authors of occult and mystical works. Preoccupation with the personal world of simple human needs can overshadow any material strivings. CAUTION: Do not spend too much time thinking—seek the company of loved ones or close friends.

## MOON IN LEO
New horizons of exciting and rather extravagant activity open up. This is the time for exhilarating entertainment, glamorous and lavish parties, and expensive shopping sprees. Any merrymaking that relies upon your generosity as a host has every chance of being a spectacular success. You should find yourself right in the center of the fun, either as the life of the party or simply as a person whom happy people like to be with. Romance thrives in this heady atmosphere and friendships are likely to explode unexpectedly into serious attachments. Children and younger people should be attracted to you and you may find yourself organizing a picnic or a visit to a fun-fair, the movies, or the beach. The sunny company and vitality of youthful companions should help you to find some unsuspected energy. In career, you could find an opening for promotion or advancement. This should be the time to make a direct approach. The period favors those engaged in original research. CAUTION: Bask in popularity, not in flattery.

## MOON IN VIRGO
Off comes the party cap and out steps the busy, practical worker. He wants to get his personal affairs straight, to rearrange them, if necessary, for more efficiency, so he will have more time for more work. He clears up his correspondence, pays outstanding bills, makes numerous phone calls. He is likely to make inquiries, or sign up for some new insurance and put money into gilt-edged investment. Thoughts probably revolve around the need for future security—to tie up loose ends and clear the decks. There may be a tendency to be "finicky," to interfere in the routine of others, particularly friends and family members. The motive may be a genuine desire to help with suggestions for updating or streamlining their affairs, but these will probably not be welcomed. Sympathy may be felt for less fortunate sections of the community and a flurry of some sort of voluntary service is likely. This may be accompanied by strong feelings of responsibility on several fronts and health may suffer from extra efforts made. CAUTION: Everyone may not want your help or advice.

## MOON IN LIBRA

These are days of harmony and agreement and you should find yourself at peace with most others. Relationships tend to be smooth and sweet-flowing. Friends may become closer and bonds deepen in mutual understanding. Hopes will be shared. Progress by cooperation could be the secret of success in every sphere. In business, established partnerships may flourish and new ones get off to a good start. Acquaintances could discover similar interests that lead to congenial discussions and rewarding exchanges of some sort. Love, as a unifying force, reaches its optimum. Marriage partners should find accord. Those who wed at this time face the prospect of a happy union. Cooperation and tolerance are felt to be stronger than dissension and impatience. The argumentative are not quite so loud in their bellowings, nor as inflexible in their attitudes. In the home, there should be a greater recognition of the other point of view and a readiness to put the wishes of the group before selfish insistence. This is a favorable time to join an art group. CAUTION: Do not be too independent—let others help you if they want to.

## MOON IN SCORPIO

Driving impulses to make money and to economize are likely to cause upsets all around. No area of expenditure is likely to be spared the ax, including the household budget. This is a time when the desire to cut down on extravagance can become near fanatical. Care must be exercised to try to keep the aim in reasonable perspective. Others may not feel the same urgent need to save and may retaliate. There is a danger that possessions of sentimental value will be sold to realize cash for investment. Buying and selling of stock for quick profit is also likely. The attention turns to organizing, reorganizing, tidying up at home and at work. Neglected jobs could suddenly be done with great bursts of energy. The desire for solitude may intervene. Self-searching thoughts could disturb. The sense of invisible and mysterious energies in play could cause some excitability. The reassurance of loves ones may help. CAUTION: Be kind to the people you love.

## MOON IN SAGITTARIUS

These are days when you are likely to be stirred and elevated by discussions and reflections of a religious and philosophical nature. Ideas of faraway places may cause unusual response and excitement. A decision may be made to visit someone overseas, perhaps a person whose influence was important to your earlier character development. There could be a strong resolution to get away from present intellectual patterns, to learn new subjects, and to meet more interesting people. The superficial may be rejected in all its forms. An impatience with old ideas and unimaginative contacts could lead to a change of companions and interests. There may be an upsurge of religious feeling and metaphysical inquiry. Even a new insight into the significance of astrology and other occult studies is likely under the curious stimulus of the Moon in Sagittarius. Physically, you may express this need for fundamental change by spending more time outdoors: sports, gardening, long walks appeal. CAUTION: Try to channel any restlessness into worthwhile study.

## MOON IN CAPRICORN
Life in these hours may seem to pivot around the importance of gaining prestige and honor in the career, as well as maintaining a spotless reputation. Ambitious urges may be excessive and could be accompanied by quite acquisitive drives for money. Effort should be directed along strictly ethical lines where there is no possibility of reproach or scandal. All endeavors are likely to be characterized by great earnestness, and an air of authority and purpose which should impress those who are looking for leadership or reliability. The desire to conform to accepted standards may extend to sharp criticism of family members. Frivolity and unconventional actions are unlikely to amuse while the Moon is in Capricorn. Moderation and seriousness are the orders of the day. Achievement and recognition in this period could come through community work or organizing for the benefit of some amateur group. CAUTION: Dignity and esteem are not always self-awarded.

## MOON IN AQUARIUS
Moon in Aquarius is in the second last sign of the Zodiac where ideas can become disturbingly fine and subtle. The result is often a mental "no-man's land" where imagination cannot be trusted with the same certitude as other times. The dangers for the individual are the extremes of optimism and pessimism. Unless the imagination is held in check, situations are likely to be misread, and rosy conclusions drawn where they do not exist. Consequences for the unwary can be costly in career and business. Best to think twice and not speak or act until you think again. Pessimism can be a cruel self-inflicted penalty for delusion at this time. Between the two extremes are strange areas of self-deception which, for example, can make the selfish person think he is actually being generous. Eerie dreams which resemble the reality and even seem to continue into the waking state are also possible. CAUTION: Look for the fact and not just for the image in your mind.

**MOON IN PISCES**
Everything seems to come to the surface now. Memory may be crystal clear, throwing up long-forgotten information which could be valuable in the career or business. Flashes of clairvoyance and intuition are possible along with sudden realizations of one's own nature, which may be used for self-improvement. A talent, never before suspected, may be discovered. Qualities not evident before in friends and marriage partners are likely to be noticed. As this is a period in which the truth seems to emerge, the discovery of false characteristics is likely to lead to disenchantment or a shift in attachments. However, when qualities are accepted, it should lead to happiness and deeper feeling. Surprise solutions could bob up for old problems. There may be a public announcement of the solving of a crime or mystery. People with secrets may find someone has "guessed" correctly. The secrets of the soul or the inner self also tend to reveal themselves. Religious and philosophical groups may make some interesting discoveries. CAUTION: Not a time for activities that depend on secrecy.

NOTE: When you read your daily forecasts, use the Moon Sign Dates that are provided in the following section of Moon Tables. Then you may want to glance back here for the Moon's influence in a given sign.

# MOON TABLES

## CORRECTION FOR NEW YORK TIME, FIVE HOURS
## WEST OF GREENWICH

Atlanta, Boston, Detroit, Miami, Washington, Montreal,
  Ottawa, Quebec, Bogota, Havana, Lima, Santiago ... Same time
Chicago, New Orleans, Houston, Winnipeg, Churchill,
  Mexico City .................................. Deduct 1 hour
Albuquerque, Denver, Phoenix, El Paso, Edmonton,
  Helena ..................................... Deduct 2 hours
Los Angeles, San Francisco, Reno, Portland,
  Seattle, Vancouver ......................... Deduct 3 hours
Honolulu, Anchorage, Fairbanks, Kodiak ........ Deduct 5 hours
Nome, Samoa, Tonga, Midway ................. Deduct 6 hours
Halifax, Bermuda, San Juan, Caracas, La Paz,
  Barbados ..................................... Add 1 hour
St. John's, Brasilia, Rio de Janeiro, Sao Paulo,
  Buenos Aires, Montevideo ..................... Add 2 hours
Azores, Cape Verde Islands ...................... Add 3 hours
Canary Islands, Madeira, Reykjavik ............... Add 4 hours
London, Paris, Amsterdam, Madrid, Lisbon,
  Gibraltar, Belfast, Raba ...................... Add 5 hours
Frankfurt, Rome, Oslo, Stockholm, Prague,
  Belgrade ..................................... Add 6 hours
Bucharest, Beirut, Tel Aviv, Athens, Istanbul, Cairo,
  Alexandria, Cape Town, Johannesburg ........... Add 7 hours
Moscow, Leningrad, Baghdad, Dhahran,
  Addis Ababa, Nairobi, Teheran, Zanzibar ........ Add 8 hours
Bombay, Calcutta, Sri Lanka ...................... Add 10$\frac{1}{2}$
Hong Kong, Shanghai, Manila, Peking, Perth ...... Add 13 hours
Tokyo, Okinawa, Darwin, Pusan ................. Add 14 hours
Sydney, Melbourne, Port Moresby, Guam ......... Add 15 hours
Auckland, Wellington, Suva, Wake .............. Add 17 hours

# 2009 MOON SIGN DATES—
# NEW YORK TIME

## JANUARY
**Day Moon Enters**

1. Pisces
2. Pisces
3. Aries 4:51 am
4. Aries
5. Taurus 10:47 am
6. Taurus
7. Gemini 1:13 pm
8. Gemini
9. Cancer 1:15 pm
10. Cancer
11. Leo 12:42 pm
12. Leo
13. Virgo 1:34 pm
14. Virgo
15. Libra 5:31 pm
16. Libra
17. Libra
18. Scorp. 1:21 am
19. Scorp.
20. Sagitt. 12:31 pm
21. Sagitt.
22. Sagitt.
23. Capric. 1:19 am
24. Capric.
25. Aquar. 1:58 pm
26. Aquar.
27. Aquar.
28. Pisces 1:13 am
29. Pisces
30. Aries 10:26 am
31. Aries

## FEBRUARY
**Day Moon Enters**

1. Taurus 5:10 pm
2. Taurus
3. Gemini 9:16 pm
4. Gemini
5. Cancer 11:07 pm
6. Cancer
7. Leo 11:44 pm
8. Leo
9. Leo
10. Virgo 12:39 am
11. Virgo
12. Libra 3:34 am
13. Libra
14. Scorp. 9:52 am
15. Scorp.
16. Sagitt. 7:54 pm
17. Sagitt.
18. Sagitt.
19. Capric. 8:26 am
20. Capric.
21. Aquar. 9:07 pm
22. Aquar.
23. Aquar.
24. Pisces 8:01 am
25. Pisces
26. Aries 4:25 pm
27. Aries
28. Taurus 10:34 pm

## MARCH
**Day Moon Enters**

1. Taurus
2. Taurus
3. Gemini 3:00 pm
4. Gemini
5. Cancer 6:08 am
6. Cancer
7. Leo 8:25 am
8. Leo
9. Virgo 10:35 am
10. Virgo
11. Libra 1:47 pm
12. Libra
13. Scorp. 7:24 pm
14. Scorp.
15. Scorp.
16. Sagitt. 4:23 am
17. Sagitt.
18. Capric. 4:20 pm
19. Capric.
20. Capric.
21. Aquar. 5:08 am
22. Aquar.
23. Pisces 4:09 pm
24. Pisces
25. Pisces
26. Aries 12:04 am
27. Aries
28. Taurus 10:10 am
29. Taurus
30. Gemini 8:37 am
31. Gemini

**Daylight saving time to be considered where applicable.**

# 2009 MOON SIGN DATES— NEW YORK TIME

| APRIL | | MAY | | JUNE | |
|---|---|---|---|---|---|
| Day Moon Enters | | Day Moon Enters | | Day Moon Enters | |
| 1. Cancer | 11:31 am | 1. Leo | | 1. Libra | 10:18 am |
| 2. Cancer | | 2. Virgo | 11:38 pm | 2. Libra | |
| 3. Leo | 2:34 pm | 3. Virgo | | 3. Scorp. | 5:45 pm |
| 4. Leo | | 4. Virgo | | 4. Scorp. | |
| 5. Virgo | 6:02 pm | 5. Libra | 4:52 am | 5. Scorp. | |
| 6. Virgo | | 6. Libra | | 6. Sagitt. | 3:25 am |
| 7. Libra | 10:23 pm | 7. Scorp. | 11:49 am | 7. Sagitt. | |
| 8. Libra | | 8. Scorp. | | 8. Capric. | 3:01 pm |
| 9. Libra | | 9. Sagitt. | 8:50 pm | 9. Capric. | |
| 10. Scorp. | 4:24 am | 10. Sagitt. | | 10. Capric. | |
| 11. Scorp. | | 11. Sagitt. | | 11. Aquar. | 3:54 am |
| 12. Sagitt. | 1:02 pm | 12. Capric. | 8:10 am | 12. Aquar. | |
| 13. Sagitt. | | 13. Capric. | | 13. Pisces | 4:33 pm |
| 14. Sagitt. | | 14. Aquar. | 9:02 pm | 14. Pisces | |
| 15. Capric. | 12:28 am | 15. Aquar. | | 15. Pisces | |
| 16. Capric. | | 16. Aquar. | | 16. Aries | 2:53 am |
| 17. Aquar. | 1:20 pm | 17. Pisces | 9:18 am | 17. Aries | |
| 18. Aquar. | | 18. Pisces | | 18. Taurus | 9:21 am |
| 19. Aquar. | | 19. Aries | 6:31 pm | 19. Taurus | |
| 20. Pisces | 12:56 am | 20. Aries | | 20. Gemini | 12:01 pm |
| 21. Pisces | | 21. Taurus | 11:41 pm | 21. Gemini | |
| 22. Aries | 9:10 am | 22. Taurus | | 22. Cancer | 12:13 pm |
| 23. Aries | | 23. Taurus | | 23. Cancer | |
| 24. Taurus | 1:47 pm | 24. Gemini | 1:35 am | 24. Leo | 11:51 pm |
| 25. Taurus | | 25. Gemini | | 25. Leo | |
| 26. Gemini | 4:03 pm | 26. Cancer | 1:59 am | 26. Virgo | 12:48 pm |
| 27. Gemini | | 27. Cancer | | 27. Virgo | |
| 28. Cancer | 5:39 pm | 28. Leo | 2:45 am | 28. Libra | 4:26 pm |
| 29. Cancer | | 29. Leo | | 29. Libra | |
| 30. Leo | 7:57 pm | 30. Virgo | 5:19 am | 30. Scorp. | 11:20 pm |
| | | 31. Virgo | | | |

**Daylight saving time to be considered where applicable.**

# 2009 MOON SIGN DATES—
# NEW YORK TIME

| JULY Day Moon Enters | | AUGUST Day Moon Enters | | SEPTEMBER Day Moon Enters | |
|---|---|---|---|---|---|
| 1. Scorp. | | 1. Sagitt. | | 1. Aquar. | |
| 2. Scorp. | | 2. Capric. | 3:09 am | 2. Aquar. | |
| 3. Sagitt. | 9:12 am | 3. Capric. | | 3. Pisces | 10:59 am |
| 4. Sagitt. | | 4. Aquar. | 5:09 pm | 4. Pisces | |
| 5. Capric. | 9:09 pm | 5. Aquar. | | 5. Aries | 9:15 pm |
| 6. Capric. | | 6. Aquar. | | 6. Aries | |
| 7. Capric. | | 7. Pisces | 4:35 pm | 7. Aries | |
| 8. Aquar. | 10:04 am | 8. Pisces | | 8. Taurus | 5:19 am |
| 9. Aquar. | | 9. Aries | 3:24 pm | 9. Taurus | |
| 10. Pisces | 10:45 pm | 10. Aries | | 10. Gemini | 11:18 am |
| 11. Pisces | | 11. Taurus | 11:51 pm | 11. Gemini | |
| 12. Pisces | | 12. Taurus | | 12. Cancer | 3:21 pm |
| 13. Aries | 9:41 am | 13. Taurus | | 13. Cancer | |
| 14. Aries | | 14. Gemini | 5:27 am | 14. Leo | 5:40 pm |
| 15. Taurus | 5:31 pm | 15. Gemini | | 15. Leo | |
| 16. Taurus | | 16. Cancer | 8:14 am | 16. Virgo | 6:57 pm |
| 17. Gemini | 9:42 pm | 17. Cancer | | 17. Virgo | |
| 18. Gemini | | 18. Leo | 8:58 am | 18. Libra | 8:27 pm |
| 19. Cancer | 10:52 pm | 19. Leo | | 19. Libra | |
| 20. Cancer | | 20. Virgo | 9:02 am | 20. Scorp. | 11:53 pm |
| 21. Leo | 10:29 pm | 21. Virgo | | 21. Scorp. | |
| 22. Leo | | 22. Libra | 10:13 am | 22. Scorp. | |
| 23. Virgo | 10:24 pm | 23. Libra | | 23. Sagitt. | 6:44 am |
| 24. Virgo | | 24. Scorp. | 2:17 pm | 24. Sagitt. | |
| 25. Virgo | | 25. Scorp. | | 25. Capric. | 5:20 pm |
| 26. Libra | 12:27 am | 26. Sagitt. | 10:17 pm | 26. Capric. | |
| 27. Libra | | 27. Sagitt. | | 27. Capric. | |
| 28. Scorp. | 5:57 am | 28. Sagitt. | | 28. Aquar. | 6:08 am |
| 29. Scorp. | | 29. Capric. | 9:45 am | 29. Aquar. | |
| 30. Sagitt. | 3:11 pm | 30. Capric. | | 30. Pisces | 6:27 pm |
| 31. Sagitt. | | 31. Aquar. | 10:44 pm | | |

**Daylight saving time to be considered where applicable.**

# 2009 MOON SIGN DATES—
## NEW YORK TIME

| OCTOBER Day Moon Enters | | NOVEMBER Day Moon Enters | | DECEMBER Day Moon Enters | |
|---|---|---|---|---|---|
| 1. Pisces | | 1. Taurus | 7:46 pm | 1. Gemini | 9:25 am |
| 2. Pisces | | 2. Taurus | | 2. Gemini | |
| 3. Aries | 4:22 am | 3. Gemini | 11:54 pm | 3. Cancer | 11:02 am |
| 4. Aries | | 4. Gemini | | 4. Cancer | |
| 5. Taurus | 11:34 am | 5. Gemini | | 5. Leo | 12:06 pm |
| 6. Taurus | | 6. Cancer | 2:44 am | 6. Leo | |
| 7. Gemini | 4:48 pm | 7. Cancer | | 7. Virgo | 2:07 pm |
| 8. Gemini | | 8. Leo | 5:24 am | 8. Virgo | |
| 9. Cancer | 8:49 pm | 9. Leo | | 9. Libra | 5:48 pm |
| 10. Cancer | | 10. Virgo | 8:31 am | 10. Libra | |
| 11. Cancer | | 11. Virgo | | 11. Scorp. | 11:33 pm |
| 12. Leo | 12:04 am | 12. Libra | 12:23 pm | 12. Scorp. | |
| 13. Leo | | 13. Libra | | 13. Scorp. | |
| 14. Virgo | 2:46 am | 14. Scorp. | 5:25 pm | 14. Sagitt. | 7:26 am |
| 15. Virgo | | 15. Scorp. | | 15. Sagitt. | |
| 16. Libra | 5:31 am | 16. Scorp. | | 16. Capric. | 5:33 pm |
| 17. Libra | | 17. Sagitt. | 12:23 am | 17. Capric. | |
| 18. Scorp. | 9:24 am | 18. Sagitt. | | 18. Capric. | |
| 19. Scorp. | | 19. Capric. | 10:02 am | 19. Aquar. | 5:40 am |
| 20. Sagitt. | 3:50 pm | 20. Capric. | | 20. Aquar. | |
| 21. Sagitt. | | 21. Aquar. | 10:12 pm | 21. Pisces | 6:43 pm |
| 22. Sagitt. | | 22. Aquar. | | 22. Pisces | |
| 23. Capric. | 1:40 am | 23. Aquar. | | 23. Pisces | |
| 24. Capric. | | 24. Pisces | 11:09 am | 24. Aries | 6:41 am |
| 25. Aquar. | 2:09 pm | 25. Pisces | | 25. Aries | |
| 26. Aquar. | | 26. Aries | 10:12 pm | 26. Taurus | 3:27 pm |
| 27. Aquar. | | 27. Aries | | 27. Taurus | |
| 28. Pisces | 2:46 am | 28. Aries | | 28. Gemini | 8:14 pm |
| 29. Pisces | | 29. Taurus | 5:35 am | 29. Gemini | |
| 30. Aries | 12:58 pm | 30. Taurus | | 30. Cancer | 9:46 pm |
| 31. Aries | | | | 31. Cancer | |

**Daylight saving time to be considered where applicable.**

## 2009 PHASES OF THE MOON— NEW YORK TIME

| New Moon | First Quarter | Full Moon | Last Quarter |
|---|---|---|---|
| Dec. 27 ('08) | Jan. 4 | Jan. 10 | Jan. 17 |
| Jan. 26 | Feb. 2 | Feb. 9 | Feb. 16 |
| Feb. 24 | March 4 | March 10 | March 18 |
| March 26 | April 2 | April 9 | April 17 |
| April 24 | May 1 | May 9 | May 17 |
| May 24 | May 30 | June 7 | June 15 |
| June 22 | June 29 | July 7 | July 15 |
| July 21 | July 28 | August 5 | August 13 |
| August 20 | August 27 | Sept. 4 | Sept. 11 |
| Sept. 18 | Sept. 26 | Oct. 4 | Oct. 11 |
| Oct. 18 | Oct. 25 | Nov. 2 | Nov. 9 |
| Nov. 16 | Nov. 24 | Dec. 2 | Dec. 8 |
| Dec. 15 | Dec. 24 | Dec. 31 | Jan. 7 ('10) |

Each phase of the Moon lasts approximately seven to eight days, during which the Moon's shape gradually changes as it comes out of one phase and goes into the next.

There will be a solar eclipse during the New Moon phase on January 26 and July 21.

There will be a lunar eclipse during the Full Moon phase on February 9, July 7, August 5, and December 31.

## 2009 FISHING GUIDE

| | Good | Best |
|---|---|---|
| January | 4-8-9-11-12-13-14-26 | 10-18 |
| February | 8-9-10-11-17 | 2-6-7-25 |
| March | 4-9-10-11-19-26 | 12-13-14-15 |
| April | 7-8-13-17-18 | 2-8-9-10-11-25 |
| May | 1-10-11-17-24-31 | 5-6-7-8-9 |
| June | 6-7-8-16-22 | 4-5-9-10-29 |
| July | 4-5-8-9-10-15-21 | 6-7-28 |
| August | 4-5-6-20-27 | 2-3-7-8-13 |
| September | 2-3-6-7-8-11 | 4-5-19-26 |
| October | 1-3-4-5-7-26-31 | 2-6-11-18-29 |
| November | 1-4-5-9-16-29 | 2-3-25-30 |
| December | 1-2-3-5-9-16-25-29-30 | 4-27-31 |

## 2009 PLANTING GUIDE

|  | Aboveground Crops | Root Crops |
|---|---|---|
| January | 1-2-6-10-29 | 16-17-18-19-23-24 |
| February | 2-3-6-7-24-25 | 12-13-14-15-20-21 |
| March | 1-2-5-6-29 | 13-14-15-16-19-20-24-25 |
| April | 2-8-9-25-29-30 | 10-11-15-16-21 |
| May | 5-6-7-8-26-27 | 13-14-18-19-22-23 |
| June | 2-3-4-5-23-29-30 | 9-10-14-15-19 |
| July | 1-2-6-27-28-29 | 7-11-16-17-20-21 |
| August | 2-3-23-24-25-26-30 | 7-8-12-13-17 |
| September | 4-19-20-21-22-26-27 | 5-9-13 |
| October | 2-18-19-23-24-28-29 | 6-10-11-17 |
| November | 2-19-20-25-30 | 3-6-7-13-14-15-16 |
| December | 17-18-22-23-27-28 | 4-10-11-12-13 |

|  | Pruning | Weeds and Pests |
|---|---|---|
| January | 18-10 | 12-13-14-15-21-22 |
| February | 14-15 | 1-11-17-18-22 |
| March | 14-15-24-25 | 16-17-21-22 |
| April | 10-11-21 | 13-14-18-23 |
| May | 17-18 | 10-11-15-16-20-21 |
| June | 14-15 | 11-12-17-21 |
| July | 12-20-21 | 9-10-13-14-18-19 |
| August | 8-9-17 | 10-11-14-15-19 |
| September | 4-13 | 6-7-11-15-16-17 |
| October | 10-11 | 8-12-13-14-15 |
| November | 6-7-15-16 | 4-5-8-9-10-11 |
| December | 4-12-13 | 1-5-6-7-8-14-15 |

## MOON'S INFLUENCE OVER PLANTS

Centuries ago it was established that seeds planted when the Moon is in signs and phases called Fruitful will produce more growth than seeds planted when the Moon is in a Barren sign.
**Fruitful Signs:** Taurus, Cancer, Libra, Scorpio, Capricorn, Pisces
**Barren Signs:** Aries, Gemini, Leo, Virgo, Sagittarius, Aquarius
**Dry Signs:** Aries, Gemini, Sagittarius, Aquarius

| Activity | Moon In |
|---|---|
| Mow lawn, trim plants | **Fruitful sign:** 1st & 2nd quarter |
| Plant flowers | **Fruitful sign:** 2nd quarter; best in Cancer and Libra |
| Prune | **Fruitful sign:** 3rd & 4th quarter |
| Destroy pests; spray | **Barren sign:** 4th quarter |
| Harvest potatoes, root crops | **Dry sign:** 3rd & 4th quarter; Taurus, Leo, and Aquarius |

# MOON'S INFLUENCE OVER YOUR HEALTH

| | |
|---|---|
| ARIES | Head, brain, face, upper jaw |
| TAURUS | Throat, neck, lower jaw |
| GEMINI | Hands, arms, lungs, shoulders, nervous system |
| CANCER | Esophagus, stomach, breasts, womb, liver |
| LEO | Heart, spine |
| VIRGO | Intestines, liver |
| LIBRA | Kidneys, lower back |
| SCORPIO | Sex and eliminative organs |
| SAGITTARIUS | Hips, thighs, liver |
| CAPRICORN | Skin, bones, teeth, knees |
| AQUARIUS | Circulatory system, lower legs |
| PISCES | Feet, tone of being |

Try to avoid work being done on that part of the body when the Moon is in the sign governing that part.

# MOON'S INFLUENCE OVER DAILY AFFAIRS

The Moon makes a complete transit of the Zodiac every 27 days 7 hours and 43 minutes. In making this transit the Moon forms different aspects with the planets and consequently has favorable or unfavorable bearings on affairs and events for persons according to the sign of the Zodiac under which they were born.

When the Moon is in conjunction with the Sun it is called a New Moon; when the Moon and Sun are in opposition it is called a Full Moon. From New Moon to Full Moon, first and second quarter— which takes about two weeks—the Moon is increasing or waxing. From Full Moon to New Moon, third and fourth quarter, the Moon is decreasing or waning.

| Activity | Moon In |
|---|---|
| Business: buying and selling new, requiring public support | Sagittarius, Aries, Gemini, Virgo 1st and 2nd quarter |
| meant to be kept quiet | 3rd and 4th quarter |
| Investigation | 3rd and 4th quarter |
| Signing documents | 1st & 2nd quarter, Cancer, Scorpio, Pisces |
| Advertising | 2nd quarter, Sagittarius |
| Journeys and trips | 1st & 2nd quarter, Gemini, Virgo |
| Renting offices, etc. | Taurus, Leo, Scorpio, Aquarius |
| Painting of house/apartment | 3rd & 4th quarter, Taurus, Scorpio, Aquarius |
| Decorating | Gemini, Libra, Aquarius |
| Buying clothes and accessories | Taurus, Virgo |
| Beauty salon or barber shop visit | 1st & 2nd quarter, Taurus, Leo, Libra, Scorpio, Aquarius |
| Weddings | 1st & 2nd quarter |

*Aquarius*

# AQUARIUS

## Character Analysis

Of all the signs of the Zodiac, Aquarius is perhaps the most progressive. People born under this sign are usually quite tolerant and broad-minded. As a rule they are unselfish and peace-loving. They are often more interested in helping others than they are in helping themselves.

This eleventh sign of the Zodiac is often known as the Water Bearer, which is the symbol for Aquarius. Aquarius pours the water of life and intelligence for humanity to drink. Aquarius thinks of humanity on a very broad scale and is interested in justice for all. All the wrongs that exist in the world appall these men and women. They may spend a lifetime trying to set things right in their own way.

Aquarius does not believe in hanging onto old, useless values. By definition the Water Bearer is for progress, for moving ahead and making a better world. It is important that peace and harmony exist in all social situations. Aquarius will accept nothing less than that.

Anything connected with the betterment of mankind interests Aquarius individuals. They are likely to have a useful hobby. In short, they have a purpose in mind. General education methods and sociology are very appealing to the Water Bearer. They do not believe that mankind should be divided into rich and poor. They feel that everyone should be entitled to the same privileges regardless of background.

More often than not, Aquarius individuals have an intellectual nature. They usually know a lot about many things and they are sure of what they know. There is nothing superficial about them. They are eager to impart what they know.

To them, it is more important to have a good mind than a full stomach. Aquarius probably feels that people will eat out of necessity, but that their mind must be properly trained in order to enjoy all that life has to offer. Aquarius holds that the world would be a better place if all people were intellectually responsible.

Aquarius men and women are years ahead of time in way of thinking. Others often find it hard to keep up with them. They are not afraid of change; on the contrary, they welcome it. New ways of living are always of interest.

The person born under this eleventh sign of the Zodiac is eager to develop along creative lines, to generate new forms of organization or thought. Even in love matters, they tend to be creative. To some they may seem slightly mad, to others they appear to have a touch of genius.

Aquarius is interested in groups—how they are structured, their behavioral patterns, and so on. They enjoy bringing people together. They want to see everyone living in peace and harmony. The individual is not the central focus for them. They think in terms of masses of people as the focal point for change.

Aquarius is a master of surprise and unpredictability. He or she always keeps other people guessing. At times, Aquarius individuals do not even know themselves what their next step in life will be.

They sometimes seem detached, impersonal, disengaged. They may be accused of sizing up everyone around them and making mental notes. But Aquarius men and women really believe in a live-and-let-live approach as an all-around way of getting on in the world.

Aquarius men and women would never try to dominate another person. They respect people for their individuality. They believe in letting people express themselves as they wish. They do not feel they have the right to direct another's lifestyle.

People find it hard to classify or categorize Aquarius. He or she seems so full of contradictions that it's difficult to say with certainty they are one thing or the other.

Aquarius men and women usually have their own set of laws to live by. Conventional rules and regulations, they feel, need not apply to them. They have their own rights and wrongs. To the average person Aquarius may seem downright unconventional, trying to gain attention by shock tactics of any kind. But this is far from the truth.

Aquarius men and women do not believe in poses. They believe in what they do and accomplish. The customs and dress of the average person say little to Aquarius. They may find it necessary to develop their own way of behaving and dressing in order to express their real nature. Every Aquarius is an individualist. Original modes of behavior and thinking are the lifeline of their survival.

Their minds are always generating interesting ideas and plans. Because Aquarius men and women are often so busy turning things over in their heads, they are apt to seem dreamy and out of it. At times, Aquarius set their hopes and expectations so high that they have to suffer the consequences of being unrealistic.

# Health

On the whole, people born under the sign of Aquarius are good to look at. They may be slight of build, yet they are strong in a wiry sort of way. They have a strong resistance against illnesses, generally. They are healthy, for the most part, and know how to take care of themselves. They are usually interested in hygiene and safety. They take all sorts of precautions so that disease never has a chance to strike them. Physically they have little to worry about. Their constitutions are strong and healthy.

Tensions and pressure, however, can cause them to become depressed, and this often has a bad effect on their overall health. But this is generally rare, for Aquarius men and women have the ability to remove themselves from things that are disturbing. They can look at anything in an objective way so that it does not really affect their spiritual balance.

It is important for Aquarius to oppose anyone who tries to dominate or drive them into a corner. They cannot allow someone to encroach upon their freedom. The strain of someone bearing down on them can have a bad influence on their well-being.

At times, disturbing conditions in the environment can make Aquarius so uptight that they are prone to nervousness. Aquarius men and women must see to it that have get the proper amount of vitamins and minerals to help counteract nervousness and anxiety. They should follow a well-balanced diet containing plenty of fresh fruit and vegetables. It is not unusual for many Aquarius to become strict vegetarians later in life.

These men and women also need peace and quiet alone a lot of the time. Being an air sign, they must have plenty of fresh air. A country place where they can retreat when the going gets rough would be ideal. Harmonious surroundings are a must.

Still and all, Aquarius men and women will not back away when someone criticizes their ideals. They will stand up for what they believe. Their objective and forthright manner will protect them from injury on many occasions.

State of mind is vital to Aquarius health. They can train themselves in mind control to some extent. So when they encounter a disturbance or setback, it does not affect them too much.

The weak parts of the Aquarius body are the ankles and calves. If there is an accident or mishap, often these areas are affected. Nervous and circulatory disorders sometimes are chronic. The Aquarius who is not careful may become the victim of low blood pressure and anemia. By taking the proper vitamins and eating the proper food, Aquarius can prevent these ailments.

# Occupation

The kind of occupation that generally interests someone born under the sign of Aquarius is work that has a bit of idealism to it—

a job that has a philosophical outlook. It is important that these men and women have jobs suited to their particular talents and character. If it is not exactly their kind of work, then it must be open-ended enough so that they can mold it to fit their particular needs.

Aquarius men and women have to be creative in their work. Suggestions and new techniques will keep them motivated. Quite often their place of business profits if they are allowed to approach the duties of their position in a creative manner.

Aquarius enjoys keeping busy. They believe in rolling up their sleeves and getting down to brass tacks immediately. They do not like to waste time when working. Quite often they are quicker than the people they work with and can finish their job in half the time it takes others to do it. They are energetic and enthusiastic in what they do. Many of their suggestions for improvements on the job are helpful. They are usually a great source of inspiration for co-workers. Responsibility does not frighten Aquarius, but they would rather not take orders from someone else.

Quite often the mind of an Aquarius is turning over new plans and ideas, even while he or she is busy at work. Their thoughts never rest. They are inventive in their way of thinking. Quite often the results of their mental endeavors benefit everyone. They are intrigued by things that are new and different. They are not afraid to try out a new work technique or method. They believe in experimentation and change.

Routine work is not apt to hold their interest for very long. Aquarius men and women like unusual tasks, something that gives them a chance to do an assignment on their own. If they are tied down to a humdrum kind of job, they are not likely to be motivated to do their best.

An employer may find Aquarius a bit difficult and unreliable. Without a challenge and facing the same old thing, they are apt to work in spurts and their attention can be easily distracted. If their work is dull, they might begin it with a bang in an attempt to get it out of the way soon as possible. But later their energy is likely to peter out, and they may even allow themselves to become careless.

If co-workers and colleagues are slow and unimaginative, Aquarius is apt to become restless and impatient. When teammates and associates do not make any effort to better themselves, the Aquarius man or woman will become scornful and keep a distance.

Social work is an occupation well suited to Aquarius. Most Water Bearers are more concerned for other people than for themselves. Their self-sacrificing way is reassuring. People under their care or counsel trust Aquarius to do what is best. Water Bearers also do well in rehabilitation work. They like to help people help themselves. Any kind of service work is ideal and often earns Aquarius men and women notable honors.

Aquarius men and women make good writers and journalists. They have sharp, acute minds. They know how to translate their thoughts into the appropriate medium so that other people can benefit from them.

Art and all things related to culture attract the average Aquarius. Some of them make good painters and musicians. They know how to be critical in a constructive way. Often they make good art or music critics.

It is important for Aquarius to put their heart and soul into their creative work if they want to attain the high goals they set. They can do well in any job where they are allowed to make use of their rich imagination. In strict business matters, they may not be able to function very well due to a tendency to dream. Some Aquarius, in spite of their good intentions, only plan during their lives and never get around to putting their ideas into action. Then when things get to be too much for them, they allow their plans to slide.

Money to the average Aquarius is nice to have for what it can do. Money in itself has little interest for them. Aquarius is neither a splurger nor a penny-pincher. They generally make use of their finances in what they feel is a practical way. They may use some of it to make progress for themselves and others easier.

Some Aquarius come by money through their inventions or discoveries. They may work night and day for a long period of time before coming up with the answer or solution of a problem. However, this sort of research or investigatory work generally intrigues them.

Aquarius is the kind of person who will work hard for success, but is more pleased if it comes as a surprise.

## Home and Family

Aquarius is generally a very sociable person. He or she feels it is important to have a nice home—one where it is pleasant to entertain friends and associates. Their taste is generally modern, although they do have a respect for old things. They are bound to have all the latest fixtures and appliances in their home. As soon as something becomes out of date or nonfunctional, they are likely to throw it out and get something that is in keeping with the times. Appliances that save on housework are a must for Aquarius homemakers. They have more important things to do than attending to the drudgery of housekeeping.

Although Aquarius are fond of having a lot of company around, they do have moments when they have to be alone. They want peace and quiet so they can think things out without being interrupted. Chances are he or she is a member of many kinds of clubs and organizations. They like people of all kinds. But they also like their privacy to be respected. When they feel that it is necessary to withdraw from the hubbub of the crowd, they do not appreciate people who try to prevent this.

Although Aquarius men and women are serious about raising a family, home life usually does not play a dominating role in their life. They will own up to their responsibilities, but they do not want to have duties constantly shoved under their noses. In other words, they do not want to feel tied down and constrained. Aquarius needs love and affection, as everyone does, but he or she needs to be independent too. At times, home and family may conflict with the need for independence.

With children, Aquarius is likely to get along very well. He or she does not treat youngsters as inferiors, but regards them as little people. Aquarius men and women know how to talk and reason with a child just as they would someone their own age. Children, in turn, generally respect Aquarius for treating them as individuals. Aquarius would never dream of oppressing children. On the contrary, children are encouraged to develop their natural talents and to express their own personalities.

Aquarius at times prefers the direct and honest company of children over that of so-called adults. Aquarius men and women know how to keep children entertained with stories and games. In spite of an ability to be permissive, the average Aquarius makes it clear to the child that they will tolerate no nonsense. Children, understanding this, never misbehave while in the company of an Aquarius adult.

## Social Relationships

The average Aquarius is cheerful and outgoing when around people. At home they may be quiet and pensive. Few people understand Aquarius very well, even though they may feel they do. Some Aquarius withdraw so often from social situations that it becomes a permanent habit. Some famous recluses were born under this eleventh sign of the Zodiac.

Because they sometimes keep themselves separate and apart, they seem standoffish and critical to anyone who does not understand them. Aquarius men and women make many friends over a lifetime, but the quality of being unconsciously aloof may make it difficult for anyone to get to know them. Close friendships may be few.

Aquarius is optimistic by nature and always tends to look on the positive or bright side of social situations. This outlook makes it possible for them to get along well with all kinds of people, even if only for a limited amount of time. Some of their friends and acquaintances may seem strange and eccentric to conventional souls and traditional folks. The Aquarius collection of friends is likely to encompass many extremes of personality types.

Aquarius is a valued friend because of their helpful qualities and tolerant disposition. They are admired by business associates as a rule, and usually sought after in the community.

The average Aquarius enjoys observing humanity in all its forms and variations. He or she is never quick to judge another, for no one is totally bad or good. Aquarius men and women will make excuses for someone if they feel the person really means well. At times, this tolerant attitude works against them. Someone may take advantage of their easygoing ways and play them for a sucker.

Aquarius men and women do not always learn from their mistakes. They are easily moved by hard-luck stories. They are always willing to give someone the benefit of a doubt.

Naturally, Aquarius individuals stick by their friends and acquaintances. Many of their friends are friends for life. Aquarius is loyal and dependable. When friends are in trouble, they can always depend on Aquarius. He or she expects a friend to respect their individuality as much as they respect a friend's. Aquarius will never meddle in someone's private affairs but will lend a helping hand if asked.

# Love and Marriage

The archetypal Aquarius man or woman may be more interested in universal love—love for all humanity—than in personal love—love on a one-to-one basis. When he or she does fall in love with someone, it is usually because of some intellectual attraction rather than for some physical or superficial quality the person may have.

Love to Aquarius is serious business. They are faithful and fair. When looking for a mate or partner, they are more interested in the person's intellectual capacities and emotional depths than in superficial personality characteristics. If a dating partner or lover does not measure up to Aquarius standards, the relationship will be ended then and there—often without any explanation from Aquarius.

Although the average Aquarius becomes deeply involved in affairs of the heart, he or she may occasionally seem cool and distant. They are difficult to understand on the playing field of love. As with other things, Aquarius individuals have particular rules that they feel they must follow.

A lover or mate may have a hard time trying to pin Aquarius

down. They won't allow themselves to be totally possessed. They believe in holding onto their sense of liberty and freedom. They would never make excessive demands of a loved one's freedom. So they expect the same consideration. In spite of this attitude, Aquarius men and women are generally affectionate and loving.

In love, Aquarius men and women do not always know what they want. They may have a good many love affairs before they decide to settle down. The idea of love may mean more to an Aquarius than the act of loving.

When he or she does marry, Aquarius is faithful and considerate. They enjoy family life, the peace and quiet of home. Their love may waver at times, but it will never stray.

# Romance and the Aquarius Woman

Some Aquarius women may seem cool and aloof while still exuding a sort of sexual warmth and charm. They may not be particularly interested in sex. They are more often than not attracted to the mental capacities of a man. The purely physical attributes, no matter how attractive they may be, hold little interest for them.

When she does fall in love, it is usually with a man who is her intellectual equal or superior. She makes a faithful wife or lover. The man to whom she gives her affection must live up to her expectations. If he does not, she is likely to drop him quite quickly.

Many men are apt to find the Aquarius woman both attractive and cold. She is not a very demonstrative person as a rule. A possessive man is apt to be in for a lot of frustration while courting her. She has her own laws to live by. She will not submit to a man who wants to fashion her to fit his own needs. Freedom and privacy are important to her even after marriage. If the man she loves respects her for her individuality and allows her what she feels are her inalienable rights, everything will run smoothly in their relationship.

She is in need of warmth and affection. The right man can help her to develop her interest in these qualities. Although she is no flirt, she may have a good many romantic adventures behind her before she consents to marry and settle down.

She makes an excellent companion, spiritually and intellectually. She makes a faithful and devoted wife. It is important to her that she have all the latest household appliances—especially those that save time—for she is not very domestically inclined. Chances are that after marriage she will want to continue her career or interests outside the home.

She is loving when dealing with her family. She must have peace and harmony in her home. She will put her foot down if things upset her. Her husband or children must not make excessive demands of her.

Home may tie her down more than she desires. She may feel the need to get out and do something for others. Her family may see this as neglectful behavior, although it is not. She holds that her family is more than just a husband and children. She relates to the community in which she lives and feels that she has obligations to it. She is very conscientious in her relationships.

As a mother, she is ideal. She understands her children and treats them as equals. She is not a scold, but her children would never step out of line anyway. They respect her too much for that.

# Romance and the Aquarius Man

The Aquarius man is generally quite broad-minded. His interests extend to the farthest horizons. Humanity means a lot to him. He is in love with people. This is more important to him, sometimes, than being in love with just one person.

He is the kind of a lover who can win a woman over by his intellectual charm. He is usually witty and a good conversationalist. His joy of life usually impresses a mate or date.

Liberty is important to him. He will take up with the woman he loves but never try to strap her down with dos and don'ts. He wants his loved one to respect his right to express himself as he desires. If she understands his deep interest in personal freedom, and accepts it, the relationship is bound to be an enjoyable one. If she becomes too possessive, he is apt to break the relationship without giving an explanation.

Chances are he will have quite a number of love affairs in his life before he thinks of marrying. Sometimes he is impulsive about love and falls for a woman quickly and without reason. Later he may regret it. He is unpredictable in love. Some Aquarius men marry their loved ones after a relatively unhappy love affair and make good husbands. They may disappoint their loved ones while courting, but after they settle down they do their best to set matters right.

He is generally affectionate, although he may not be very demonstrative. He is kind and considerate; he would never take advantage of another's feelings. Every time he is in love he is serious—even if the affair is short-lived.

He is fair in all things. He is likely to treat strangers with the same courtesy and kindness as he treats his family. Everyone is equal to him. He won't act one way with one person, another way with another. He's honest and always the same as far as his personality is concerned.

He is a faithful husband and a responsible parent. His interests outside may take him away from home affairs quite often. However, he will never neglect his basic duties as a provider. He may have to be coaxed to stay home more often.

Children love him. He is tolerant with them and enjoys seeing them developing their own personalities. He is not a disciplinarian; he does not have to be. He guides the youngsters with ease.

# Woman—Man

### AQUARIUS WOMAN
### ARIES MAN

You will appreciate the intellectual friskiness of the Aries man. He has an insatiable thirst for knowledge. He's ambitious and is apt to have his finger in many pies. He can go far with a woman like you—someone attractive, studious, and smart.

He is not interested in a clinging vine kind of wife. He wants someone who is there when he needs her, someone who listens and understands what he says, someone who can give advice if he should ever need it—which is not likely to be often.

The Aries man wants a woman who will look good on his arm without hanging on it too heavily. He is looking for a woman who has both feet on the ground and yet is mysterious and enticing—a kind of domestic Helen of Troy whose face or fine dinner can launch a thousand business deals if need be. That woman he's in search of sounds a little like you, doesn't she? If the shoe fits, put it on. You won't regret it.

The Aries man makes a good husband. He is faithful and attentive. He is affectionate and amorous. He'll make you feel needed and loved. Love is a serious matter for the Aries man. He does not believe in flirting or playing the field, especially after he's found the woman of his dreams. He'll expect you to be as constant in your affection as he is in his. He'll expect you to be one hundred percent his. He won't put up with any nonsense while romancing you.

The Aries man may be as progressive and modern about many things as you are. But when it comes to pants wearing, he's downright conventional: it's strictly male attire. The best role you can take in the relationship is a supporting one. He's the boss and that's that. If an Aquarius woman can learn to accept that, the going will be easy.

The Aries man, with his endless energy and drive, likes to relax in the comfort of his home at the end of the day. The good homemaker can be sure of holding his love. He's an avid follower of current events and politics, which you will like. If you see to it that everything in the house is where he expects to find it, you'll have no difficulty keeping the relationship on an even keel.

Life and love with an Aries man may be just the medicine you need. He'll be a good provider. He'll spoil you if he's financially able.

The Aries father is young at heart and can get along easily with children. His ability to jump from one activity to another will suit a youngster's attention span. Aries will spoil the children every chance he gets. You must teach them how to finish what they start.

## AQUARIUS WOMAN
## TAURUS MAN

If you've got your heart set on a man born under the sign of Taurus, you'll have to learn the art of being patient. Taurus men take their time about everything—even love.

The steady and deliberate Taurus man is a little slow on the draw. It may take him quite a while before he gets around to popping that question. For the woman who doesn't mind twiddling her thumbs, the waiting and anticipating almost always pays off in the end. Taurus men want to make sure that every step they take is a good one—particularly if they feel that the path they're on is one that leads to the altar.

If you are in the mood for a whirlwind romance, you had better cast your net in shallower waters. Moreover, most Taurus prefer to do the angling themselves. They are afraid if a woman takes the lead. Once she does, he might drop her like a dead fish. If you let yourself get caught on his terms, you'll find that he's fallen for you—hook, line, and sinker.

The Taurus man is fond of a comfortable home life. It is very important to him. If you keep those home fires burning, you will have no trouble keeping that flame in your Taurus lover's heart aglow. You have a talent for homemaking; use it. Your taste in furnishings is excellent. You know how to make a house come to life with bold splashes of color and design.

Taurus, the strong, steady, and protective Bull, may not be your idea of a man on the move. Still, he's reliable. Perhaps he could be the anchor for your dreams and plans. He could help you to acquire a more balanced outlook and approach to your life. If you're given to impulsiveness, he could help you to curb it. He's the man who is always there when you need him.

When you tie the knot with a man born under Taurus, you can put away fears about creditors pounding on the front door. Taurus are practical about everything including bill paying. When he carries you over that threshold, you can be certain that the entire house is paid for, not only the doorsill.

As a wife, you won't have to worry about putting aside your many interests for the sake of back-breaking household chores. Your Taurus hubby will make sure that you have all the latest time-saving appliances and comforts.

Your Taurus husband will see to it that the children are obedient and respectful. He doesn't believe in spoiling the kids or in letting them run the household. With a Taurus father, the youngsters will learn to take their place in company of all kinds.

## AQUARIUS WOMAN
## GEMINI MAN

The Gemini man is quite a catch. Many a woman has set her cap for him and failed to bag him. Generally, Gemini men are intelligent, witty, and outgoing. Many of them are versatile in several areas. The Gemini man could easily wind up being your better half.

One thing that causes a Twin's mind and affection to wander is a bore. But it is unlikely that the active, with-it Aquarius woman would ever be accused of being boring. The Gemini man who has caught your heart will admire you for your ideas and intellect— perhaps even more than for your homemaking talents and good looks.

The woman who hitches up with a Twin needn't feel that once she's made her marriage vows she'll have to store her interests and ambition in the attic somewhere. The Gemini man will admire you for your zeal and liveliness and participation in community life. He's a guy who won't scowl if you let him shift for himself in the kitchen. He'll enjoy the challenge of wrestling with pots and pans and recipes. Chances are that he might turn out to be a better cook than you—that is, if he isn't already.

There aren't many women who have enough pep to keep up with an on-the-move Gemini. But this should be no problem for a pro-gressive, unconventional Aquarius woman.

The Gemini man is a dreamer, planner, and idealist. A woman with a strong personality could easily fill the role of rudder for her Gemini's ship-without-a-sail. If you are a cultivated, purposeful woman, he won't mind it too much. The intelligent Twin is often aware of his shortcomings and doesn't resent it if someone with better bearings than himself gives him a shove in the right direction—when it's needed. The average Gemini does not have serious ego hang-ups and will even accept a well-deserved chewing out from his mate quite good-naturedly.

When you team up with a Gemini man, you'll probably always have a houseful of people to entertain—interesting people, too. Geminis find it hard to tolerate narrow minds and passive disposi-tions.

Geminis generally have two sides to their natures, as different as night and day. It's very easy for them to be happy-go-lucky one minute, then down in the dumps the next. They hate to be bored and will generally do anything to make their lives interesting, vivid, and action-packed.

Gemini men are always attractive to the opposite sex. He'll flirt occasionally, but it will never amount to anything serious.

The Gemini father is a pushover for children. He loves them so much, he generally lets them do what they want. Gemini's sense of humor is quickly adopted by the youngsters. Like you, he creates a light and airy quality that makes the household vibrant with curiosity and learning.

## AQUARIUS WOMAN
## CANCER MAN

Chances are you won't hit it off too well with the man born under Cancer if your plans are love. But then Cupid has been known to do some pretty unlikely things. The Cancer man is very sensitive, thin-skinned, and occasionally moody. You've got to keep on your toes—and not step on his—if you're determined to make a go of the relationship.

The Cancer man may be lacking in some of the dynamic, electric qualities you seek in a man. But when it comes to being faithful and being a good provider, he's hard to beat.

The perceptive woman will not mistake the Crab's quietness for sullenness or his thriftiness for penny-pinching. In some respects, he is like that wise old owl out on a limb. He may look like he's dozing, but actually he hasn't missed a thing.

Cancers often possess a well of knowledge about human behavior. They can come across with some pretty helpful advice to those in trouble or in need. He can certainly guide you in making investments both in time and money. He may not say much, but he's always got his wits about him.

The Crab may not be the match or catch for a woman like you. At times, you are likely to find him downright dull. True to his sign, he can be fairly cranky and crabby when handled the wrong way. He is perhaps more sensitive than he should be.

If you're smarter than your Cancer friend, be smart enough not to let him know. Never give him the idea that you think he's a little short on brainpower. It would send him scurrying back into his shell. And all that ground lost in the relationship will perhaps never be recovered.

The Crab is happiest at home. Once settled down for the night or the weekend, wild horses couldn't drag him any farther than the gatepost—that is, unless those wild horses were dispatched by his mother. The Crab is sometimes a Momma's boy. If his mate does not put her foot down, he will see to it that his mother always comes first. No self-respecting wife would ever allow herself to play second fiddle to her mother-in-law.

With a little tact, you can slip into the number-one position as easy as pie—that legendary pie his mother used to bake. If you pamper your Cancer man, you'll find that "Mother" turns up increasingly less at the front door as well as in conversations.

Cancers make proud, patient, and protective fathers. But they can be a little too protective. Sheltering may interfere with a youngster's growing need for freedom, a view you independent Aquarius women share with the kids. Still, the Cancer father usually knows what's best for the brood.

## AQUARIUS WOMAN
## LEO MAN

To know a man born under the sign of the Lion is not necessarily to love him, even though the temptation may be great for you. After all, Aquarius and Leo are zodiacal mates—but you're also zodiacal opposites. And Aquarius can usually see through Leo's showy facade.

You are a little too sensible to allow yourself to be bowled over by a regal strut and roar. Still, there's no denying that Leo has a way with women. Once he's swept a lover off her feet, it may be hard for her to scramble upright again. But you are no pushover for romantic charm, especially if you feel it's all show.

He'll wine you and dine you in the fanciest places. He'll croon to you under the moon and shower you with diamonds if he can get a hold of them. Still, it would be wise to find out just how long that shower is going to last before consenting to be his wife.

Lions in love are hard to ignore, let alone brush off. Your resistance will have a way of nudging him on until he feels he has you completely under his spell. Once mesmerized by this romantic powerhouse, you will most likely find yourself doing things you never dreamed of.

Leos can be vain pussycats when involved romantically. They like to be pampered and petted. This may not be your cup of tea. But when he fixes you with his leonine double-whammy, your heart will go pitter-pat and your spirit will soar. You'll adore doing things to make your Leo purr.

Although he may be big and magnanimous while trying to win you, he'll let out a blood-curdling roar if he thinks he's not getting the tender love and care he feels is his due. If you keep him well supplied with affection, you can be sure his eyes will never look for someone else and his heart will never wander.

Leo men often tend to be authoritarian. They are born to lord it over others in one way or another, it seems. If he is the top banana at his firm, he'll most likely do everything he can to stay on top. If he's not number one, he's most likely working on it and will be sitting on the throne before long.

You'll have more security than you can use if he is in a position to support you in the manner to which he feels you should be accustomed. He is apt to be too lavish, though, at least by your standards.

You'll always have plenty of friends when you have a Leo for a mate. He's a natural-born friendmaker and entertainer. He loves to kick up his heels at a party.

Leo fathers feel close to the children and often spoil them. But he can be strict when he thinks the rules of the royal kingdom are being broken. You'll have to do your best to smooth over the children's hurt feelings. A dose of your famous objectivity would placate both the children and the Leo father.

## AQUARIUS WOMAN
## VIRGO MAN

The Virgo man is all business. At least he may seem so to you. He is usually very cool, calm, and collected. He's perhaps too much of a fussbudget to wake up deep romantic interests in an unconventional woman like you. Torrid romancing to him is sentimental mush. He can do without it and can make that quickly evident.

Virgo finds honor in chastity. If necessary, he can lead a sedentary, sexless life without caring too much about the fun others think he's missing. You might find him a first-class dud. He doesn't have much of an imagination. Fights of fancy don't interest him. He is always correct and likes to be handled correctly. Almost everything about him is orderly. There's a place for everything, and everything in its place—including love, romance, and sex.

He does have an honest-to-goodness heart, believe it or not. The woman who finds herself strangely attracted to his cool, feet-flat-on-the-ground ways will discover that his is a constant heart, not one that goes in for flings or sordid affairs. Virgos take an awfully long time to warm up to someone. A practical man, even in matters of the heart, he wants to know just what kind of person you are before he takes a chance on you.

The impulsive woman had better not make the mistake of kissing her Virgo friend on the street—even if it's only a peck on the cheek. He's not at all demonstrative and hates public displays of affection. Love, according to him, should be kept within the confines of one's home with the curtains drawn.

Once he believes that you are on the level with him as far as your love is concerned, you'll see how fast he can lose his cool. Virgos are considerate, gentle lovers. He'll spend a long time, though, getting to know you. He'll like you before he loves you.

A romance with a Virgo man can be a sometime—or, rather, a one-time—thing. If the bottom ever falls out, don't bother reaching for the adhesive tape. Nine times out of ten he won't care about patching up. He's a once-burnt twice-shy guy. When he crosses your telephone number out of his address book, he's crossing you out of his life for good.

Neat as a pin, he's thumbs-down on what he considers sloppy housekeeping. An ashtray with just one stubbed out cigarette in it can annoy him even if it's only two seconds old. And he'll lecture anyone about smoking because he always tries to correct habits harmful to one's health.

A Virgo man puts great emphasis on the health, hygiene, and safety of the children. He may try to restrict their freedom, a tendency you can easily counteract. He also wants the youngsters to be kind and courteous and always helpful to the neighbors—community values that you will appreciate and share.

## AQUARIUS WOMAN
## LIBRA MAN

If there's a Libra in your life, you are most likely a very happy woman. Men born under this sign have a way with women. You'll always feel at ease in a Libra's company. You can be yourself when you're with him.

The Libra man can be moody at times. His moodiness is often puzzling. One moment he comes on hard and strong with declaration of his love, the next moment you find that he's left you like yesterday's mashed potatoes. He'll come back, though; don't worry. Libras are like that. Deep down inside he really knows what he wants, even though he may not appear to.

You'll appreciate his admiration of beauty and harmony. If you're dressed to the teeth and never looked lovelier, you'll get a ready compliment—and one that's really meant. Libras don't indulge in idle flattery. If they don't like something, they are tactful enough to remain silent.

Libras will go to great lengths to preserve peace and harmony, even by telling a fat lie if necessary. They don't like showdowns or disagreeable confrontations. The frank woman is all for getting whatever is bothering her off her chest and out into the open, even if it comes out all wrong. To Libra making a clean breast of everything seems like sheer folly sometimes.

You may lose your patience while waiting for your Libra friend to make up his mind. It takes him ages sometimes to make a decision. He weighs both sides carefully before committing himself to anything. You seldom dillydally—at least about small things. So it's likely that you will find it difficult to see eye-to-eye with a hesitating Libra when it comes to decision making.

All in all, though, he is kind, considerate, and fair. He is interested in the real truth. He'll try to balance everything out until he has all the correct answers. It's not difficult for him to see both sides of a story.

He's a peace-loving man who seeks equilibrium and equality in a tolerant, nonviolent environment.

Libras are not show-offs. Generally, they are well-balanced, modest people. Honest, wholesome, and affectionate, they are serious about every love encounter they have. If he should find that the woman he's dating is not really suited to him, he will end the relationship in such a tactful manner that no hard feelings will come about.

The Libra father is patient and fair. Although he can be a harsh judge at times, he seldom exercises undue strictness or discipline. He can be firm without making the children feel restricted or repressed. His gentle, airy manner helps to make the household a harmonious one. You will appreciate the lessons of tolerance he teaches the children.

## AQUARIUS WOMAN
## SCORPIO MAN

The Scorpio moodiness and the Aquarius unpredictability are a fragile combination, giving rise to frequent bursts of temperament and explosive scenes. Many find the Scorpio's sting a fate worse than death. When his anger breaks loose, you will want to flee the vicinity as soon as possible.

The average Scorpio may strike you as a brute. He'll stick pins into the balloons of your plans and dreams if they don't line up with what he thinks is right. If you do anything to irritate him, he'll pick a quarrel that could go on for hours. Both of you, being fixed signs, are stubborn by nature. So you are likely to match any verbal onslaught with telling accusations of your own.

The Scorpio man hates being tied down to home life. He would rather be out on the battlefield of life, belting away at whatever he feels is a just and worthy cause, instead of staying home nestled in a comfortable armchair with the evening papers. If you have a home-making streak, don't keep those home fires burning too brightly too long. You may run out of firewood.

As passionate as he is in business affairs and politics, the Scorpio man still has plenty of dynamism stored away for lovemaking. Most women are quickly attracted to him. Perhaps you are no exception.

Those who allow a man born under this sign to sweep them off their feet soon find that they're dealing with a pepper pot of seething excitement.

The Scorpio man is passionate with a capital P, you can be sure of that. But he's capable of wounding you with words. Scorpio is blunt. An insult is likely to whiz out of his mouth quicker than a compliment.

If you're the kind of woman who can keep a stiff upper lip, take it on the chin, turn a deaf ear, and all of that, because you feel you are still under his love spell in spite of everything—lots of luck.

If you have decided to take the bitter with the sweet, prepare yourself for a lot of ups and downs. Chances are you won't have as much time for your own affairs and interests as you'd like. The Scorpio's love of power may cause you to be at his constant beck and call.

Scorpio likes fathering large families. He loves children, but often he fails to live up to his responsibilities as a parent. When he takes his fatherly duties seriously, he is a proud and patient parent. He is wonderful with difficult and challenged youngsters because he knows how to tap the best in each child.

## AQUARIUS WOMAN
## SAGITTARIUS MAN

If you've set your cap for a man born under the sign of Sagittarius, you may have to apply an awful lot of strategy before you can persuade him to get down on bended knee. Although some Sagittarius may be marriage-shy, they're not ones to skitter away from romance. You'll find a love relationship with a Sagittarius—whether a fling or the real thing—a very enjoyable experience.

As a rule, Sagittarius men are bright, happy, and healthy people. They have a strong sense of fair play. Often they are a source of inspiration to others. They are full of drive and ideas.

You'll be taken by the Archer's infectious grin and his light-hearted friendly nature. If you do wind up being the woman in his life, you'll find that he may treat you more like a buddy than the love of his life. It's just his way. Sagittarius are often more chummy than romantic.

You'll admire his broad-mindedness in most matters, including those of the heart. If, while dating you, he claims that he still wants to play the field, he'll expect you to enjoy the same liberty. Once he's promised to love, honor, and obey, however, he does just that. Marriage for him, once he's taken that big step, is very serious business.

The Sagittarius man is quick-witted. He has a genuine interest in equality. He hates prejudice and injustice. Generally, Sagittarius are good at sports. They love the great outdoors and respect wildlife in all its forms.

He's not much of a homebody. Quite often he's occupied with far-away places either in his daydreams or in reality. He enjoys being on the move. He's got ants in his pants and refuses to sit still for long stretches at a time. Humdrum routine, especially at home, bores him. At the drop of a hat, he may ask you to take off on some wild trip for an unspecified length of time. He likes to surprise people.

He'll take great pride in showing you off to his friends. He'll always be considerate where your feelings are concerned. He will never embarrass or disappoint you intentionally.

His friendly, sunshiny nature is capable of attracting many people. Like you, he's very tolerant when it comes to friends. You will most likely spend a great deal of time helping him entertain people.

The Sagittarius father will dote on any infant son or daughter, but he feels clumsy handling them. As soon as the children are old enough to walk and talk, the Sagittarius dad feels comfortable enough to play with them. He will encourage all their skills and will participate in their education.

## AQUARIUS WOMAN
## CAPRICORN MAN

A with-it gal like you is likely to find the average Capricorn man a bit of a drag. The man born under the sign of the Goat is often a closed person and difficult to get to know. Even if you do get to know him, you may not find him very interesting.

In romance, Capricorn men are a little on the rusty side. You'll probably have to make all the passes.

You may find his plodding manner irritating and his conservative, traditional ways downright maddening. He's not one to take chances on anything. If it was good enough for his father, it's good enough for him. He follows a way that is tried and true.

Whenever adventure rears its tantalizing head, the Goat will find excuses to stay rooted to a secure, comfortable place. Adventure can be a little scary to this conservative, cautious man.

He may be just as ambitious as you are, perhaps even more so. But his ways of accomplishing his aims are more subterranean or at least seem so. He operates from the background a good deal of the time. At a gathering you may never even notice him. But he's there, taking in everything, sizing everyone up, planning his next careful move.

Although Capricorns may be intellectual to a degree, it is not generally the kind of intelligence you appreciate. He may not be as quick or as bright as you. It may take him ages to understand a simple joke.

If you do decide to take up with a man born under this sign, you ought to be pretty good in the cheering up department. The Capricorn man often acts as though he's constantly being followed by a cloud of gloom.

The Capricorn man is happiest when in the comfort and privacy of his own home. The security possible within four walls can make him a happy man. He'll spend as much time as he can at home. If he is loaded down with extra work, he'll bring it home instead of working overtime at the office.

You'll most likely find yourself frequently confronted by his relatives. Family is very important to the Capricorn—his family, that is. They had better take a pretty important place in your life, too, if you want to keep your home a happy one.

Although his caution in most matters may drive you up the wall, you'll find his concerned way with money justified most of the time. He'll plan everything down to the last penny.

The Capricorn father can be quite a scold with children at times. You'll have to step in and ease their anxiety. But the Capricorn father is steady and serious, always acting in the best interests of the youngsters. He will build their character and prepare them for the world of work.

## AQUARIUS WOMAN
## AQUARIUS MAN

Aquarius is extremely friendly and open, even with another Aquarius. Of all the signs, they are perhaps the most tolerant. In the thinking department they are often miles ahead of others, and with very little effort, it seems.

As an Aquarius yourself, you will most likely find your Aquarius friend intriguing, and the relationship between two Aquarius is likely to be twice as challenging. Your own high respect for intelligence and fair play may be reason enough to settle your heart on another Water Bearer.

Aquarius individuals love everybody, even their worst enemies sometimes. Through your relationship with another Aquarius, you'll find yourself running into all sorts of people, ranging from near-genius to downright insane. And these are all friends that you'll share in common.

In the holding hands stage of your romance your Water Bearer friend may have cold feet that may take quite a bit of warming up. More than likely, he'll just want to be your pal in the beginning. For him, as for you, that's an important step in any relationship—even love. The poetry and flowers stage will come later, perhaps some years later.

Aquarius is all heart. Still, when it comes to tying himself down to one person and for keeps, he hesitates. He may even try to get out of it if you give him half a chance. And as an Aquarius, you may be inclined to do just that. He's no Valentino and wouldn't want to be, but then a Valentino isn't quite what you're looking for either. In fact, as an Aquarius, you are bound to understand his hesitation—more or less. You are also likely to be more attracted by his broad-mindedness and high moral standards than by his abilities to romance you.

You won't find it difficult to look up to a man born under your sign, and the challenge is certain to be exciting. He can pierce through the most complicated problem as if it were a matter of two plus two. Others may find him too lofty or high-minded, but you're pretty much that way yourself.

In marriage you need never be afraid that his affection will wander. It stays put once he's hitched. He'll certainly admire you for your intelligence, and don't think that you have to stick close to the kitchen. Once you're married, he'll want you to pursue whatever you want in your quest for knowledge. You'll most likely have a minor squabble with him now and then, but never anything serious.

Still, even you may find his forgetfulness (added to your own) a little bothersome. His head is so full of ideas and plans that sometimes he seems like the absentminded professor. Kids love him and vice versa. He's tolerant and open-minded with everybody, from the very young to the very old.

The Aquarius father sees the children as individuals in their own right, not as possessions or as extensions of himself. Like you, he can fascinate the youngsters with a variety of topics and activities. Children of Aquarius-Aquarius parents learn tolerance and equality at an early age.

## AQUARIUS WOMAN
## PISCES MAN

The man born under Pisces is quite a dreamer. Sometime he's so wrapped up in his dreams that he's difficult to reach. To the ambitious woman, he may seem a little passive.

He's easygoing most of the time. He seems to take things in his stride. He'll entertain all kinds of views and opinions from just about anyone, nodding or smiling vaguely, giving the impression that he's with them one hundred percent while that may not be the case at all. His attitude may be why bother when he is confronted with someone wrong who thinks he's right. The Pisces man will seldom speak his mind if he thinks he'll be rigidly opposed.

The Pisces man is oversensitive at times. He's afraid of getting his feelings hurt. He'll sometimes imagine a personal affront when none's been made. Chances are you'll find this complex of his maddening. You may feel like giving him a swift kick where it hurts the most. It won't do any good, though. It would just add fuel to the fire of his complex.

One thing you will admire about Pisces is his concern for people who are sick or troubled. He'll make his shoulder available to anyone in the mood for a good cry. He can listen to one hard-luck story after another without seeming to tire. When his advice is asked, he is capable of coming across with some pretty important words of wisdom.

He often knows what's bothering someone before that person is aware of it himself. It's almost intuitive with Pisces, it seems. Still, at the end of the day, he looks forward to some peace and quiet. If you've got a problem on your mind, don't dump it into his lap at the end of the day. If you do, you'll find him short-tempered. He's a good listener, but he can only take so much.

Pisces men are not aimless although they may seem so at times. The positive sort of Pisces man is quite often successful in his profession and is likely to wind up rich and influential. Material gain, however, is not a direct goal for the Fishes.

The weaker Pisces is usually content to stay put on the level where he happens to find himself. He won't complain too much if the roof leaks or the fence is in need of repair. He'll just shrug it off as a minor inconvenience. He's thinking and dreaming about more important things.

The Pisces father, with his live-and-let-live-attitude, is immensely popular with children. He plays the double role of confidant and playmate for the kids. It will never enter his mind to discipline a child, no matter how spoiled or incorrigible that youngster becomes.

# Man—Woman

## AQUARIUS MAN
## ARIES WOMAN

The Aries woman is quite a charmer. When she tugs at the strings of your heart, you'll know it. She's a woman who's in search of a knight in shining armor. She is a very particular person with very high ideals. She won't accept anyone but the man of her dreams.

The Aries woman never plays around with passion. She means business when it comes to love. She is proud and capable of being quite jealous. While you're with her, never cast your eye in another woman's direction. It could spell disaster for your relationship. The Aries woman won't put up with romantic nonsense when her heart is at stake.

Don't get the idea that she's a dewy-eyed damsel. She isn't. In fact, she can be pretty practical and to the point when she wants. She's a gal with plenty of drive and ambition. With an Aries woman behind you, you can go far in life. She knows how to help her man get ahead. She's full of wise advice; you only have to ask.

Enterprising and inventive, the Aries woman has a keen business sense. Many of them become successful career women. There is nothing hesitant or retiring about her. She is equipped with a good brain and she knows how to use it.

Your union with her could be something strong, secure, and romantic. If both of you have your sights fixed in the same direction, there is almost nothing that you could not accomplish.

If the Aries woman backs you up in your business affairs, you can be sure of succeeding. However, if she only is interested in advancing her own career and puts her interests before yours, she can be sure of rocking the boat. It will put a strain on the relationship. The overambitious Aries woman can be a pain in the neck and make you forget you were once in love with her.

The cultivated Aries woman makes a wonderful wife and mother. She has a natural talent for homemaking. With a pot of paint and some wallpaper, she can transform the dreariest domicile into an abode of beauty and snug comfort. The perfect hostess—even when friends just happen by—she knows how to make guests feel at home.

You'll also admire your Aries because she knows how to stand on her own two feet. Hers is an independent nature. She won't break down and cry when things go wrong. She'll pick herself up and try to patch up matters.

The Aries woman is an affectionate mother although she is not keen on burdensome responsibilities. She is skilled at juggling both a career and motherhood, so her kids will never feel that she is an absentee parent. In fact, as the youngsters grow older, they might want some of the liberation that is so important to her—and on which you place great value.

## AQUARIUS MAN
## TAURUS WOMAN

The woman born under the sign of Taurus may lack a little of the sparkle and bubble you often like to find in a woman. The Taurus woman is generally down to earth and never flighty. It's important to her that she keep both feet flat on the ground. She is not fond of bounding all over the place, especially if she's under the impression that there's no profit in it.

On the other hand, if you hit it off with a Taurus woman, you won't be disappointed at all in the romance area. The Taurus woman is all woman and proud of it, too. She can be very devoted and loving once she decides that her relationship with you is no fly-by-night romance.

Basically, she's a passionate person. In sex, she's direct and to the point. If she really loves you, she'll let you know she's yours—and without reservations. Better not flirt with other women once you've committed yourself to her. She can be jealous and possessive.

She'll stick by you through thick and thin. It's almost certain that if the going ever gets rough, she'll not go running home to her mother. She can adjust to hard times just as graciously as she can to the good times.

Taurus are fairly even-tempered. They like to be treated with kindness. Luxurious surroundings and beautiful things provide the softness and graciousness they desire in a home life.

You may find her a little slow and deliberate. She likes to be safe and sure about everything. Let her plod along if she likes; don't coax her but just let her take her own sweet time. Everything she does is done thoroughly and, generally, it is done without mistakes.

Don't deride her for being a slowpoke. It could lead to an explosive scene. The Taurus woman doesn't anger readily. But when prodded often enough, she's capable of letting loose with a cyclone of ill will. If you treat her with kindness and consideration, you'll have no cause for complaint.

The Taurus woman loves doing things for her man. She's a whiz in the kitchen and can whip up feasts fit for a king if she thinks they'll be royally appreciated. She may not fully understand you, but she'll adore you and be faithful to you if she feels you're worthy of it.

The Taurus woman will make a wonderful mother. She knows how to keep her children well-loved, cuddled, and warm. She may find them difficult to manage, however, when they reach adolescence. Despite their resentment as teenagers, the youngsters of a Taurus mother are thankful in later life that they were brought up so conscientiously and properly.

## AQUARIUS MAN
## GEMINI WOMAN

You may find a romance with a woman born under the sign of the Twins a many-splendored thing. In her you can find the intellectual companionship you often look for in a friend or mate. A Gemini, as an air sign like you, can appreciate your aims and desires because she travels pretty much the same road as you do intellectually—that is, at least part of the way. She may share your interest but she will lack your tenacity.

She suffers from itchy feet. She can be here, there, all over the place and at the same time, or so it would seem. Her eagerness to move may make you dizzy. Still, you'll enjoy and appreciate her liveliness and mental agility.

Geminis have sparkling personalities. You'll be attracted by her bubble and bounce. While she's on your arm, you'll probably notice that many male eyes are drawn to her. She may even return a gaze or two, but don't let that worry you. All women born under this sign have nothing against a harmless flirt once in a while. They enjoy the attention. If she feels she is already spoken for, however, she will never let it get out of hand.

In the kitchen she's as much in a hurry as you are. You won't feel like she's cheating if she breaks out the instant mashed potatoes or the frozen peas. She may not spend a lot of time cooking, but she is clever. With a dash of this and a suggestion of that, she can make an uninteresting TV dinner taste like a gourmet meal. Then, again, maybe you've struck it rich and have a Gemini mate who finds complicated recipes a challenge to her intellect. If so, you'll find every meal a tantalizing and mouth-watering surprise.

When you're beating your brains out over a crossword puzzle and find yourself stuck, just ask your Gemini partner. She'll give you all the right answers without batting an eyelash.

Like you, she loves all kinds of people. You may even find that you're a bit more particular than she. Often all that a Gemini requires is that her friends be interesting—and stay interesting. One thing she's not able to abide is a dullard.

Leave the party organizing to your Gemini sweetheart or mate, and you'll never have a chance to know what a dull moment is. She'll bring the swinger out in you if you give her half a chance.

A Gemini mother enjoys her children. Like them, she's often restless, adventurous, and easily bored. She will never complain about their fleeting interests because she understands the changes they will go through as they mature. And she instinctively knows how to maintain the youngsters' individuality as they grow toward adulthood.

## AQUARIUS MAN
## CANCER WOMAN

If you fall in love with a Cancer woman, be prepared for anything. Cancers are sometimes difficult to understand when it comes to love. In one hour, she can unravel a whole gamut of emotions that will leave you in a tizzy. She'll keep you guessing, that's for sure.

You may find her a little too uncertain and sensitive for your liking. You'll most likely spend a good deal of time encouraging her—helping her to erase her foolish fears. Tell her she's a living doll a dozen times a day, and you'll be well loved in return.

Be careful of the jokes you make when in her company. Don't let any of them revolve around her, her personal interests, or her family. If you do, you'll most likely reduce her to tears. She can't stand being made fun of. It will take bushels of roses and tons of chocolates—not to mention the apologies—to get her to come back out of her shell.

In matters of money managing she may not easily come around to your way of thinking. Money will never burn a hole in her pocket. You may get the notion that your Cancer sweetheart or mate is a direct descendent of Scrooge. If she has her way, she'll hang onto that first dollar you earned. She's not only that way with money, but with everything right on up from bakery string to jelly jars. She's a saver; she never throws anything away, no matter how trivial.

Once she declares her love for you, you'll have an affectionate, self-scarificing, and devoted woman. Her love for you will never alter unless you want it to. She'll put you high upon a pedestal and will do everything—even if it's against your will—to keep you up there.

Cancer women love home life. For them, marriage is an easy step. They're domestic with a capital D. She'll do her best to make your home comfortable and cozy. She, herself, is more at ease at home than anywhere else. She makes an excellent hostess. The best in her comes out when she is in her own environment.

Cancer woman make the best mothers of all the signs of the Zodiac. She'll consider every complaint of her child a major catastrophe. With her, children always come first. If you're lucky, you'll run a close second. You'll perhaps see her as too devoted to the children. You may have a hard time convincing her that her apron strings are a little too long and that the youngsters need some of the freedom you value so highly.

## AQUARIUS MAN
## LEO WOMAN

In the astrological scheme of things, Aquarius and Leo are zodiacal partners as well as zodiacal opposites. You will admire the Leo woman's differences from you, although they can be maddening at times.

If you can manage a woman who likes to kick up her heels every now and again, then the Leo woman was made for you. You'll have to learn to put away jealous fears, or at least forget about them. Leo makes heads turn and tongues wag. You don't necessarily have to believe any of what you hear. It's most likely just jealous gossip or wishful thinking. Take up with a Leo woman, and you'll be taking off on a romance full of fire and ice. Be prepared to take the good things with the bad, the bitter with the sweet.

The Leo woman has more than a fair share of grace and glamour. She is aware of her charms and knows how to put them to good use. Needless to say, other women in her vicinity turn green with envy and will try anything in order to put her out of commission.

If she's captured your heart and fancy, woo her full force if your intention is to eventually win her. Shower her with expensive gifts and promise her the moon—if you're in a position to go that far. Then you'll find her resistance beginning to weaken. It's not that she's such a difficult cookie. She'll probably make a big fuss over you once she's decided you're the man for her. But she does enjoy a lot of attention. And she feels she's entitled to it.

Her mild arrogance, though, is becoming. The Leo woman knows how to transform the crime of excessive pride into a very charming misdemeanor. It sweeps most men right off their feet. Those who do not succumb to her leonine charm are few and far between.

If you've got an important business deal to clinch and you have doubts as to whether or not it will go over well, bring your Leo lover along to that business luncheon. It's a cinch the contract will be yours. She won't have to do or say anything, just be there at your side. The grouchiest oil magnate can be transformed into a gushing, obedient schoolboy if there's a Leo woman in the room.

If you're rich and want to stay that way, don't give your Leo mate a free hand with the charge accounts and credit cards. If you're poor, the luxury-loving Leo will most likely never enter your life.

The Leo mother is strict yet, like you, easygoing with the children. She wants her youngsters to follow the rules, and she is a patient teacher. She loves to pal around with the kids, proudly showing them off on every occasion. She can be so proud of the children that she sometimes is blind to their faults.

## AQUARIUS MAN
## VIRGO WOMAN

The Virgo woman may be a little too difficult for you to understand at first. Her waters run deep. Even when you think you know her, don't take any bets on it. She's capable of keeping things hidden in the deep recesses of her womanly soul—things she'll only release when she's sure you're the man she's been looking for.

It may take her some time to come around to this decision. Virgo women are finicky about almost everything. Everything has to be letter-perfect before they're satisfied. Many of them have the idea that the only people who can do things correctly are Virgos.

Nothing offends a Virgo woman more than slovenly dress, sloppy character, or a careless display of affection. Make sure your tie is not crooked and your shoes sport a bright shine before you go calling on this lady. Take her arm when crossing the street.

Don't rush the romance. Trying to corner her in the back of a cab may be one way of striking out. Never criticize the way she looks.

In fact, the best policy would be to agree with her as much as possible. Still, there's just so much a man can take. All those dos and don'ts you'll have to observe if you want to get to first base with a Virgo may be just a little too much to ask of you. After a few dates, you may come to the conclusion that she just isn't worth all that trouble.

However, the Virgo woman is mysterious enough to keep her men running back for more. Chances are you'll be intrigued by her airs and graces.

If lovemaking means a lot to you, you'll be disappointed at first in the cool ways of your Virgo partner. However, under her glacial facade lies a hot cauldron of seething excitement. If you're patient and artful in your romantic approach, you'll find that all the caution was well worth the trouble. When Virgos love, they don't stint. It's all or nothing as far as they're concerned. Once they're convinced that they love you, they toss all cares to the wind.

One thing a Virgo woman can't stand in love is hypocrisy. They don't give a hoot about what the neighbors say if their hearts tell them to go ahead. They're very concerned with human truths. If their hearts stumble upon another fancy, they will be true to that new heartthrob and leave you standing in the rain.

She's honest to her heart and will be as true to you as you are with her. Do her wrong once, however, and it's farewell.

The Virgo mother has high expectations for her children, and she will strive to bring out the very best in them. She is more tender than strict, though, and will nag rather than discipline. But youngsters sense her unconditional love for them, and usually turn out to be model citizens just as she hoped they would.

## AQUARIUS MAN
## LIBRA WOMAN

You'll probably find that the woman born under the sign of Libra is worth more than her weight in gold. She's a woman after your own heart.

With her, you'll always come first—make no mistake about that. She'll always be behind you one hundred percent, no matter what you do. When you ask her advice about almost anything, you'll most likely get a very balanced and realistic opinion. She is good at thinking things out and never lets her emotions run away with her when clear logic is called for.

As a homemaker Libra is hard to beat. She is very concerned with harmony and balance. You can be sure she'll make your house a joy to live in. She'll see to it that the house is tastefully furnished and decorated. Libra cannot stand filth or disarray. Anything that does not radiate harmony goes against her orderly grain.

She is chock-full of charm and womanly ways. She can sweep just about any man off his feet with one winning smile. When it comes to using her brains, she can outthink almost anyone and, sometimes, with half the effort. She is diplomatic enough, though, never to let this become glaringly apparent. She may even turn the conversation around so that you think you were the one who did all the brain work. She couldn't care less, really, just as long as you wind up doing what is right.

The Libra woman will put you up on a pedestal. You are her man and her idol. She'll leave all the decision making, large or small, up to you. She's not interested in running things and will only offer her assistance if she feels you really need it.

Some find her approach to reason masculine. However, in the areas of love and affection the Libra woman is all woman. She'll literally shower you with love and kisses during your romance with her. She doesn't believe in holding out. You shouldn't, either, if you want to hang onto her.

She likes to snuggle up to you in front of the fire on chilly autumn nights. She will bring you breakfast in bed on Sunday. She'll be very thoughtful about anything that concerns you. If anyone dares suggest you're not the grandest guy in the world, she'll give that person what-for. She'll defend you with her dying breath. The Libra woman will be everything you want her to be.

The Libra mother is sensitive and tolerant, with a talent for creating a sharing environment in which children feel important and equal. She will see to it that they develop refined tastes and sensibilities. Her youngsters will never lack for anything that could make their lives easier and richer.

## AQUARIUS MAN
## SCORPIO WOMAN

The Scorpio woman can be a whirlwind of passion, perhaps too much passion to suit the impersonal Aquarius man. When her temper flies, you'd better lock up the family heirlooms and take cover. When she chooses to be sweet, you might think it's a pose. But it isn't. Scorpio is a creature of moods.

The Scorpio woman can be as hot as a tamale or as cool as a cucumber. But whatever mood she's in, she's in it for real. She does not believe in pretense or putting on airs.

The Scorpio woman is often sultry and seductive. Her femme fatale charm can pierce through the hardest of hearts like a laser ray. She may not look like Mata Hari (quite often Scorpios resemble the tomboy next door) but once she's fixed you with her tantalizing eyes, you're a goner.

Life with the Scorpio woman will not be all smiles and smooth sailing. When prompted she can unleash a gale of venom. Generally, she'll have the good grace to keep family battles within the walls of your home. When company visits, she's apt to give the impression that married life with you is one great big joyride. It's just one of her ways of expressing her loyalty to you, at least in front of others. She may fight you tooth and nail in the confines of your living room, but during an evening out she'll hang on your arm and have stars in her eyes.

Scorpio women are good at keeping secrets. She may even keep a few buried from you if she feels like it.

Never cross her on even the smallest thing. When it comes to revenge, she's an eye-for-an-eye woman. She's not too keen on forgiveness, especially when she feels she's been wronged unjustly. You'd be well-advised not to give her any cause to be jealous. When the Scorpio woman sees green, your life will be made far from rosy. Once she's put you in the doghouse, you can be sure you'll stay there a long time.

You may find life with the Scorpio woman too emotionally draining. She may not be the woman you'd like to spend the rest of your natural life with. You'd prefer someone gentler and not so hot-tempered, someone who can take the highs with the lows and not bellyache, someone who is flexible and understanding. If you've got your sights set on a shapely Scorpio, forget about that sweet ideal of your dreams. A woman born under Scorpio can be heavenly, but she can also be the very devil when she chooses.

The Scorpio mother is devoted to developing her youngsters' talents without putting the children on a pedestal. She is encouraging yet protective. Under her skillful guidance, the children will learn how to cope with life's adversity. She will teach them to be steadfast and courageous.

## AQUARIUS MAN
## SAGITTARIUS WOMAN

You'll may never come across a more good-natured gal than the one born under the sign of Sagittarius. They're full of bounce and good cheer. Their sunny disposition seems almost permanent and can be relied upon on the rainiest of days.

Sagittarius women are almost never malicious. If ever they seem to be, it is only seeming. Sagittarius are often a little short on tact and say literally anything that comes into their heads no matter what the occasion. Sometimes the words that tumble out of their mouths seem downright cutting and cruel. Still, no matter what she says, she means well. The Sagittarius woman is quite capable of losing some of her friends, and perhaps even some of yours, through a careless slip of the lip.

On the other hand, you will appreciate her honesty and good intentions. To you, qualities of this sort play an important part in life. With a little patience and practice, you can probably help cure your Sagittarius of her loose tongue. In most cases, she'll give in to your better judgment and try to follow your advice.

Chances are she'll be the outdoors type of partner. Long hikes, fishing trips, and white-water canoeing will most likely appeal to her. She's a busy person; no one could ever call her a slouch. She sets great store in mobility. Her feet are itchy and she won't sit still for a minute if she doesn't have to.

She is great company most of the time and lots of fun. Even if your buddies drop by for poker and beer, she won't have any trouble fitting in.

On the whole, the Sagittarius woman is very kind and sympathetic. If she feels she's made a mistake, she'll be the first to call your attention to it. She's not afraid to own up to her faults and shortcomings. You might lose your patience with her once or twice. After she's seen how upset her shortsightedness or bluntness has made you, she'll do her best to straighten up.

The Sagittarius woman is not the kind who will pry into your business affairs. But she'll always be there, ready to offer advice if you need it. If you come home with red stains on your collar and you say it's paint and not lipstick, she'll believe you. She'll seldom be suspicious; your word will almost always be good enough for her.

The Sagittarius mother is a wonderful and loving friend to her children. Like you, she places great emphasis on freedom and equality. She is not afraid if the youngsters come home with some strange ideas. She will round out their knowledge and encourage them to form their own opinions.

## AQUARIUS MAN
## CAPRICORN WOMAN

If you are not a successful businessman or at least on your way to success, it's quite possible that a Capricorn woman will have no interest in entering your life. Generally, she is a very security-minded female. She'll see to it that she invests her time only in sure things.

Men who whittle away their time with one unsuccessful scheme or another seldom attract a Capricorn. Men who are interested in getting somewhere in life and keep their noses close to the grindstone quite often have a Capricorn woman behind them, helping them to get ahead.

Although she may be an opportunist or a social climber, she is not what you could call cruel or hard-hearted. Beneath that cool, seemingly calculating exterior there's a warm and desirable woman. She just happens to think that it is as easy to fall in love with a rich or ambitious man as it is with a poor or lazy one. She's practical.

The Capricorn woman may be intent on rising to the top, but she'll never be aggressive about it. She'll seldom step on someone's feet or nudge competitors away with her elbows. She's quiet about her desires. She sits, waits, and watches. When an opening or opportunity does appear, she'll latch onto it.

For an on-the-move man, an ambitious Capricorn wife or lover can be quite an asset. She can probably give you some very good advice about business matters. When you invite the boss and his wife for dinner, she'll charm them both right off the ground.

The Capricorn woman is thorough in whatever she does: cooking, cleaning, making a success out of life. Capricorns make excellent hostesses as well as guests. Generally, they are very well mannered and gracious, no matter what their backgrounds are. They seem to have a built-in sense of what is right. Crude behavior or a careless faux pas can offend them no end.

If you should marry a woman born under Capricorn, you need never worry about her going on a wild shopping spree. Capricorns are careful with every cent that comes into their hands. They understand the value of money better than most women and have no room in their lives for careless spending.

Capricorns are usually very fond of family—their own, that is. With them, family ties run very deep. Don't make jokes about her relatives; she won't stand for it. You'd better check her family out before you get down on bended knee. After your marriage you'll undoubtedly be seeing lots of them.

The Capricorn mother wants her children to have every advantage in life. She is very ambitious for the children. She sees to it that they will benefit from things she perhaps lacked as a child. She will train the youngsters to be poised, polite, and prepared to get ahead in the world.

## AQUARIUS MAN
## AQUARIUS WOMAN

There should be no problem when two Aquarius get together in a love match. You think along the same lines and often have the same goals. Both of you like a life full of action and purpose, filled with the company of other people. Because love to both of you is more a matter of mind than of physical attraction, this union can survive many challenges and changes and endure as a lasting friendship.

The Aquarius woman is like a rainbow, full of bright and shining hues. There is something elusive about her, something delightfully mysterious. You may never be able to put your finger on it. It's not calculated, either. There is nothing phony about the Aquarius charm.

There will never be a dull moment in your life with this Water Bearer woman. She seems to radiate adventure and magic. She'll most likely be the most open-minded and tolerant woman you've ever met. She has a strong dislike for injustice and prejudice. Narrow-mindedness runs against her grain.

She is very independent by nature and quite capable of shifting for herself if necessary. She may receive many proposals for marriage from all sorts of people without ever really taking them seriously. Marriage is a very big step for her. She wants to be sure she knows what she's getting into. If she thinks that it will seriously curb her independence and love of freedom, she will return the engagement ring—if indeed she's let the romance get that far.

The line between friendship and romance is a pretty fuzzy one for an Aquarius. It's not difficult for her to remain buddy-buddy with an ex-lover. She's tolerant, like you. So if you should see her on the arm of an old love, don't jump to any hasty conclusions.

She's not a jealous person herself and doesn't expect you to be either. You'll find her a free spirit most of the time. Just when you think you know her inside out, you'll discover that you don't really know her at all.

She'll seldom be suspicious even if she has every right to be. If she loves a man, she'll forgive him just about anything. If he allows himself a little fling, chances are she'll just turn her head the other way. Her tolerance does have its limits, however, and her man should never press his luck.

The Aquarius mother is open-minded, loving, and generous. She seldom refuses her children anything. But there is little chance that the youngsters will become spoiled or selfish because she emphasizes giving to others. With two Aquarius parents, children grow up to be kindhearted, considerate, and humane.

## AQUARIUS MAN
## PISCES WOMAN

Many a man dreams of an alluring Pisces woman. You're perhaps no exception. She's soft and cuddly and very domestic. She'll let you be the brains of the family; she's contented to play a behind-the-scenes role in order to help you achieve your goals. The illusion that you are the master of the household is the kind of magic that the Pisces woman is adept at creating.

She can be very ladylike and proper. Your business associates and friends will be dazzled by her warmth and femininity. Although she's a charmer, there is a lot more to her than just a pretty exterior. There is a brain ticking away behind that soft, womanly facade. You may never become aware of it—that is, until you're married to her. It's no cause for alarm, however; she'll most likely never use it against you, only to help you and possibly set you on a more successful path.

If she feels you're botching up your married life through careless behavior or if she feels you could be earning more money than you do, she'll tell you about it. But any wife would, really. She will never try to usurp your position as head and breadwinner of the family.

No one had better dare say one uncomplimentary word about you in her presence. It's likely to cause her to break into tears. Pisces women are usually very sensitive beings. Their reaction to adversity, frustration, or anger is just a plain, good, old-fashioned cry. They can weep buckets when inclined.

She can do wonders with a house. She is very fond of dramatic and beautiful things. There will always be plenty of fresh-cut flowers around the house. She will choose charming artwork and antiques, if they are affordable. She'll see to it that the house is decorated in a dazzling yet welcoming style.

She'll have an extra special dinner prepared for you when you come home from an important business meeting. Don't dwell on the boring details of the meeting, though. But if you need that grand vision, the big idea, to seal a contract or make a conquest, your Pisces woman is sure to confide a secret that will guarantee your success. She is canny and shrewd with money, and once you are on her wavelength you can manage the intricacies on your own.

Treat her with tenderness and generosity and your relationship will be an enjoyable one. She's most likely fond of chocolates. A bunch of beautiful flowers will never fail to make her eyes light up. See to it that you never forget her birthday or your anniversary. These things are very important to her. If you let them slip your mind, you'll send her into a crying fit that could last a considerable length of time.

If you are patient and kind, you can keep a Pisces woman happy for a lifetime. She, however, is not without her faults. Her sensitivity may get on your nerves after awhile. You may find her lacking in practicality and good old-fashioned stoicism. You may even feel that she uses her tears as a method of getting her own way.

The Pisces mother has great faith in her children. She is a strong, self-sacrificing mother. She will teach the youngsters the value of service to the community while not letting them lose their individuality. Her notion of universal love, which also is an Aquarius ideal, will be an inspiration to the children.

# AQUARIUS
# LUCKY NUMBERS 2009

Lucky numbers and astrology can be linked through the movements of the Moon. Each phase of the thirteen Moon cycles
vibrates with a sequence of numbers for your Sign of the Zodiac
over the course of the year. Using your lucky numbers is a fun system that connects you with tradition.

| New Moon | First Quarter | Full Moon | Last Quarter |
|---|---|---|---|
| Dec. 27 ('08) | Jan. 4 | Jan. 10 | Jan. 17 |
| 8 2 3 1 | 0 1 6 4 | 7 7 8 9 | 2 6 8 4 |
| Jan. 26 | Feb. 2 | Feb. 9 | Feb. 16 |
| 5 7 2 4 | 7 8 6 7 | 6 1 9 5 | 5 3 3 5 |
| Feb. 24 | March 4 | March 10 | March 18 |
| 5 7 0 1 | 2 1 0 9 | 0 9 4 3 | 6 8 7 8 |
| March 26 | April 2 | April 9 | April 17 |
| 0 7 9 3 | 4 3 2 2 | 2 6 5 8 | 9 9 1 3 |
| April 24 | May 1 | May 9 | May 17 |
| 7 6 9 1 | 8 8 3 2 | 5 6 7 1 | 9 4 6 8 |
| May 24 | May 30 | June 7 | June 15 |
| 9 8 7 7 | 7 2 1 0 | 4 4 5 6 | 3 5 8 9 |
| June 22 | June 29 | July 7 | July 15 |
| 0 6 5 4 | 8 7 1 8 | 8 3 5 9 | 2 5 6 5 |
| July 21 | July 28 | August 5 | August 13 |
| 5 4 3 8 | 6 9 1 0 | 2 4 8 1 | 4 5 4 3 |
| August 20 | August 27 | Sept. 4 | Sept. 11 |
| 3 7 6 1 | 4 4 5 6 | 8 3 5 3 | 9 8 7 7 |
| Sept. 18 | Sept. 26 | Oct. 4 | Oct. 11 |
| 2 1 4 5 | 5 6 7 9 | 4 6 9 1 | 0 9 8 3 |
| Oct. 18 | Oct. 25 | Nov. 2 | Nov. 9 |
| 3 2 5 6 | 7 1 3 7 | 0 3 4 2 | 2 6 5 5 |
| Nov. 16 | Nov. 24 | Dec. 2 | Dec. 8 |
| 8 9 1 3 | 3 6 1 3 | 6 7 6 5 | 9 8 2 2 |
| Dec. 15 | Dec. 24 | Dec. 31 | Jan. 7 ('10) |
| 2 2 3 4 | 6 8 2 3 | 1 0 1 6 | 6 4 7 7 |

# AQUARIUS
# YEARLY FORECAST 2009

*Forecast for 2009 Concerning Business
and Financial Affairs, Job Prospects,
Travel, Health, Romance and Marriage
for Persons Born with the Sun
in the Zodiacal Sign of Aquarius.
January 20–February 18*

A mixed yet powerful year is promised for those born under the influence of the Sun in the zodiacal sign of Aquarius, ruled by Saturn, the planet associated with discipline and structure, and by Uranus, the planet of excitement and chaos. With a number of diverse trends being sent by the universe, you can expect a roller-coaster journey of mayhem, mystery, and achievement. The year begins with Venus, Mercury, and Neptune gracing your sign of Aquarius and impacting your first house of self and personality. These three planets as well as Chiron here will encourage a positive move toward personal growth and self-advancement.

Jupiter, the planet of abundance, begins the year in Capricorn, your twelfth house of secrets, sorrows, and solitary activities. But Jupiter quickly moves into your own sign of Aquarius, potentially sending personal magnetism to a high level. Self-beautification through changes of personal image and appearance may be an important ongoing theme all year. Moderation will be essential in such areas of your life as food, drink, money, and leisure. Gambling, spending, and speculating require restraint, certainly care. Overconfidence can be a big plus in some areas but a downfall in others.

Health and general well-being should improve this year as you display a more optimistic and outgoing demeanor. Sensitive areas ruled by Aquarius are the shins, ankles, heart, and circulatory system, all of which will benefit from consistent nurturing. Nurture your nervous system, too. Make sure you get enough sleep. Beware pushing yourself too hard. Counteract nervousness by implementing such stress busters as regular massage, yoga classes, or a sporting

**129**

activity. This year favors plans to upstyle your image and persona. Be fastidious about personal grooming. Avoiding overindulgence may be an issue because Jupiter is the planet of expansion, which includes your waistline. It isn't the best year to begin a strict diet or try to lose weight. If this is something that must be done, hire a personal trainer, join a gym, or hook up with exercise buddies who will provide the motivation you need to stay on track.

Travel, whether for pleasure, business, or education, is likely to call loudly. You could also be drawn toward foreign folk and want to experience the customs and cultures of faraway places. Allergies and viruses may be more prevalent as you journey out of your familiar environment. So dress appropriately to ward off ailments. When restlessness or anxiety threatens to become overwhelming, find some familiar territory to concentrate on and remember all that you have in life to be grateful for.

Your traditional ruler Saturn begins 2009 in Virgo, your house of shared assets, sex, and rebirth. Saturn transits Virgo until the end of October. During these ten months gains can be made by implementing a savings plan and continuing to increase your financial worth. Reducing or paying off debts quicker will also raise your economic status. Taking on new debt should be avoided except to purchase a home, investment property, or commercial real estate. Investing in blue-chip stocks and bonds may be lucrative, but steer clear of any risky investments.

A major cosmic influence occurs on October 29 when your coruler Saturn moves into Libra, your house of higher education and philosophical beliefs. Many Aquarius folk will feel as if a burden has been lifted off your shoulders as money pressures ease up. Paying off a home mortgage or reducing credit card debt to a more manageable level will be a relief. With Saturn in Libra formal academic study could become more appealing. You are likely to enroll in college or university classes to increase your knowledge and skills. Traveling overseas to learn more or to receive specialized training is foreseen. Taking up an academic post or a religious pledge is a possibility for some Aquarius.

Saturn in Libra discloses that older people or an authority figure may provide guidance for you in a legal or educational matter. Overseas connections can assist your career and professional development. Because of Saturn's restrictive influence you may become frustrated and feel that it is difficult to move ahead as desired. Step back and look at perceived obstacles from a distance. That way you should discover methods to improve your chances. Those of you in business might need to look to the past to see what you did right or wrong as clues to future success. Behind-the-scenes competition will require all of your skills and determination to rise above any challenges presented. Looking for alternative methods of doing business will pay dividends and assist in wealth creation.

Settling into a permanent relationship either overseas or with someone from another country is a possibility this year. Loving Venus and inspirational Neptune begin 2009 conjunct in your sign of Aquarius. Love affairs will be a strong force in the year ahead. Those of you currently single may be seeking that perfect but elusive soul mate. Reviving the romance and vigor in a committed union will be important for partnered Aquarius folk. As was the case last year, this year also cautions against involvement in a clandestine relationship. The chances of being found out are high. Marriage and parenthood are strong possibilities for those of you in a committed relationship. The fruition of deep personal goals is foreseen. From March 6 to April 17 the love planet Venus is retrograde in Aries, then Pisces. Venus retrograde here increases the likelihood of meeting an ex-lover or a romantic link from the past. Also, there may be problems communicating with a partner or a loved one who will be frustrated by your elusive nature. A relationship breakup or a protracted separation could occur if a rocky patch is ongoing.

Your modern-day ruler Uranus continues to light up Pisces, your house of personal finances and possessions. You should expect an ebb and flow in generating income. Sudden fluctuations might increase or decrease personal wealth. The timing of property settlements is an example. Patience will be required if expected money from a legacy, an insurance claim, or a home sale is delayed or tied up way longer than originally advised. Self-employed Aquarius could find that money doesn't come in as quickly or as steadily as you would like. However, your bank balance should remain fairly buoyant. The manner in which you earn your living may change. Some of you will experience the ups and downs of employment appearing and disappearing periodically, especially if you work on a contract basis. This is a good year to develop your innate skills, whether these are creative talents that can generate extra income or hobby pursuits that provide the chance to rest, relax, and unwind. Learning the fine art of budgeting will help you manage the ebb and flow of income.

Mystic Neptune still calls the tune while continuing to transit your sign of Aquarius, thereby making waves in your first house of self. Don't sit back and wait to be recognized for your achievements. Blow your own horn because people may be inclined to take you for granted. Be assertive. Consistently put yourself in a place where others cannot fail to notice you. Otherwise, you might be overlooked for a promotion or leadership responsibilities. As an Aquarius you are prone to detachment and distraction. These characteristics are enhanced this year. You need to make more of an effort to focus, be more attentive, and listen closely to others, especially the boss. Fortunately, your self-esteem and self-confidence will also be enhanced this year.

Transformational Pluto is settled in Capricorn, your twelfth house of all that is hidden. There is a greater chance of secrets coming to light and of other folk revealing your personal confidences. If you don't want your secrets shared with the world, in general keep mum and trust only your closest friends. You can expect plenty of action to happen behind closed doors all year. Charitable or humanitarian work will be of interest, and you are apt to spend more time volunteering your services to help people. There may be more involvement with hospitals, facilities for the aged, or government organizations. Pluto in Capricorn encourages you to look deep into your psyche and to acknowledge every part of your being. Even qualities that are not as attractive as you would like should be examined and changes implemented to help you become a new you. This is a year when a number of your long-held views and opinions might change as your knowledge and your wisdom grow.

To the uninitiated, a retrograde planet seems to stop before apparently moving backward in the zodiac. All planets except the Sun and Moon appear to go through this optical illusion of retreating, which in astrology is called retrograde motion. It is planet Mercury that causes the most chaos when retrograde. Misunderstandings, delays, and confusion are possible. Breakdowns in electronic equipment, communication, and transportation are also possible. Making decisions, signing important paperwork, and purchasing expensive items are not recommended. However, you don't need to hibernate during a Mercury retrograde. Instead, review, rethink, and reconsider situations, choices, and current goals to ensure that you are working toward your main aim. Mercury usually goes retrograde three times a year, but in 2009 Mercury is retrograde four times: January 11–February 1, May 7–30, September 7–29, December 26–January 15, 2010.

The phases of the Moon can be a guide to decision making and appropriate action. Beginning a venture during the New Moon phase can increase the chances of obtaining a fruitful conclusion. Completing a venture during the Full Moon phase can bring the desired end results. People, including yourself, are likely to be cranky and agitated during Full Moon phase. This is the time to steer clear of risky behavior.

Planning and precision are the keys to moving through the many cosmic ups and downs that Aquarius individuals are likely to experience this year. Building a strong financial foundation and learning to manage all your material resources will put you on the road to success, and keep you there.

# AQUARIUS
# DAILY FORECAST

## January–December 2009

# JANUARY

**1. THURSDAY. Confident.** As 2009 begins, Venus, goddess of love and beauty, remains in your own sign and boosts your confidence, morale, and the feeling that you are beautiful and desirable. If single, take advantage of a romantic potential who is looking your way. Don't hesitate to make the first move because this person may be reluctant to do so. Your ability to charm people is high, and you can now reap the rewards from a cheerful demeanor. It is time to follow your good natural instincts and remain firm in regard to decisions already made. Chatty Mercury moves into your solar Aquarius house of self, bringing an urge to launch a new personal plan or aim to ensure making headway in 2009.

**2. FRIDAY. Quiet.** With four of the planets placed in Capricorn, your solar twelfth house of secrets, sorrow, and solitude, Aquarius folk may prefer to spend time at home on the couch or in front of the computer rather than going out to socialize. You need to recoup and regroup. Get back in touch with yourself, with social intermission as your reward. This is reinforced by the position of the Moon in the placid sign of Pisces. Spiritual pursuits, yoga, or meditation could be a relaxing medium if you have the day or the evening free of other commitments. The energetic could find the New Year sales offer great purchasing power, allowing more to be bought than usual for a budget sum of money.

**3. SATURDAY. Positive.** Finances should improve over the next few weeks, especially if you cut back on expenses and implement strategies to keep within your budget. Venus, the goddess of love and money, now enters the sign of Pisces, putting your personal finances and possessions in the spotlight. This planetary influence indicates that boosting both your income and bank balance should be easier over the next few weeks. An offer of a new job could come your way, with a bigger take-home package than you are now receiving. Creative Aquarius could experience an urge to write after hours, and this could turn into a way to earn some money on the side.

**4. SUNDAY. Happy.** The stars are favoring you, and with the right effort many areas of your life should be falling into place. Desire and romance make a welcome return as saucy Venus happily greets passionate Pluto. This is an excellent day to spend with your significant other to cement loving bonds. Creative juices should be flowing. Your natural ability to grasp innovative ideas and concepts is an added incentive to stretch yourself. Have a go at something you have always wanted to do but haven't had the confidence or time to try. Aquarius folk who are inclined to socialize will find that this is a good day to enjoy the company of special friends.

**5. MONDAY. Major.** As increased energy kicks in, you will be encouraged to move into top gear and get down to duties that you have been putting off. Family or property matters could be of particular concern. As an Aquarius you usually go with the flow without a problem, but today care is needed not to make mountains out of molehills when it comes to domestic issues. A turning point is occurring in your life as one cycle comes to an end and another begins. Abundant Jupiter enters your sign and remains there for the next twelve months. During this period you will have the opportunity to expand your horizons and test your capabilities and skills by tackling new projects.

**6. TUESDAY. Tricky.** This isn't the easiest of days. You could experience a sense of being lost or alienated from the mainstream. The best way to handle this unsettled energy is by dealing with daily duties in a practical, routine manner. Be aware of the possibility of deception. Something could be happening behind the scenes that you aren't yet aware of. However, also guard against jumping to conclusions because more than likely you will come up with the wrong scenario. If going out, remember to drink in moderation, and don't get behind the wheel of a car if you have been imbibing. Soothing music, a relaxing bath, and time on the couch could set the scene for a night of comfort and pleasure.

**7. WEDNESDAY. Soothing.** With Jupiter settled in your sign and your first house, Aquarius folk who are prone to gaining weight will need to be more careful with diet and consumption of food and alcohol. Jupiter rules expansion and growth, so whenever this planet visits the house of the physical you can't ignore the chance of an expanding waistline. As an Aquarius you value independence, and this planetary placement increases the urge to be free from limitations and issues that keep you in one place for too long. This evening other people could make a number of demands that frustrate you. Establish firm boundaries or you may feel that your good nature is being taken for granted.

**8. THURSDAY. Frustrating.** Issues with a child, lover, or a creative project could find you running around in circles. Because there may be certain restrictions or delays, this isn't the best time to attempt to understand or settle outstanding problems. On the social scene, try to keep discussions upbeat and not very serious rather than launching into intense conversations. Your imagination is likely to run high, although putting ideas into usable form could prove more difficult than usual. The focus in on fun and socializing, but it might be wise to wait until the weekend because you may be disappointed with the entertainment that is available tonight.

**9. FRIDAY. Sensitive.** The universe brings a finely tuned sensitivity to your emotional nature and personality. Restlessness and an urge to go off to explore the wild blue yonder will need to be dampened down if you have urgent tasks to accomplish. It may be intuition or a premonition that impels you to turn from one path of action in favor of another. Acting spontaneously should produce favorable results. The self-employed may want to consider changing accountants or credit arrangements if difficulties are being experienced receiving payment for goods or services rendered. Guard against conflicts with coworkers midafternoon.

**10. SATURDAY. Edgy.** Toil and trouble may be the theme of today. Superpowered emotions and instincts are likely. There is also the potential to overdo with sensitivity and heightened feelings. The Full Moon falls in the sign of family-oriented Cancer, accentuating your house of health and employment conditions. A tricky situation with a coworker or employee will require careful handling to keep emotions under control. More attention to your teeth or a certain dental problem might be required, especially if you are suffering from a general health condition. Past secrets or skeletons in the closet could come to light sometime during the next two weeks.

**11. SUNDAY. Revealing.** The Moon is moving through the warm and regal sign of Leo, highlighting your zone of partnerships and the important others in your life. This energy can be difficult for you because as an Aquarius you are normally cool and detached, not inclined to warm and very emotional feelings. Don't be afraid to see what happens if you do allow your emotions to flow freely. Mercury now goes into retrograde motion, which happens approximately three or four times a year, for around three weeks each time. As a result, difficulties can arise with everyday communications and verbal skills. Be prepared for mistakes, misunderstandings, delays, as well as computer and transportation problems.

**12. MONDAY. Diverse.** If you experience a boost of energy, grasp the chance to harness it productively rather than wasting an opportunity to accomplish something of importance. Networking increases the likelihood of cultivating powerful alliances. Group and teamwork success will be measured by the effort exerted, so do your best and you could be a winner. Touchy moments are likely with a personal or business partner who becomes angry about a matter that you consider minor. Refrain from bringing up old emotional baggage in any discussion. Instead, state your views in a calm, rational manner.

**13. TUESDAY. Worrisome.** You may be in a downbeat mood and could do with some cheering up. Rather than giving in to current negative circumstances, try to find the positive in each situation that arises. Someone who has been misbehaving could decide to turn over a new leaf and might need guidance and moral support. Give this person a second chance and you should be well rewarded. Financial constraints could rain on your parade, forcing you to limit spending in order to keep within the budget. Don't overcommit yourself to whatever of interest comes your way. This is a time when you could land in trouble if you open your mouth before thinking.

**14. WEDNESDAY. Stressful.** It may be a tough having to meet a deadline or handle a financial deal. Resilience will be required to effectively overcome possible obstacles, disruptions, delays, or criticism. However, if you are able to do so, respect from other people should soar. Consider clearing out books, magazines, clothes, and nonessential items to reduce clutter in your environment. Give away or donate pre-loved items; someone will be happy to own your old treasures that you no longer need or use. To avoid the pos-

sibility of conflict, discuss plans with your business or personal partner before going ahead.

**15. THURSDAY. Manageable.** For much of the day issues surrounding joint finances will claim attention. However, you shouldn't
have many problems resolving difficulties, and there may even be
a boost to your bank account. Long-distance travel is indicated;
this could be a dream trip on a luxury cruise ship or flying overseas
to visit a loved one or family members. Philosophical ideas may
seem more interesting, and new knowledge could be obtained by
studying a topic that has captured your attention. You might prefer to remain at home this evening to read about various belief
systems or to study the customs and cultures of those living in distant places.

**16. FRIDAY. Stimulating.** Your mind is apt to be stimulated, encouraging you to talk or write about what you are thinking. The key
to making this worthwhile is to maintain focus. If you succumb to
being overwhelmed or are unable to concentrate, you may as well
pack up and go home because accomplishing anything of value
could be limited. Unless you can sidestep any foolish arguments
that erupt quickly, your whole day could be disrupted. Sharing
problems with a friend could help ease any anxiety you are currently experiencing. Heed the warning that money and in-laws are
not a good mix this evening. Going to bed early can be a positive
way to escape potential conflict later tonight.

**17. SATURDAY. Disquieting.** It may be difficult to settle your
emotions. Impatience and a wandering mind are apt to limit your
ability to accomplish anything of a practical nature. Researching
different cultures or looking into the possibility of overseas travel
could be an attractive option. If you have urgent or important duties to attend to, concentrate and exercise self-discipline so you can
meet responsibilities and obligations. Your elusive nature might be
the cause of stress for your significant other; this may have been
ongoing for some time due to Neptune moving through your sign
of Aquarius. If you value the relationship, make an effort to move
emotionally closer by opening up your heart more.

**18. SUNDAY. Starred.** This should be a memorable day, with a general feeling of good fortune prevailing. Your popularity is steadily increasing as other people send invitations or turn to you for guidance
and advice. New associations could be formed at a social gathering,

with the possibility of benefits enhancing your career or your public image. Buy a lottery ticket, begin planning how to achieve personal goals, or organize a trip to a locale you have never visited before. A public speaking engagement could propel you into the limelight. First-time authors can make headway with writing that can lead to future fame and wealth.

**19. MONDAY. Favorable.** If life has seemed a little dull lately, consider ways of introducing a dash of excitement. Your ability to speak up for yourself is enhanced, and you should have little difficulty finding your voice. Be alert for opportunities to advance your professional and public standing. The Sun enters your sign, impacting your first house of self and personality, and will give you a huge boost of energy and vitality. This is your time to shine. Act on tasks that will raise your profile as well as allowing other people to view your capabilities. Health and energy rise, and tasks that require strenuous effort can be carried out with ease.

**20. TUESDAY. Helpful.** Balance your emotions and keep your ego under control. Treat yourself to something special and don't hold back, especially if you deserve a little extra indulgence. Planning new projects and creative enterprises can begin now, but wait until the beginning of February before putting ideas into practice. Finding various ways to improve skills and expertise should be easier and can be an excellent way to move quickly up the ladder of success. A trusted friend who shares a common interest could provide motivation and inspiration for you. Aim to make headway in your activity of choice.

**21. WEDNESDAY. Moderate.** Entertaining grandiose illusions and ideas would be unwise right now. Moderation is required. If someone advises you to be more cautious or conservative, heed the warning. Spending money to increase warmth, love, and affection from other people should be unnecessary. If you must give a loved one a gift, make it simple and inexpensive. With Mercury still in reverse, this isn't the time to shop for expensive or big-ticket items because more than likely you will end up purchasing a lemon or the item will be overpriced. Refrain from signing an important contract, and carefully read through documents or any paperwork before passing them on.

**22. THURSDAY. Promising.** The currently single could unexpectedly meet an interesting romantic potential. However, this isn't a good time to make a permanent commitment. Have fun, enjoy loving moments, but be ready to move on when the affair has run its course, as it probably will. An unexpected windfall could come your way providing welcome relief if you have been falling short covering current bills and expenditures. Aquarius who have spent some time devising strategies to increase income could be in for a pleasant surprise. Be sure to put some money in a savings account rather than spending every cent as fast as it comes in.

**23. FRIDAY. Restful.** This is the time of the month when strenuous tasks should be placed on the back burner. Rest, relax, and recharge your batteries as the Moon slips through your Capricorn twelfth sector. If you have recently encountered a number of obstacles and hurdles, you need a break so you can renew your vim and vitality. As an Aquarius you are more future-oriented than locked in the past, but over the next few days you can gain inspiration by looking backward even for a short period of time. Keep to your established health routine to ensure that you remain strong mentally and physically. Eat light and right, even if going out tonight.

**24. SATURDAY. Varied.** Today's mixed influences increase lucky vibes and romantic inclinations, but also send out warning bells where finances are concerned. Avoid taking a pessimistic approach to money matters; a positive attitude could provide the necessary answers. Use the energy of the day to plan and strategize instead of feeling weighed down by fiscal pressures. Reminiscing could be a pleasant pastime, allowing memories and feelings of long ago to surface. Love and romance should be in plentiful supply. Those who are single and looking for a partner may be helped by going where other solo folks congregate.

**25. SUNDAY. Vital.** Emotions as well as vim and vitality should be stronger now that the Moon has returned to your sign. Problems will be easier to resolve thanks to a more optimistic approach. Giving as well as receiving works well for the Water Bearer, and today you have plenty of good humor, love, and compassion to share with those in your immediate environment and beyond. Curiosity peaks, and the discovery of interesting new ideas can both enlighten and entertain. Go to the movies or to an art exhibit if a large social gathering is not your style. Aquarius parents may find that a local museum will keep children amused and be educational as well.

**26. MONDAY. Renewing.** Whether ready or not, you are bound to be pushed to center stage. A New Moon in your own sign of

Aquarius, plus a bundle of planetary influences culminating over the next few days, can serve as the catalyst to take charge of your life and make a bevy of new decisions. If your job is no longer providing the emotional gratification you expect, seriously consider moving on. However, take your time with this. As an Aquarius you are prone to jumping the gun and rushing into situations and choices before giving them sufficient thought. A journal in which you can write your thoughts for future examination can be helpful.

**27. TUESDAY. Optimistic.** Grabbing the spotlight seems assured again today as you go about your daily business. If you continue to put your best foot forward, you are bound to receive rewards, whether a promotion or pay raise from a boss or compliments and increased business from a client. Creative juices should soar. The impulse to produce new work and to experiment with new ideas in your field can assist the climb up the career ladder or lead to having your name go up in lights. Look at all opportunities without making any commitments, either verbally or in writing, until next week. A lecture or an encouraging talk should be well received by an attentive audience.

**28. WEDNESDAY. Fine.** The good times continue to roll, although focus is likely to shift to matters concerning money and values. There shouldn't be any unpleasant surprises in the mail. Finances should be looking up, or at least fairly stable. The only way you could hurt your capacity to pay bills on time is by acting impulsively and buying items you can do without right now. Be alert if shopping for special objects. If traveling you could discover something of value. Your influence over other people may be stronger than usual, and with this energy you could be an agent for making overall improvements or improving the life of someone in need.

**29. THURSDAY. Good.** Revising your values or coming up with a new household budget may be where energy is needed. Ensure that everything is in order and remains on track. The morning hours are more likely to produce good results than later in the day, as the lunar goddess sends helpful vibes to support your efforts. A delightful surprise, gift, or gesture could bring a sense of emotional comfort and the realization that other people appreciate your efforts, even if they are not usually vocal or demonstrative in displaying this to you. Later in the day issues surrounding joint finances could surface, and it would be wise to step back and wait rather than trying to charge ahead.

**30. FRIDAY. Bewildering.** As Jupiter clashes with your traditional ruler Saturn, you could feel that you are standing still. Right now this may be your best course of action because trying to push or pull against the tide will cause frustration and stress. Use humor and wit to cover anxiety and help ease unsettled feelings, especially in conversation with other people. Avoiding a financial issue won't make it disappear. If you need to sort out a loan or a bill, do so first thing this morning rather than putting it off, which will only raise your stress level even higher. Brace yourself for changes linked to a group or an organization that you are a member of.

**31. SATURDAY. Enterprising.** Expect lively action as the Moon rushes through the impulsive sign of Aries. If you have a creative idea or an innovative venture that could increase your income, now is the time to get the ball rolling by at least putting plans down on paper. A neighbor could surprise you with a kind gesture, making you feel that there are still many folk willing to lend a hand when needed. However, don't be surprised if you encounter more emotional outbursts or anger from those in close proximity to you. Safety precautions should be heeded precisely. A tendency to rush in or act in haste means you could repent at leisure, especially if you drive or walk too fast.

# FEBRUARY

**1. SUNDAY. Fruitful.** New ventures and projects can be started now that messenger Mercury is once again in forward motion. Delays and obstacles should begin to disappear as cosmic energy slowly returns to normal. As an Aquarius friendships are inherently important to you, so don't be surprised if you begin having second thoughts about a particular friend. In deciding whether to continue the relationship, it would be wise to wait a little longer before making any conclusive decision because you could change your mind later on. Seek entertainment that stretches your mental facilities and provides the stimulation you require. You could also enjoy a get-together with neighbors or schoolmates.

**2. MONDAY. Touchy.** If you have been neglecting your duties around the house, you may have to do some fast catching up. Someone is not happy and is very prepared to tell you so. Relations with a woman in the domestic environment may be strained and stressful, but today is not the best time to try to resolve a serious concern. You or another person may be a little hotheaded, so it would be wise to switch into cruise control and just go with the flow. Tonight Venus slides into your solar zone of impulsive Aries, putting verbal expression and communication in the limelight. This is a good time to begin a short course or to finish educational studies.

**3. TUESDAY. Good.** Home life and domestic routines are to the fore. Whether completing chores around home base or chauffeuring children to their various activities, family members and loved ones are likely to feature strongly in your day. Step in quickly to get household repairs and maintenance work done, particularly if there are safety factors to consider. A vacation might be due. If you intend to visit distant shores, consider studying the appropriate foreign language to enhance your stay away from home. A child may be stubborn or willful, requiring careful handling to restore harmony. Enjoy some tasty home cooking to round out the evening.

**4. WEDNESDAY. Enjoyable.** When the Moon enters the sign of movable Gemini, it is play time for Aquarius folk. Routine tasks or tedious activities are unlikely to interest you. Whatever is on your schedule, be sure to add a dash of fun and humor to keep motivation high and to increase your enjoyment of the day. Aquarius who are part of a couple should be innovative in adding spice to make love more exciting. Children could feature once again in your day. Parents are likely to be busy running errands or involved in school activities. Let relaxing oils or incense increase your relaxation and comfort this evening. Don't put off bedtime.

**5. THURSDAY. Restrained.** During the next week do whatever you can to avoid power struggles with other people. Guard against becoming too caught up with worries and concerns. Panicking about something that might or might not happen is a senseless waste of time, and this can also hinder your ability to find the best course of action to resolve issues. Warrior Mars has now entered your sign and your first house of self and personality, boosting courage and perseverance to begin something new just for you. Singles who have met someone interesting should be bold; make the first move because you have nothing to lose and possibly a lot to gain.

**6. FRIDAY. Cautious.** Tolerance is the key to getting through the day without too many problems to slow your progress. The lunar goddess isn't sending many positive trends, so you need to move carefully, especially on the job. Clashes with an employee or with coworkers are likely because you may get carried away and end up dominating a conversation, to your detriment. Be prepared to donate some of your time and energy as a way of providing service to someone in need or to a volunteer group. This is a good period to make that appointment for a checkup, especially if you have been putting off this task. Romantic desire burns strongly.

**7. SATURDAY. Fair.** Some areas of your life will begin with a bang and then go downhill. This morning you could be the star of your own show, but later on there may be a number of issues to confront. Romantic vibes are heightened. If connecting with your significant other is a main priority, loving feelings can be pleasantly experienced. Activities conducted behind the scenes should work in your favor. Aquarius who are involved in creative fields could meet with almost instant success. A family function or a large gathering may be a wonderful occasion to renew old friendships and to take a trip down memory lane.

**8. SUNDAY. Caring.** Sleeping late and a leisurely breakfast could be the ideal way to begin the day on a pleasant note. You will benefit from making extra time for love even if there are a hundred other things clamoring for your attention. You are apt to be very reliant on your mate or partner. Try to take life as it comes, especially if you value your current one-on-one relationship. The Sun and your traditional ruler Saturn are causing friction while also reducing the vim and vitality at your disposal. Avoid conflict with older people. If socializing, use your sharp intellect to advantage by defusing potential disagreements, not igniting them.

**9. MONDAY. Emotional.** Be careful in choosing which activities to undertake. The next few days could be more difficult than usual. Although as an Aquarius you are not typically known for being sensitive, the prevailing energy of receptive awareness could even make you sit up and take notice. Today's eclipsed Full Moon in Leo urges Aquarius to place partnership issues in the forefront. You may gain insight about a partner's feelings and needs, or realize that something you want badly will have to take second place to your mate's current desires or requirements. Efforts to complete a project should be successful if you can maintain focus.

**10. TUESDAY. Tricky.** On this challenging day you need to make the best of situations presented. New ways of acquiring money that once seemed bountiful could meet with obstacles, requiring more effort than you envisioned. A recent purchase may be causing stress and discontent. If you have changed your mind, take the item back and replace it with something you prefer before it is too late. Leave a competitive demeanor at work when you walk out the door because your loved one is likely to strongly object to an overly assertive approach. Singles may be attracted to a neighbor or someone who works in the same office, but this relationship may not be what it seems so proceed with care.

**11. WEDNESDAY. Challenging.** A personal or business partner could be moody throughout the day, making the atmosphere downbeat. You may have little patience or tolerance for this type of behavior, so it would be wise if you can go off on your own and avoid interruptions. Money is apt to be on your mind, perhaps more than necessary, which could also increase unsettled feelings. Acting on impulse without serious consideration is never wise, even for the spontaneous Aquarius, so slow down and refrain from making rash decisions. Use your natural talents to get a grip on what you need to do, or not do, to resolve current issues.

**12. THURSDAY. Variable.** Control any urge to take risks. This isn't the time to test your luck. Unless you keep life as simple as possible, you may become lost in details, erroneous information, or bad advice given by other people. If your actions are planned well today, benefits can come your way tomorrow. Creative juices should be flowing freely. Through experimentation you could discover a new talent or could experience one of your trademark flashes of inspiration that can help achieve a special aim. A problem that had seemed insurmountable could be taken off your hands, leaving you free to focus on your own plans.

**13. FRIDAY. Steady.** Don't be concerned about negative connotations of today's date. There aren't many unpleasant cosmic trends in force. A new endeavor could take you on an adventure, which is exactly what you may desire. Performing the same tasks on a daily basis can be tedious as well as reducing motivation. If you have been working harder than ever, schedule some time off so that you can chill out at home or enjoy a cozy weekend retreat for two, moving closer to that special person. Those who covet the good life need to take care this evening because social expenses could quickly spiral out of control.

**14. SATURDAY. Happy.** Life remains steady and on track. If you haven't finalized plans for a romantic Valentine's Day, make arrangements as early as possible. Or you may prefer to entertain your mate or partner at home, preparing a feast that will tantalize the taste buds and set the scene for a romantic evening. Mercury, the messenger of the gods, zooms into your sign of Aquarius, joining the Sun and Neptune there for a three-week stay. At this time of the year the focus should be on making personal plans and plotting future aims. Don't settle for anything less than what you really want.

**15. SUNDAY. Dreamy.** Romance could play second fiddle to other activities today. Although generally your mind will be active, quick, and impulsive, emotionally your thoughts may be clouded by a lack of clear vision. This isn't the day to make any decisions regarding your love life because friction between Venus and Neptune is causing lack of clarity and poor judgment. Also beware making rash moves with financial matters. Even if you have a strong desire for retail therapy, steer clear of high-class shopping malls and leave credit cards at home. Social activities could squeeze the household budget or bank account to the limit unless you take a moderate approach.

**16. MONDAY. Constructive.** Although your business and career skills might not be as sharp as usual, good vibes prevail. Don't hesitate to ask questions or seek answers in order to gain more knowledge and act in the best possible manner. Affectionate Venus is making positive vibes to Mars and Jupiter over the next few days, increasing loving feelings for Aquarius folks of all ages. Focusing on your dreams can increase your chances of manifesting deepest desires and wishes. Reading, writing, and expressing your views come to the fore. Students, or those with a special assignment to complete, should find such tasks become easier.

**17. TUESDAY. Inspiring.** Venus and Jupiter, the two cosmic energies associated with the good life, are conspiring together today. So the urge to overdo and overindulge increases. There is no need to deprive yourself, but it is time to be sensible and moderate so that you don't have regrets later. A happy romantic surprise could have put you on cloud nine. If you are part of a loving couple, take the time to celebrate your relationship and further cement those bonds. Currently single Aquarius should be in luck. You may discover someone who makes your heart beat faster. If so, let this person know that they have captured your attention, but don't come on so strong that you risk scaring them off.

**18. WEDNESDAY. Auspicious.** Good fortune and vigorous social and romantic influences make this an action-packed day. However, there is also a tendency to be overanxious or inclined to brood more than usual. If you can overcome this tendency, a great day looms on the horizon. Otherwise a minor health issue could dominate your thoughts. A lottery ticket or a small flutter at the racetrack may give you even more reason to smile. Hold down spending on superfluous items. If considering buying a large-ticket item such as a new computer, car, or electronic system, find out about all the many styles and designs that suit your budget.

**19. THURSDAY. Helpful.** Ideally you should continue to concentrate on ways to make your future dreams and goals come true. Today you may be content to escape from reality and invest in some soul searching. Even if you are busy, give yourself time and space to retreat for a short period to help revitalize your energy and clear your mind. The Sun is now residing in the sign of Pisces, which will heighten your ambitions and the urge to generate more income. Your self-worth could receive a boost, possibly due to a wage increase or a promotion. This is also a great day to analyze ways to reduce household expenditures.

**20. FRIDAY. Restful.** Although as an Aquarius you are a social sign, there are many times when you prefer to hide out of sight from the world at large. Other people are probably used to you going off by yourself for periods of inner growth, research, or just to think. This urge increases whenever the Moon rolls through your solitary twelfth house of Capricorn, as it does today. Avoid excessive physical strain because your energy could be below par, making you more likely to catch a minor infection or a cold. Something hidden, confidential, or pushed out of the way could require urgent action, whether you like it or not. Hiding away with a special person could be the highlight of the day.

**21. SATURDAY. Low-key.** If you are on the job, keep a low profile and work behind the scenes on career or business plans. Put all of life's many demands in perspective. This is another day when you need to understand that at times you must recharge rundown batteries. An unexpected development could require a quick change of plans. A friend could experience money problems, but be careful not to become too involved. Although this person might only be asking for advice and not a loan, extend sympathy but don't provide financial advice unless qualified to do so. Keep your plans sim-

ple tonight. It may be late evening before you have an urge to socialize and mingle with other people.

**22. SUNDAY. Pleasing.** Low-key activities are recommended this
morning until helpful planetary trends take over after lunch. Someone's disproval could increase your stress level, especially if you
are seeking agreement to ensure that you are on the right track.
With the Moon now in your own sign, Aquarius charm and charisma
should be on display. This is an ideal time to invite friends over for
a meal or a good laugh about past or present actions. If venturing
out to socialize, once again the desire to overindulge in the goodies
of life needs to be contained.

**23. MONDAY. Vigorous.** The cosmos swings into high gear, making
this another day of high activity and excitement. Your mind and
physical energy should be in great shape, which can increase the
tendency to take on more than you should. Knowing what you are
letting yourself in for before assuming too much responsibility will
reduce the chance of not fulfilling a promise. Before assuming an
obligation that could prove tricky, let other people know in advance of any uncertainties so you are not left trying to meet an impossible deadline. With your genuine concern for the welfare of
others, make a donation to your favorite charity if you don't have
time to volunteer your services.

**24. TUESDAY. Buoyant.** Confidence receives a boost from the universe today. Mental clarity is strengthened and your ability to make
plans and implement new projects is enhanced. Lucky trends also
exist, so don't hesitate to enter a competition, buy a lottery ticket,
or ask for special favors. Incentive for success is high as tonight's
New Moon culminates in Pisces, your solar house of personal finances and possessions. You should have sufficient money or the
opportunity to generate extra wealth over the next few weeks. If
fiscal management has been poor in the past, now is the time to
reevaluate your priorities and make the necessary adjustments.

**25. WEDNESDAY. Active.** Stellar patterns form with Mercury, the
planet of communication, perfectly aligned with Venus, the planet
of money. If you make lists and keep busy, you should be delighted
with your accomplishments by the end of the day. Easy negotiations in any potential deal or collaborative effort will assist career,
business, or personal matters. There is the potential of wanting and

desiring more than your bank account can handle, so make sure your whims are kept under control. Balance the checkbook and other accounts to get a clear idea of your current fiscal status. Express your love in a special way tonight.

**26. THURSDAY. Enterprising.** Money matters will again consume much of your thoughts. This can be an active and industrious period, especially if you are developing a passion for creative writing, poetry, or music. You could compose a hit song or write an inspirational novel or play. Writing a letter to the editor detailing concerns for people who are less fortunate than you could put you in the spotlight. This can be an excellent period to raise your public profile. A decision might need to be made that involves the pursuit of a dream or a special goal. Providing you take a realistic attitude, moving in the right direction is more than likely.

**27. FRIDAY. Slow.** Move slowly today, and put safety above all else. Keep your nose to the grindstone and retain a sense of what can be accomplished and what will have to be postponed. Extra work or business emergencies could interrupt scheduled plans, but this shouldn't disrupt your weekend if you exert extra effort. Contact with a friend may fill you with longing that borders on romantic desire. If the atmosphere seems right, perhaps it is time to reveal your feelings in a subtle manner. Let close relatives know that you view them in the same light as your close friends so that they don't feel neglected.

**28. SATURDAY. Diverse.** As an Aquarius you often display a stubborn demeanor. Today you may choose to be more obstinate, fixed in your views, and less tolerant than usual. Don't reject the ideas and plans of other people without first examining their views and the reasons behind them. Difficult or frustrating events could require that you take a different approach. Misunderstandings with a relative or neighbor are foreseen due to different levels of understanding. Unless you are ready to argue, try to be understanding and to accept the foibles of other people as they attempt to understand yours.

# MARCH

**1. SUNDAY. Sensitive.** Sleep late if possible. You'll need some extra effort to rise above today's negative atmosphere. If you allow either your own pessimistic thoughts or those of other people to derail your efforts and spoil the day, problems and issues are likely to seem more serious than they really are. Be alert in case someone at home is feeling neglected or is lacking direction and don't know how to bring up their problems with you. Find a way to help a loved one open up and explain. Your public speaking powers are enhanced, and you should excel if talking in front of an audience. Just be sure to keep your remarks brief and to the point.

**2. MONDAY. Useful.** Aquarius verbal skills remain sharp and fluent, which will help if you are attending a meeting, presenting a report, or negotiating a deal. If a change of residence or some other real estate transaction would increase your level of security and comfort, consider taking action now. Working from home requires taking a little extra care with safety precautions to reduce the possibility of a minor mishap or accident. Save yourself time and trouble by doing extra advance planning and decision making; otherwise you could end up doing a project more than once. Clear the decks and act on one thing at a time. Romance can be outstanding if you are prepared to let your honey know your innermost feelings.

**3. TUESDAY. Upbeat.** Positive trends continue, and a spot of good luck is likely to arrive on your doorstep. If you have been neglecting your personal needs, take a long, hard look to see what you can do to make life even sweeter. Aquarius caring for children could sense their frustration regarding a certain situation this morning. Try to help ease their upset so that they can settle down and relax, as youngsters should. A surprise outing after school or one that is in the planning stage could restore harmonious vibes. Leisure pursuits may be more of the physical variety than the relaxing kind, but this can be a great way to unload accumulated stress and pressure.

**4. WEDNESDAY. Loving.** Romance tops your list, and today you may be making a decision in that regard. Aquarius who are now in a committed relationship can share happy accord. Your imagination is stimulated, benefiting spare-time activities that require creative input, such as cooking, acting, or sports. Guard against becoming involved in issues that are none of your business. Although your curiosity could be piqued, other people might not appreciate your interference. Happiness shouldn't depend on how much money you have; the more you have, the more you might want. Try to control spending if your budget can't handle another shock right now.

**5. THURSDAY. Dreamy.** With today's easygoing mood you may prefer to be around folk who are gentle and understanding rather than noisy and demanding. Mercury and Neptune are in happy alignment, bringing your imagination and creative juices to the fore. Aquarius who write fiction, music, or poetry could significantly increase their output, and designers could come up with novel plans and schemes. This isn't the day to make clear and purposeful decisions because you are more inclined to be dreamy or indecisive, making it difficult to reach a definite choice. Be careful if issuing instructions or passing on important messages. Misunderstandings can occur unless your communication is clear and concise.

**6. FRIDAY. Interesting.** Domestic and social pursuits focus on health and fitness activities. Joining a gym, participating in a sports event, or hosting a group meeting discussing cooking and preparing healthy meals can be productive, especially for those who desire a change of lifestyle. Venus the planet of harmony, begins retreating through Aries and will be retrograde until April 17. This increases the chance of meeting old connections from the past. If there have been problems communicating with your partner or a loved one, the cosmos now provides a chance to resolve outstanding issues. Don't be caught flat-footed if social arrangements go haywire over the next few months.

**7. SATURDAY. Mixed.** As far as your relationships are concerned, this can be a good or not so good day depending on your attitude. The Moon makes its way through your opposite sign of Leo, which can increase an emotional attachment to your significant other and provide an ideal chance to improve intimacy and affection. It would be best to postpone any major decisions because you may succumb to dramatics. If you act on one task at a time rather than your usual dozen or so, you should be able to accomplish a great deal. Socially you are likely to be in the thick of all that is going on, with other people clamoring for your attendance at various functions and events.

**8. SUNDAY. Lethargic.** Refrain from making decisions again today because a more negative atmosphere now prevails. With your physical energy limited, this is a good day to rest and take it easy. Choosing entertainment that is relaxing rather than rushing from place to place will minimize stress and make you feel as though you had a day off. Family members and other people in your immediate environment may be more restrictive, and any ideas you put forward are likely to be vetoed without much discussion. Financial issues may arise and cause a dispute with your mate or partner, especially if one of you has been spending without telling the other person.

**9. MONDAY. Unsettled.** Hiding your emotions could be difficult this morning as anger and unsettled feelings erupt. People close to you could try to reason with you, which may upset you even more unless you make an effort to remain cool and calm. Mercury moves into Pisces, which will generate new discussions and plans regarding finances and possessions. Scheming and dreaming are also likely, so make sure you remain realistic. Refrain from ignoring a problem in the hope that it will just disappear. Money matters might require some change over the next three weeks because an activity you have been doing for a while could be altered unexpectedly.

**10. TUESDAY. Revealing.** Aquarius concentration remains on fiscal arrangements. Something that has been hidden could come to light. Over the next few days your appeal for support or a special favor from someone in authority could be granted. All types of communication are under auspicious vibes, and you can now convey powerful messages to other people. A Full Moon in perfectionist Virgo will bring a money matter to the surface. It may be time to rethink an old strategy, especially if it doesn't appear to be working anymore. A promised payment that has been delayed could be causing increased anxiety.

**11. WEDNESDAY. Fortunate.** Happy trends ensure that the atmosphere remains light and easygoing. Take advantage of surrounding good fortune by grasping opportunities and chances that come your way. Travel and cultural matters assume importance. Short trips for business or pleasure can produce financial gains as well as personal rewards. If involved in selling, you should experience a bonanza of orders as your powers of persuasion increase. Keeping to a set limit in any sphere of life could be very difficult now as Venus, goddess of the good times, entwines with excessive Jupiter. Unless you make moderation the theme over the next few days, overindulgence could make your life a little more problematical.

**12. THURSDAY. Exciting.** Life has an adventurous feel to it, and routine activities are unlikely to be very rewarding or enjoyable. The Pisces Sun merges with your modern ruler, unpredictable Uranus. Although most Aquarius folk never know what to expect on a daily basis, this is even more prevalent today. Remain flexible and be prepared for anything to happen, and you won't be disappointed. Becoming involved in activities that are outside your usual orbit will keep stimulation and motivation high. Explore new surroundings even if this is just a shopping mall that you haven't visited before or a restaurant that just opened for business.

**13. FRIDAY. Good.** This is another Friday the thirteenth that shouldn't cause any problems. Buy a lottery chance or a raffle ticket and you could receive a small windfall. This is a favorable period to examine a new enterprise that has the potential to make money. Dealing with someone associated with the law, such as a lawyer, arbitrator, or judge, should proceed smoothly. For Aquarius who are involved in any legal activities, a favorable result is likely. If you require assistance, don't be too proud to ask for help or guidance. If you have been under pressure lately, this is an excellent period to take off on a long-distance trip or to research the Internet to see what vacation packages are available at discount prices.

**14. SATURDAY. Agreeable.** If finances have been on your mind a lot over the past few weeks, this trend is likely to continue. A major new moneymaking scheme could claim your attention. Assertive Mars now enters Pisces, your house of finances, increasing your desire to help other people in a material manner. Just make sure that you don't take on commitments that will stretch you too far right now, as the tendency for self-sacrifice is heightened. If you are considering putting money into a building or domestic project, first come up with a budget so you know how much can be spent before beginning the job. For Aquarius shoppers, the best bargains are likely to be found during the afternoon hours.

**15. SUNDAY. Busy.** Life could be hectic today, although your preference will be to chill out and do your own thing. Keep a strict eye on the pluses and minuses when it comes to money matters, and don't allow debts to mount up. This isn't a good time to rely on the generosity of other people if money is an issue. It will be up to you to cover your own expenses. Follow the middle path and everything should work out well. If you haven't done some thorough spring

cleaning consider starting now even if you only get to a few draws
or a closet. Items that are no longer of use, including children's toys
or clothes, could be sold or given to a local charity.

**16. MONDAY. Easygoing.** As an Aquarius you should be displaying a kinder, more generous nature now. Even if there have been
disputes and heated debates, you will now be more willing to back
down and keep the peace, particularly when it comes to minor incidents. With the Moon zooming through independent Sagittarius,
duties that require an idealistic touch will fare better than those
that need a practical approach. Your ability to generate enthusiasm
and to make others laugh is a gift that is sure to increase your popularity. The artist within you could be trying to get out, so find your
medium and begin to create your masterpiece.

**17. TUESDAY. Favorable.** Sometimes life proceeds particularly
smoothly because of the people you know, which may be the case
right now. Being friendly with a wide assortment of people can give
you a jump-start and make all the difference to a career or business
goal. Ideas and promising plans should be flowing freely. A decision
is looming that may involve friends, money, or your long-term
goals. Providing you are realistic, you shouldn't experience much
difficulty arriving at the right choice for you. Check your bank balance and credit card limit before heading out tonight because socializing with friends could be costly.

**18. WEDNESDAY. Fair.** As mischievous Mercury challenges your
traditional ruler Saturn, you can expect a serious tone to dominate
throughout the day. However, it shouldn't be all work and no play.
You should also experience some lighthearted moments along the
way. You may lack energy throughout the daylight hours due to reduced motivation and enthusiasm to attempt anything physical.
This evening you'll be inclined to curl up on the couch and block
out the rest of the world. A relaxing foot massage or a long soak in
the tub may be very appealing if you have been working long hours
or if you have a mental dilemma to mull over.

**19. THURSDAY. Obliging.** Even though the Moon is in Capricorn,
your twelfth house of solitary activity, influences are sending a huge
boost of energy through the alignment of action-packed Mars and
powerful Pluto. Your persistence to stick with plans, along with the
ability to tackle difficult tasks, will be strengthened, assisting even
the most ambitious projects. Performing routine, practical chores

shouldn't be overly boring because you will want to complete all tasks that are on your agenda. Self-employed and business-oriented Aquarius could discover that mixing business with pleasure doesn't deliver as much as you envisioned, although this could still help bring your name into prominence.

**20. FRIDAY. Industrious.** Your strength comes from mixing with people who live nearby. The Sun now enters the pioneering sign of Aries, accentuating your solar sector of communication and transport, and will remain in Aries until April 19. This is an ideal period to reestablish contact with friends and acquaintances you may have been neglecting. If you are not totally into the technical age, consider enrolling in a course or purchasing a new computer or other electronic equipment to advance your knowledge. Planning a short trip to a place you haven't visited before, or not for a long time, could be a pleasant and memorable experience.

**21. SATURDAY. Good.** Your ability to spot opportunities is heightened with the advent of the Moon racing through your sign of Aquarius. Clever ideas and schemes abound, improving your chance of achieving ambitions and increasing income. Getting together with friends and associates should provide pleasant social interaction along with the chance to unwind for a few hours. If life seems too predictable, plan an adventurous trip or weekend retreat where you can meet people who have interests and ideas different from yours. When it comes to love and romance, singles could meet a few interesting potentials.

**22. SUNDAY. Steady.** Your vim and vitality should be high, but you may nevertheless prefer to rest and relax instead of venturing out for the whole day. Give yourself a break and stretch out on the couch to catch up on your reading. Or make personal tasks a priority, at least for part of the day. Refuse to allow anyone to pressure you into taking on their obligations or chores, especially if this is a regular occurence. Shopping could beckon if you need to buy a special outfit or purchase new skin care products. Be careful when it comes to volunteering your time or donating money because you may have an overly idealist view of your limits. Friends could be a good buffer later in the day, so spend some time interacting, chatting, and catching up on the latest gossip.

**23. MONDAY. Diverse.** An interesting day lies ahead for Water Bearers as a number of planetary aspects will create pleasant although intense events. An undercurrent of energy is likely as the Sun challenges passionate Pluto. You will need to use your power and control wisely. A neighbor or relative could be in a very inquisitive mood, refusing to stop badgering you until they have learned whatever they want to know. If you don't want them to know your personal business, resist their efforts at giving you the third degree. Enjoy taking part in a group activity, but don't be surprised if you are asked to contribute more than your fair share.

**24. TUESDAY. Satisfactory.** As insight and intuition increase, you need to listen to signals and follow your intuition when confronted by situations, events, or people you are not sure about. With the Moon sailing through Pisces, money matters will become more important over the next few days. There is a chance of a salary increase that could make you and your credit card bank very happy. However, there is also a tendency to give in to the urge to spend on a whim unless you apply discipline and control. This may not be what you want to hear right now, but being fiscally conservative will make you happier in the long run as your savings begin to grow instead of disappearing.

**25. WEDNESDAY. Stimulating.** You should be in a lively and outgoing mood. Powerful energies are gathering in your communication zone as Mercury trips in to visit Aries, joining the Sun and Venus there until April 9. Other people are likely to be suitably impressed by your communication skills and ability to act quickly as situations arise. Aquarius students should find that study and retaining knowledge is easier; your mind is more receptive to receiving and retaining information. If taking an exam or learning new skills, you will also benefit from increased ability to absorb and process data. Introduce plenty of variety into your daily activities to ensure that restlessness doesn't hinder progress.

**26. THURSDAY. Refreshing.** Watch the tendency to be outspoken over the next few days. This isn't the time to be alone. You are likely to jump at the chance to get together with people who share your interests. Taking a trip out of town could appeal. Aquarius who travel for business purposes should find that sales rise and contacts become more helpful. Attending a cultural event or a local neighborhood function could be an eye-opener for the community-minded Aquarius. Sometimes it is relaxing just to be alone with your own thoughts, and this could appeal tonight if you have experienced a busy day.

**27. FRIDAY. Variable.** Mixed cosmic influences are in force throughout the day. You could find yourself in a strange mood, while other people close to you experience similar unsettled feelings. Try to tone down any aggressive tendencies, and avoid people who are inclined to throw their weight around. If a loved one is intent on letting off some steam, do your best to ignore their comments until they have calmed down. Love and romance should be on the agenda. Excitement escalates for those setting off to visit a special friend residing some distance away. Be open to all possibilities.

**28. SATURDAY. Vibrant.** Your energy to complete chores around the house is high. Home owners with an inclination to begin do-it-yourself repairs or renovations could make good progress. Even if your ambitions only run to a few new pillows or an indoor plant, your ability to find what looks good is enhanced. What begins as a small gathering among neighbors or friends could turn into a full-scale party, so be prepared for a late, very enjoyable evening. Singles should stick close to home. A romantic encounter could walk up to your door, sending you into a delighted spin. A pet could help you meet a potential new love.

**29. SUNDAY. Jovial.** Pleasant vibes continue for most of the day. Take advantage of the current trends and leisurely read the Sunday newspaper, wash your hair, or soak in a bath longer than usual. You could be a little nostalgic, especially if attending a family function. Be sure to take along your camera so you can snap photos of the whole clan and later share these with everyone. If seeking a new residence you could find a number of potential places to buy or lease that would suit your current requirements. Interviewing possible roommates to share household expenses should meet with success.

**30. MONDAY. Productive.** A sharp mind, with ideas flowing easily, is the gift being sent to you by current trends. Communications and negotiations of all kinds are favored as the Sun and Mercury meet together in the sign of Aries. Other people should be pleased by the opinions, views, and suggestions that you put forward now. If you are presenting a lecture, you will receive due appreciation from an enthusiastic audience. The ability to persuade and cajole will assist those who sell for a living. Writers and journalists may be delighted by today's output and productivity. Follow your hunches and refuse to be drawn into anything that could be a sham.

**31. TUESDAY. Guarded.** Be wary of becoming bogged down in issues that are not covered by your job description. There may be a number of obstacles to slow down progress for much of the working day, but later vibes promise a much smoother evening. A male child could require guidance or special attention from parents. Although improvement is apt to be noted in a special situation, this isn't the time to rest on your laurels. Continue applying pressure and rewards will follow. Investments or any form of gambling should be off limits throughout the day. Invite company for a casual meal or drinks if socializing appeals tonight.

# APRIL

**1. WEDNESDAY. Surprising.** Keep your busy schedule flexible to make way for an impromptu invitation that could be a delightful diversion from the usual. With Venus, the goddess of love and beauty, still in reverse motion, a previous romance could begin to blossom once again. Review why the relationship faltered in the past before becoming too involved in a renewed love affair. Currently unattached Aquarius could meet someone new but will need to go into any situation with eyes wide open. Restraint is required, especially if you are currently watching your weight or trying to give up a habit you know is bad for you.

**2. THURSDAY. Sensitive.** Your mood is apt to be more serious today than yesterday, but refrain from giving into discontentment or doom and gloom. It might be wiser for you and a coworker to agree to disagree rather than arguing and debating and just going around in circles. You and a relative might not be in accord, perhaps disagreeing about a petty task that one of you should have completed. Instead of becoming bogged down in who was right or wrong, resolve the issue calmly and quickly to lessen the chance of a lingering argument developing. Call an old friend or a grandparent if you need advice that a parent cannot supply.

**3. FRIDAY. Wary.** Take it easy over the next few days, when there could be a clash with a official that results in a minor or major fine depending on whether you flaunt the law or just park in the wrong area. Take extra care if driving or traveling, staying aware of appropriate safety measures to guard against a mishap or injury. Meals will be an important feature of the day; you may be in the mood for a tasty family recipe or a romantic dinner for two. Someone close to you could be ill or stressed out and might need a healthy dose of tender loving care. Although you may want to forge ahead with your romantic desires, life could be a little difficult in this area.

**4. SATURDAY. Major.** A pessimistic attitude could drag down your mate or partner, draining both of you of energy and essential vitality. Love and romance could continue to spiral downhill if power and domination are an integral part of your relationship. Desire is strong, and this is a time to make love not war. Planet Pluto is now retrograde in Capricorn, your twelfth house, until September 11. This is an excellent period to take a walk down memory lane and revisit things that occurred in the past. Also review where you are right now. Issues involving transformation and rebirth might surface, and you will need to dig deep below the surface to discover the gift of this current planetary influence.

**5. SUNDAY. Sluggish.** Attitude will play a part in keeping the atmosphere low-key if not somber. It will be tempting to display a couldn't-care-less approach. Domestic concerns may impact your daily activities. Tension with a relative or in-law could erupt quickly, particularly if something said as a joke doesn't come across that way. Apologize and explain your words, but belaboring the point will only further highlight your faux pas. Aquarius energy may be at a low level, reducing your enthusiasm and drive. A visit to a qualified astrologer could fill in some missing blanks in your life.

**6. MONDAY. Positive.** If you are seeking financial aid for a business venture, this could be your lucky day. Dealing with a loan association or other financial organization should be easier, with favorable results more than likely. It would be advisable to keep your schedule flexible to accommodate a spur-of-the-moment meeting or a casual get-together. This evening a parent, father figure, or older relative could try to control a situation in which you are involved. Accept the help until and unless it becomes overbearing or against your wishes. Money prospects are improving, but balancing the books and paying bills could require juggling funds.

**7. TUESDAY. Inspired.** A dreamy, creative quality pervades the air as Mercury combines happily with imaginative Neptune. Keep complex tasks to a minimum or, if possible, shelve them for another day. Thoughts of talents you no longer use could inspire you to again work at producing art, writing verse, or playing music. If all work and little time for play are combining to make you into a dull Water Bearer, now is the day to stop and smell the roses, reconnecting with Mother Earth. A walk in the park or a bike ride around the community could enhance your efforts to commune with nature. Plan a romantic evening at home.

**8. WEDNESDAY. Tricky.** Revised travel or vacation plans could be disappointing at the onset. However, the alternatives presented should make you happy once you get over the initial upset. An inspired spark could bring creative ideas, plans, and designs to the surface. Be ready to record these for future reference if you are unable to utilize them immediately. Aquarius students could suffer from study overload, so it might be time to take a break for a day or two to allow information to process. Attending a lecture or filling your head with more details may make it that much harder to retain what you have already been taught. Legal affairs are unlikely to be decided in your favor.

**9. THURSDAY. Emotional.** Diverse cosmic influences prevail throughout the day. Aquarius involved in reading and researching could find that concentration is at low ebb. In fact, very little productive work will be accomplished over the next few days. Around midday is a perfect time to set off on a vacation trip abroad. This is also an excellent period to apply for a passport or a visa or to purchase a new set of luggage. A Full Moon in Libra brings emotions to the surface. Be aware that people who are normally inclined to sensitive feelings may be hypersensitive today, and before you know it tears could flow if words are not spoken gently and with care.

**10. FRIDAY. Lucky.** Although Full Moon influences will continue to affect emotions, the alignment of the Sun and Jupiter can lighten and brighten your mood and that of other people. Gratitude is the key to the day. Luck shines your way, and a sense of humor will certainly not be wasted. A situation that you thought was too premature to respond to could require immediate action now, not later. Confident moves are likely to attract the right investors, so show the world your innovative plans and designs. If you take the time to learn and develop a new skill, doors could open that will positively advance your career and economic situation.

**11. SATURDAY. Fruitful.** What was started two weeks ago under the energy of the New Moon should now begin showing signs of bearing fruit. Although a thorough investigation into a business proposition could be time consuming, it could provide information required to make an informed decision. If you are thinking about applying for a home loan or bank overdraft, this is a good day to gather essential paperwork required for the application. If it has been a while since your personal and joint possessions were valued for insurance purposes, follow up on this task now to obtain peace of mind in case anything occurs to damage or destroy your treasures.

**12. SUNDAY. Mixed.** You are likely to muddle through the morning hours with confusion and delusion a common thread. You may decide to stay close to home base at least until lunchtime. As the day unfolds you could receive secondhand news or hear from a former friend; being back in touch could lift your mood for the rest of the day. The more sociable Aquarius might prefer to invite friends to enjoy a casual meal and to share good company and stimulating conversation. Hosting the boss could be a good way to move up the career ladder as long as you actually enjoy socializing together.

**13. MONDAY. Tense.** Employed Aquarius who work for a boss might wish to be self-employed, or at least to have a large measure of autonomy. Restlessness could make you want to be free and independent in order to handle tasks in your own good time instead of according to deadlines set for you. If you have vacation time due you, consider taking off for the day to roam freely and do your own thing. Upsets are likely when it comes to finances. A friend may be thin-skinned regarding a particular monetary matter, so proceed with care if you get into a discussion. Don't reveal your income or how much money you have in the bank.

**14. TUESDAY. Volatile.** This is another day when unsettled feelings could increase the stress level of those born under the sign of Aquarius. If you can introduce a dash of excitement into the day's proceedings or can give yourself a special treat, energy should flow reasonably calmly. There may be unexpected expenses that you are required to cover, which could put a damper on good humor. Be prepared if a friend or an associate balks at the cost of an outing or deliberately delays the negotiation process. Meeting new people will give you pleasure, and later in the day you may meet someone who sparks your interest.

**15. WEDNESDAY. Varied.** Diverse planetary trends exist. Energy sizzles, but be careful of taking risks or acting impulsively. Upset could be the result of a personal obligation that you resent due to having to spend more time on that tiring activity instead of on something you love to do. Roaming around and experiencing different adventures always makes Aquarius folk very happy, and this will provide pleasure now as well. Drivers should slow down. Even if you are cautious when behind the wheel, the need for speed may give you an unhealthy adrenaline rush. Inspiration comes easily for writers, teachers, and public speakers.

**16. THURSDAY. Calm.** Expect a quieter interlude today as the Moon moves through the sign of Capricorn. Signals from your body may be suggesting that you need more rest and relaxation instead of the usual rushing around and active pursuits. Secrets and mysteries could be of special interest. Digging deep into whatever is buried beneath the surface always fascinates the inquisitive Water Bearer. This isn't the time to begin new projects because the results are unlikely to develop as you envisioned. Instead focus on completing outstanding chores, especially the ones that have been waiting on the back burner for your attention. Opt for a night spent enjoying all the comforts of home.

**17. FRIDAY. Insightful.** You might encounter someone who needs your help or spiritual insight. As an Aquarius you will instinctively know the most practical and effective way to offer assistance and to guide them through their current tough times. Although you might be busy yourself, lending a helping hand is sure to provide emotional gratification. The goddess Venus steps out of reverse motion today, and those of you who have been hiding away from social interaction should find that things begin to change. Delays involving a wage increase or an expected check in the mail should start to clear up. You can now get back into the mainstream of life.

**18. SATURDAY. Constructive.** The return of the Moon to your own sign of Aquarius usually brings a boost of vim and vitality. This comes just in time to begin the weekend on a high note. Personal considerations and aims should be your main priority. Make an appointment to change your hair color or style, purchase an outfit you have had your eye on for some time, or pay for a gym membership so you can improve your fitness level before summer begins. If there has been a problem in your love life, you can expect a solution now. There could be good reason to celebrate with the notification that someone close to you will receive a bonus, pay increase, or promotion.

**19. SUNDAY. Pleasant.** A friendly approach will help keep you out of trouble as various planetary patterns form today. Communication issues could be strained as someone insists on having their say. Give other people a chance to state their views and you may hear something you didn't know or weren't aware of. The glowing Sun moves into Taurus now, putting home and property matters in the fore. As a result you may be tempted to purchase something large or expensive to increase home comforts. The urge to move into more pleasant surroundings could also be aroused, although this is not the time to move precipitously.

**20. MONDAY. Diverse.** Mixed trends prevail throughout this first day of the new working week. You could feel slightly under par, which will have more to do with the Sun and Saturn in dispute rather than the fact that it is a Monday. Reassessing your values and priorities takes precedence. What once seemed to be very important might have lost some of its luster. Acquiring material possessions remains important, although quality may be more significant than quantity. Your appreciation of items of value and beauty is enhanced. Aquarius with an eye for a quality bargain could find something of considerable worth at a reasonable price. Romance remains on the agenda, so prepare for a happy evening.

**21. TUESDAY. Diligent.** Persistence is required when it comes to financial issues. Although saving may appear to be an uphill battle, finances can receive a boost from your innovative and inspired ideas. You will soon notice cost savings and realize that your efforts to generate more income were definitely worthwhile. Aquarius who collect money for a living or are due a payment for services rendered should step warily because it will be all too easy to get into an altercation when it comes to fiscal matters. Opportunities for love and romance should be bountiful, and singles could have a multitude of potentials from which to choose.

**22. WEDNESDAY. Expansive.** Take care with your manner of speech and body language, resisting a tendency to go over the top. What you may consider a lighthearted affair could be developing into something more serious or important, but it is still wise to move slowly. Aquarius with a committed partner should find joy in displaying love and affection, receiving due appreciation in return.

Now mighty Mars zooms into Aries, your zone of communication, education, and transportation. So mental stimulation and increased communication will be desired. Prepare for a lot of interaction from now until the end of May.

**23. THURSDAY. Energetic.** The grass is unlikely to grow under your feet as you keep busy running from one place to another. Errands and short trips could take up much of your time, and you will appreciate the chance to escape from the office, shop, or house even for a short period. Just ensure that you use your time constructively and do not scatter your energy all over the place. Vigorous activity should be enjoyed. Pushing yourself in some manual labor or in an exercise workout will make you feel you are making progress. Property matters are highlighted. Your ability to persuade other people is strong and can be used to your best advantage.

**24. FRIDAY. Refreshing.** On this very busy day in the cosmic sky there are bound to be plenty of plans and ideas buzzing around in your head. However, it would be wise to write them down to act on at a later date. Restless energy could plague you and, unless your day has a good measure of variety, boredom could hinder achievement. Guard against carelessness when it comes to speaking out in a potentially stressful situation. Unless you think first, the feelings of other people could be hurt, even if unintentional. A beneficial atmosphere spreads over your home and domestic life as a New Moon culminates in your solar zone of Taurus.

**25. SATURDAY. Artistic.** Rewards for your willingness to put imagination to work could come your way. This is a better day to spend on creative pursuits or a favored pastime rather than any mental exercise. Confusion and forgetfulness could permeate your thoughts, hindering completing any work of real value. Also make extra effort to keep facts and figures straight and to avoid the deceptive influences of other people. With a strong urge to connect to your heritage, this can be a starred day to spend time researching the facts and stories of your ancestral past. If thoughts of moving are gathering momentum, start looking for a new place by checking newspaper or Internet ads.

**26. SUNDAY. Satisfactory.** Family finances and money matters are under scrutiny. Aquarius folk looking to buy or sell property could make steady progress. Home improvement projects are also favored. Renovating or expanding your living quarters can be liberating as long as you are making the effort for the right reasons. Don't enter into a competition with the neighbors just so you can keep up with them; doing so could damage your bank balance. If you are involved in any vigorous or high-risk activity, take extra precautions because you are in the middle of an accident-prone period. Romance is well starred tonight.

**27. MONDAY. Cautious.** Dusting, cleaning closets, and tackling other boring household tasks should be easier now. Keep in mind that you don't have to be a slave to other people, especially if you share living arrangements. Ask for assistance, or insist that responsibilities be divided equally. If driving be extra careful on the roads and avoid angry responses to avert the possibility of an accident due to road rage. Walk with company, don't run, and steer clear of any neighborhood that is known to have a criminal element. Gambling or speculative investments are unlikely to increase your bank balance and could empty it if you don't protect what you have.

**28. TUESDAY. Active.** This busy day is likely to suit those who prefer surprises over routine chores. Beware impulsive spending this morning, when an inclination to buy first and think about the consequences later is enhanced. Meditation or a yoga class could bring calmness to those suffering from nervous anxiety and built-up pressure. Issues with an employee or coworkers are likely for those working a late shift unless tact and diplomacy are on display. A quick home-cooked meal could be just what you need to unwind after a busy day. Switch off your phone this evening so you have time to destress.

**29. WEDNESDAY. Helpful.** This is a day to review current treatment for an ongoing ailment. Seek a second opinion if your condition doesn't seem to be improving. If health and diet are an issue, hiring a personal trainer or making an appointment with a dietician may be helpful. Make sure your working environment is spick-and-span. File away paperwork no longer required, clean the surface of your desk, and buy an indoor plant to improve air quality. Someone you know may try to obtain something for nothing, but don't encourage anyone to take you or your assistance for granted.

**30. THURSDAY. Sentimental.** Nurturing and home comforts continue to take priority as the Moon treks through Cancer. Family-based activities are likely to claim your attention. You could be a little more sensitive than usual. The focus also turns toward your house of leisure, pleasure, and treasure as talkative Mercury moves on to take up residence in the sign of Gemini. Expect to be hearing more from the love of your life or your children. This is a good time to express love and affection verbally or through written prose. Send a card or fancy e-mail to a family member, adult child, or special friend to remind them once more how much they are loved and cherished.

# MAY

**1. FRIDAY. Cooperative.** The key to success today is teamwork and cooperation. The early part of the day is very promising for communication, particularly if you need to deliver a sharp and concise presentation, report, or lecture. As this new month begins you can expect romance to be more amorous than usual. This is a great time to spice up your love life if there has been a letup in this area. An open mind and a dash of patience should assist important decision making regarding a personal issue that you hope will work out in your favor. Keep all of your options open before committing to anything concrete.

**2. SATURDAY. Uneasy.** In most areas of your life unsettled feelings are likely to hinder forward movement. If you have been preoccupied, involved with what other people are doing, or not feeling up to par, put off important tasks until your emotions are less on edge. Your love life should be all fired up, which can be a blessing. If there has been neglect in this area due to personal or work issues, showering more attention on your significant other should work wonders for romance. Aquarius prone to jealousy or possessiveness should take extra care to keep these characteristics under control throughout the next few days.

**3. SUNDAY. Interactive.** Today's lunar influences are more likely to create minor obstructions than forward movement. With the Taurus Sun impacting your sector of family and domestic concerns, the focus continues on home and property matters. This is an excellent day to contact a real estate agent if you are currently considering relocating in order to upgrade, consolidate, or purchase a new home. A meeting involving a hobby or social group may be held at short notice. Romantic trends are strong, with a touch of volatility that should increase desire for those who are in a committed, happy relationship.

**4. MONDAY. Tense.** It is essential to release negative energy in a constructive manner. This is a day to be guarded with speech, action, and body language. Before speaking out, mull over what you are about to say so that you don't discover that you have landed on the firing line big-time. You or other people may become upset quickly, which won't make this the best beginning to the new working week if cooperation is required from workmates or other associates. A neighbor or family member could be in need of advice. Normally you would impart sage counsel without too many problems, but today you might revert to a know-it-all approach unless you take extra care to be patient.

**5. TUESDAY. Constructive.** This is an excellent day to deal with professional developments, home renovations, or purchasing and negotiating for real estate. If the lack of money has been an ongoing cause of concern, work out a new household budget that is both realistic and easy to oversee. Someone in a position of authority could let you know how pleased they are with your latest innovative ideas and plans, raising your status among peers and higher-ups. Participating in a cultural experience or adventure, or just getting to know someone from abroad, could expand your world.

**6. WEDNESDAY. Informative.** Ways for you to absorb and gain more knowledge are likely to appeal. Aquarius students studying for exams or writing a special homework project should get to work early, when lunar trends are more supportive. Plans for a pleasant journey or vacation can be finalized providing you understand any special clauses or exclusions added into a total package. A loved one may be anxious to know what secrets you are harboring, and sharing confidences may help move your relationship to another level. Your love life should be settling down into a more peaceful but still passionate routine.

**7. THURSDAY. Misleading.** Confusion, uncertainty, and the possibility of other people trying to put a fast one over on you are problems likely to be experienced today. Although your inclination may be to sit down and discuss concerns and upsets, finding answers and solutions might be difficult. Mercury, the planet that holds sway over communication and transportation, will be moving backward in Gemini, your house of love, children, and creative expression, for the next three weeks. Be on guard if a contract, lease, or formal paperwork is presented for your signature. Promises may be made in good faith, but that doesn't ensure they will be carried out.

**8. FRIDAY. Bothersome.** This is apt to be a very tiresome day due to the prevailing current energy. Emotions are likely to be highly charged as a Full Moon occurs in the fixed sign of Scorpio, increasing stress both at home and on the job. Pressure to complete a demanding employment project could create angst and nervousness, reducing your ability to focus and function effectively. Ignoring disruptive elements and remaining cool and calm will give you the best chance of finishing tasks to the expected standard. Keep a low profile and beware highly inflated egos belonging to self-described experts.

**9. SATURDAY. Playful.** Seek pleasure and play even if you must be on the job for most of the daylight hours. Participate in new and different activities in order to keep motivation and stimulation high. Otherwise boredom could result in limited fun and companionship. The universe sends words of caution: Beware being misled. You may be inclined to jump into action without taking necessary care and analyzing facts, figures, and the behavior of other people. The urge to socialize increases early this evening when the Moon slips into fun-loving Sagittarius. Meet up with special friends and get ready to party. Be discerning with words spoken to a friend around midnight, when your thoughts may pour forth too freely.

**10. SUNDAY. Refreshing.** A pleasant and social day is promised by current planetary vibes. Rules and regulations get on an Aquarius person's nerves at the best of times, and even more so today. Keep household chores to a minimum, or handle urgent duties early so you can do whatever will increase your happiness and popularity. The family-oriented could arrange a picnic or barbecue outdoors so that all the clan can gather and enjoy each other's company. Or a day spent alone with that special person, exploring interesting new vistas, could appeal to partnered Aquarius. To quell a restless mood, go for a bike ride or a walk around the park to improve fitness and commune with nature.

**11. MONDAY. Tricky.** It might not be particularly easy to be friendly and sociable because your energy and enthusiasm are likely to flag. If planning to apply for a bank loan for a major purchase such as a new car, put this task off for a few days. Moving ahead with the application now increases the risk of delays and frustrating obstacles. Difficult questions could be posed to you, which doesn't bode well if you are going on an interview or are involved in a legal matter. Exams could be harder than envisioned, needing more thought and detail than you would normally give. Expressing your opinions is fine as long as you are prepared for unexpected responses.

**12. TUESDAY. Slow.** By midmorning you may be inclined to slack off when your energy begins to plummet. Handle urgent tasks early, and put off duties requiring intensive effort until the end of the week in order to conserve energy. The Moon is slipping through Capricorn, which is the time to rest and restore run-down batteries. Practical changes that don't require a lot of input can be made, but following up could be an issue due to lethargy. Saying what needs to be said is not a problem today, and at most times, providing it can be done without causing an argument or creating many waves. Now, however, take care if you decide to speak out.

**13. WEDNESDAY. Chancy.** Feelings could be easily wounded, and these could be yours or those of a loved one. Your behavior or recent effort may be disappointing, but if you did your best under existing circumstances there isn't any need to feel you have let other people down. Your enthusiasm for what is normal and routine is likely to remain at a low level, at least until late tomorrow evening, suggesting that it would be wiser to complete chores rather than begin anything new. If you work steadily and quietly you will achieve what you set out to do. This is a favorable period to follow your hunches; intuition is strong and shouldn't fail you.

**14. THURSDAY. Good.** A moderate approach is the best course to follow. A serious mood prevails, and practical matters can be attended to with ease. Behind-the-scenes activities are likely to progress smoothly. Any matters of a confidential nature can be conducted with more assurance that matters will develop as envisioned. Expressing more compassion could inspire Aquarius those with an interest in humanitarian causes to volunteer to help with a special event or take on an ongoing commitment. Just make sure you know exactly what you are letting yourself in for before agreeing to too many outside tasks.

**15. FRIDAY. Spirited.** Your spirits and energy should be soaring now that Moon has entered into your own sign of quirky Aquarius. Extra vitality allows you to attack daily tasks with plenty of vim and gusto. Spring cleaning might be on your mind, and catching up around the house can produce emotional fulfillment. Your head may be buzzing with bright ideas, although time to act on many of them could be limited. Consider asking other people to help implement the pick of the best plans. Friends and colleagues are likely to offer plenty of physical support. Take off the rose-colored glasses when it comes to a mix of love and money.

**16. SATURDAY. Major.** A number of planetary trends prevail, with the Sun cranky at jolly Jupiter but good friends with your modern-day ruler, erratic Uranus. Physical resources are improved, and there shouldn't be much that you can't succeed at if you set your mind to it. Aquarius folk who have had difficulty finding the right real estate investment or commercial property could have a change of luck and be presented with a couple of suitable potential acquisitions. Your traditional ruler Saturn now moves forward in Virgo, your house of shared assets and resources, so any delays regarding joint finances should begin to disappear.

**17. SUNDAY. Dreamy.** Zoom through domestic duties this morning while your energy remains at a high peak. By midmorning the Moon slips into dreamy Pisces and you could become more into daydreaming than serious work. It can be very relaxing to spend time in fantasyland, indulging your imagination providing urgent and practical chores are not on the agenda. Shoppers should continue to steer clear of a large mall or expensive boutiques because the inclination to spend first and think later remains enhanced. Refrain from signing any legal document or agreement unless you have thoroughly read the fine print or had it checked by a legal adviser.

**18. MONDAY. Practical.** It is back to work today, and you should be happy to get a move on and handle set tasks. Finding a practical solution to problems and keeping a level head will be aided as the Sun and Mercury now combine. Your organizational skills are also enhanced, making this an excellent period to make plans. You could become penny-wise and pound-foolish unless you place priorities in the right order. If it is not necessary to purchase household essentials, try to keep away from the stores. Otherwise your bank balance could be severely depleted, especially if retail therapy is conducted during the afternoon hours.

**19. TUESDAY. Satisfactory.** Financial matters receive a boost, and money that is owed to you should be repaid. Be prepared for a few unexpected surprises that will bring a gleam to your eye. Morning vibes will be quieter and less hectic, but by evening there should be plenty of action as the Moon zips through active Aries, your sector of communication and movement. Motivation and the urge to speak out will increase over the next couple of days, enabling Aquarius prone to shyness to articulate opinions and theories. Be wary if in charge of any type of vehicle; don't ignore the speed limit or disregard other rules of the road.

**20. WEDNESDAY. Restless.** You could have problems trying to settle down into any sort of routine. The likelihood of unclear vision increases now as talkative Mercury challenges imaginative Neptune. Misunderstandings, miscommunication, and confusion may reign supreme over the next few days. Care is needed because someone could try to deceive you in some manner. Love and romance could also be under a cloud. This isn't the time to initiate important discussions with your mate, partner, or a child. Differences of opinion may arise regarding the final details of a plan. Postpone purchasing any major items; receiving value for your money is unlikely right now.

**21. THURSDAY. Fine.** The Sun is now residing in Gemini, your house of treasure and pleasure. The Gemini Sun will release creative expression during the next four weeks. Romance comes to the fore. You could be inclined to take more risks than usual. You should also be more energized to go out and enjoy yourself by participating in favorite pastimes and pursuits. If you find yourself locked into a boring routine, stop and think about what you are doing. Try to see current possibilities with fresh eyes. This isn't the time to make impulsive decisions or act in a rash manner. Creative and artistic ventures receive a dash of imagination that can make a huge difference to the completed project.

**22. FRIDAY. Stimulating.** Unexpected, exciting situations could occur in relation to money and property. Aquarius waiting for a reply regarding a house purchase should be thrilled with news received. You could decide on a refreshing new look for your living environment. If you are money conscious, enjoy doing the painting and redecorating yourself, saving money and knowing that the work is being executed to your high standards. For the solo Aquarius, a first or blind date might not turn out as hoped, and it may be necessary to give the relationship more time to develop and blossom.

**23. SATURDAY. Vexing.** Patience is unlikely to be your most endearing quality today as a volatile trend prevails. Relaxing and enjoying the day as it unfolds can reduce the onset of stress and anxiety. If you are on the job or have a special project to complete, working alone should help you concentrate and quickly finish required chores. There may be a clash with an authority figure if overblown egos could soar out of control. Aquarius participating in a recreational pastime that requires equipment or machinery should be prepared for a possible breakdown or malfunction. Sports-minded Aquarius could find that competitors are not inclined to fight fairly.

**24. SUNDAY. Revitalizing.** Similar vibes to yesterday exist, although you can expect a more sociable mood. Fewer obstacles will make the day seem a lot smoother than it really is. Try to retain a good balance between what you want to do and the preferred pastimes of other people, so that you are not left participating in activities that are of little interest. Aquarius parents could find children more demanding unless kept continually amused. A New Moon in Gemini brings a surge of renewal for your romantic relationship. Taking part in a team or individual sport could find you winning a substantial trophy or receiving a lucrative sponsorship deal.

**25. MONDAY. Pleasant.** Your passion and commitment for a leisure-time activity may be contagious when other people see how much fun you have. Consider turning a pleasurable hobby into a group gathering. Aquarius parents need to be prepared for temper tantrums from an emotional child who isn't ready or willing to go to bed when told to do so. Be firm; if you give in now, the bedtime situation could worsen in the future. Love could enter your life, especially if currently unattached. If partnered, spend quality time with your honey. Don't sign up for a costly future outing or social occasion. Look for ways to save by sharing.

**26. TUESDAY. Bountiful.** The stars are shining blissfully on Aquarius folk. A witty sense of humor, sharper mind, and inspired imagination are likely. Knowledge gathered over time is an important tool to help increase your bank balance. You could experience the urge to take a trip just for the adventure, a great idea for those with time and money to spare. You could meet someone who inspires you and urges you to move on to bolder, greater things. Conversely, your actions and behavior may be the catalyst that spurs other people to pursue some of their special goals and desires.

**27. WEDNESDAY. Supportive.** This is another day when motivation and imagination are at a high peak. Aquarius inclined toward spiritual or artistic work should have a wonderful day of increased productivity and inspired thought. Flowing creative juices allow you to seek perfection in everything you attempt. You may lack some direction and understanding when it comes to matters relating to a health condition. It would be wise to wait for results from a doctor or dietician before making any long-term decisions. Agree to disagree with a colleague if you find that you are on opposing wavelengths. Or concede to the popular vote if a group decision differs from what you want.

**28. THURSDAY. Significant.** Foggy Neptune goes retrograde in your sign from tonight until November 4, putting the focus on your house of self and identity. This is the time to face up to unrealistic aims and illusions. Take a long, hard look at who you really are, without pretense. It is also essential to look at the truth of current situations instead of hoping that everything will turn out as you desire. Remain alert; someone who is not as honest as you could try to take advantage. Relationships with other people should be mainly pleasant, aiding group endeavors and team activities. A loving night at home with your significant other is sure to increase your emotional comfort.

**29. FRIDAY. Helpful.** Career activities should be looking up, especially if you are involved in any financial negotiations and transactions. Collaborative efforts should bring expected results, making this a stellar day to finalize special deals. Slight tension could be felt midafternoon with your personal or business partner, so keep a low profile then and refrain from bringing up contentious subjects. Complaints from clients or customers could also create anxiety. However, it shouldn't take too long for the innovative Aquarius to resolve and restore harmonious vibes. Socializing with family members, neighbors, or those you work with should be enjoyable this evening.

**30. SATURDAY. Diverse.** The Moon slides through Virgo, your sector of sexual drive and joint finances, bringing these matters to the fore. A more intense and picky mood is likely, so watch what you say and how you say it. By enjoying love and passion instead of creating disharmony around your home base, you can create a mainly happy day. If you have been waiting for news of a property settlement, your wait is nearly over as Mercury stops, ready to move in forward motion once more. If work around the house has been stalled or is moving at a snail's pace, you should find that people you hired are now ready to finish what they started.

**31. SUNDAY. Stable.** A more serious atmosphere prevails for much of the day. If you have important activities or chores to complete, you can make good headway, particularly with tasks that need practical input. Active Mars moves into Taurus, your sector of home and the domestic scene, so prepare for lots of movement and activity centering on your living quarters. Conflict with other household members could also rise because tempers may be on a shorter fuse than usual. Aquarius who own property can constructively utilize this energy by adding value to assets through improvements, renovations, and repairs. An updated kitchen, new garage, or landscaped yard could be a good place to begin.

# JUNE

**1. MONDAY. Positive.** Expect an easygoing, pleasant day. The month begins in a positive phase that awakens Aquarius creativity as well as allowing positive expression of your many vast talents and skills. With the Sun shining in the sign of chatty Gemini, discussions and meetings are starred. Any form of negotiating and mediation should produce an excellent outcome. Matters that have been dragging along should move forward, but don't expect immediate benefits. Results could still take a little longer, so be patient and remain positive.

**2. TUESDAY. Inspired.** A stellar day dawns as Venus connects happily to Jupiter, Uranus, and Neptune. Passion and drive can be successfully utilized in creative enterprises and artistic projects. Your ability to fantasize and to use imagination in a unique way can also find you inspired in the area of love and romance. Quality time spent with that special person can pay dividends as loving bonds are forged and strengthened. New information concerning a field of interest could lead to browsing the Web and thumbing through resource material in order to gain more knowledge and understanding. Philosophy, history, or a spiritual topic might appeal.

**3. WEDNESDAY. Motivating.** Distant and foreign places are important. Aquarius who have loved ones living abroad could receive good news. A special friend may reveal a planned trip through your town and hint about staying with you for a few days. Refrain from discussions centering on politics, religion, or other controversial subjects. These topics could produce misunderstanding or even angry retorts from people who disagree with your views or who just like to argue. Physical resources should zoom to a high level due to the link between dynamic Mars and powerful Pluto. This is the time to perform duties and obligations that require strenuous effort.

**4. THURSDAY. Scattered.** You are apt to feel like you are all over the place today, with the result that not much will be accomplished. While you are performing required tasks, focus on what you are doing to reduce the likelihood of mistakes creeping into your work. There is a strong possibility of conflict with a colleague unless you can remain above discord and tension. A friend might have a number of bright ideas and try to persuade you to go along with their plans. Don't refuse without giving serious thought; their novel approach may be worth a second look and possibly some financial investment.

**5. FRIDAY. Frustrating.** The Sun is challenging restrictive Saturn, your traditional ruler, producing limitations with matters regarding joint finances and assets. If you are currently involved in a property settlement due to divorce or a legacy, expect more delays that will only increase frustration and irritation. Tackle situations one at a time rather than trying to do a number of jobs all at once. If you take on too much, your energy, or at least enthusiasm, is likely to slump, and a sense of being overwhelmed could further hinder progress. A friend is unlikely to be impressed by an attempt to change their attitude or behavior to a certain situation, so save your breath.

**6. SATURDAY. Quiet.** Another day dawns when it would be wiser not to push yourself or other people too hard. If you have a lot to do or a task that requires physical labor, pace activities to reduce the possibility of running out of steam before the job is completed. Once the planetary trends are more supportive, vim and vitality should return and chores can be successfully finished. Worry about a particular matter could be thankfully resolved with a little boost from a benefactor. Venus, the goddess of love and money, floats into your Taurus sector of home and family, bringing a more tranquil atmosphere to the household and also adding a dash of magic to your primary one-on-one relationship.

**7. SUNDAY. Problematic.** For Aquarius involved with a large group of people, problems could arise that are not easily solved. It might be wise to put off making definite decisions if a consensus cannot be reached. Something could come to an end as the Full Moon culminates in your Sagittarius house of friendships, groups, and organizations. This may be rather emotional even for the detached Aquarius. However, this is likely to open the door to new opportunities and exciting beginnings. A volunteer commitment might need to be reviewed if too much of your free time is being spent outside the home, reducing leisure periods that could be spent with family members.

**8. MONDAY. Supportive.** The heavens are very supportive of your efforts, so take advantage. Love and romance are especially starred. This is an excellent time to make a permanent commitment to that special person in your life. Matters that were left unfinished, either from last week or yesterday, should be completed today so you can keep the slate as clean as possible. This will make the day more hectic than usual but should lessen the load for later in the week. If a close friendship is not providing the same emotional comfort and support as in the past, it may be time to consider cultivating new friends who share more in common with you.

**9. TUESDAY. Erratic.** Romance and desire remain dominant, and couples should experience very happy rapport. Generally this is a tricky day as a number of mixed messages and false starts create confusion and annoyance. Normally this would be a good time to sit back and let the world flow by, or to go in search of an exciting adventure. However, there may be too much going on right now for you to relax and do nothing. Asserting your authority shouldn't be a problem; there will be more strength to your words. Other people are likely to instantly know that you mean what you say and will follow through as promised.

**10. WEDNESDAY. Prickly.** Set aside decisions regarding your home or personal life over the next few days. Thinking Mercury challenges jolly Jupiter, which could inflate your ego and lead to an overly optimistic approach that produces impaired judgment. This is a day when you are better left on your own because you will be more reserved and detached than normal. Other people could come up with some great ideas, proving that very often two heads are better than one. Be sure to give credit for their ingenuity if you go ahead and implement their ideas. A sick or lonely friend could benefit greatly from your generosity, and taking time to visit can lead to an unexpected reward.

**11. THURSDAY. Bright.** With the Moon now in your own sign of Aquarius, today shouldn't be dull or boring. The inclination to express yourself more will naturally increase, and you can draw and attract other folks who can help improve your present circumstances. Be wary of anyone who tends to promise more than they can probably deliver. Also stop and think before committing to a project or venture if this will reduce quality time available to spend with loved ones. Although a busy day, try to set some time aside for self-nurturing. Benefits will come from indulging in a full-body massage or a prolonged session at the local beauty salon.

**12. FRIDAY. Sparkling.** This is another day when Aquarius can shine in the spotlight. However, you will have to look really hard for opportunities, which may be limited by unhelpful lunar trends. Your revitalized energy will at least assist optimism, and this in turn can provide a powerful boost to energy and confidence. Getting work done, whether minor or major, shouldn't be a problem. Even routine tasks performed now will probably not feel like a chore. If you have exciting social events looming on the horizon, head for the boutiques or a preferred shopping mall and purchase a few outfits or accessories to update your wardrobe and make you feel like a million dollars when all dressed up.

**13. SATURDAY. Active.** On this busy day your spirit and vitality should be on top of the world. A course or workshop that teaches self-empowerment and how to build confidence could provide valuable information to help those who currently lack self-assurance. Financial gains are foreseen. Although as an Aquarius you are not always practical and realistic, today your mood favors being sensible and matter-of-fact. Messenger Mercury reenters your Gemini house of recreational and self-expression, assisting creative writers and those who are preparing to speak in public.

Relax tonight with one or more friends who always make you feel good about yourself.

**14. SUNDAY. Outgoing.** Don't be afraid to be yourself. Money matters are improving, but to stay ahead of bills and expenses it is important to pay close attention to your budget. Go over income and expenditures to ensure that you are aware of your current financial status. Raising funds for a good cause that is close to your heart could raise your profile while producing a sizable donation for the charitable organization. Entertaining at home with a casual barbecue lunch or more formal evening meal may appeal if you are eager to display culinary skills and hospitality to friends and family members. A newcomer could tempt you in a memorable way.

**15. MONDAY. Disconcerting.** An obsessive atmosphere prevails. It may be all too easy to overspend if you are not careful. Remain steady and realistic to reduce the chance of overindulging in too much retail therapy. A strong desire for change might cause you to act prematurely. Any vehicle or equipment problem should be attended to quickly to avoid more serious issues that could take a long time to fix. Abundant planet Jupiter will be retrograde in your sign of Aquarius from now until October 12. This gives you a chance to review personal aims and goals. Travel and educational plans could stall or have to be put on hold for a few months.

**16. TUESDAY. Confident.** As an Aquarius you are unlikely to be timid when it comes to expressing your views and opinions. However, today tact and diplomacy may be in short supply, so be careful with what you say and the words you choose. Prepare to do a lot of extra running around, with many errands unplanned. Changing your residence could be contemplated because of something that irritates you a great deal. If you won't be able to rest until alterations are carried out, don't postpone the inevitable. You could be playing host to out-of-town visitors, or you could decide to take a short trip yourself to catch up with friends. An unexpected compliment will make your day.

**17. WEDNESDAY. Expansive.** With today's lively planetary activity, Aquarius should expect the unexpected and wait to see what eventually happens. A profusion of good fortune is swirling around, ready for you to take advantage. Even though you could receive an unexpected windfall, this isn't the time to become involved in a speculative investment or to risk money in any project that seems too good to be true. The dream of a special vacation getaway by the ocean or of a luxury cruise may be moving closer, and soon you could be packing your bags ready to set off on the trip of a lifetime. An unresolved situation with a special person requires sorting out. Apologize even if you were only partly at fault.

**18. THURSDAY. Lucky.** Good fortune and edginess continue to pervade the air. Communication is enhanced first thing this morning, when you are apt to be involved in lots of discussions, meetings, and talk fests. Domestic affairs come into the frame by midmorning and may become quite complex as your chores begin to pile up. If you are unable to delegate a few duties or find someone to lend a hand, divide your to-do list to work on over several days. Time and energy devoted to a do-it-yourself project should be successful, increasing the comfort of your current living arrangements as well as the overall ambience.

**19. FRIDAY. Advantageous.** Plan on another day when changes to your home decor occupy time and energy. Generally this should be a good day. Aquarius with an interest in selling or purchasing real estate should meet with success. If looking for a new roommate or a new residence, the local newspaper could provide good information to help. Watching a movie at home with your significant other, or entertaining guests in the comfortable surroundings of your house, could appeal more than going out on the town. If you are hosting houseguests, you may be experiencing a sense that your visitors have overstayed their welcome and it is time for them to move on.

**20. SATURDAY. Stimulating.** If you are planning to invest in property, you should be pleased with today's results. This morning is the best period to view properties you are considering purchasing for yourself or to rent out. Aquarius parents could be suffering withdrawal due to a youngster embarking on their first adventure alone or leaving the nest for the first time. Creative pursuits or sports can be therapeutic and relaxing. Love and romance are high on your agenda, and this is a great time to strengthen loving ties. Don't stay home tonight. Accept an invitation to a social event, and enjoy yourself in the company of other people.

**21. SUNDAY. Entertaining.** Socializing with friends or family members should be a priority again today. You may be lucky enough to have more invitations than you can comfortably accept. For those in a happy romantic union, the day is perfect for passion and endearments. If single, you could become involved in flirting with an interesting possibility who could eventually become someone special in your life. Today marks the summer solstice for those living in the northern hemisphere as the Sun moves into the sign of canny Cancer and your solar sector of daily undertakings and employment conditions.

**22. MONDAY. Enriching.** Saturn, the traditional ruler of your Sun sign, is positively linked to lover Venus and energetic Mars, bringing a practical and sensible approach to love and money. You could be ready to form a permanent union with a special partner, through an engagement, marriage, or setting up house together. A fresh New Moon in Cancer places the spotlight in the sector of work, health, and service. Any time during the next two weeks will be an excellent period to take action to improve conditions in any of those three areas. Giving up an unhealthy habit, implementing a new exercise regime, or beginning a new diet stands a good chance of success.

**23. TUESDAY. Complex.** Expect a tricky day ahead with the possibility of rampaging egos and issues associated with power and control. If you work for a boss, put your best foot forward but in a quiet way, remaining out of the firing line in case trouble erupts. The self-employed should experience an industrious urge. This is a good time to sort through files and miscellaneous paperwork, plan upcoming jobs, and stock up on essential items needed to complete employment tasks. Before beginning any strenuous exercise warm up your muscles to lessen the chance of a strain or injury.

**24. WEDNESDAY. Discordant.** Conflict around home base may be encountered, and you might even need to be the mediator between other family members. If conventional medicine doesn't seem to be working on a chronic ailment, consider consulting a naturopath or alternative practitioner for a second opinion. Relationship issues that arise with a personal or professional partner may require in-depth discussions to restore harmonious trends. Note that it might not be your mate or partner who needs to change in order to make you happy. There may be a lack of compatibility that should be analyzed and addressed in order to restore happiness.

**25. THURSDAY. Slow.** Your mind might not be as quick or as sharp as usual. Mercury, planet of the thinking processes, is challenging your old-time ruler, serious Saturn. On the job unforced errors are likely to occur, which will make completing tasks more difficult than usual. It might be wise to keep a low profile without hiding away totally. You are unlikely to be in the mood for fun and games. Take extra care when dealing with customers or clients who are known to be difficult. Complaints regarding an offhand attitude or unhelpful approach could be leveled at you, upsetting the boss or supervisor. Go out of your way to be of service even if you have to fake it.

**26. FRIDAY. Stressful.** A solemn atmosphere prevails and could bring the mood down, resulting in a gloomy outlook. Reaching agreement with a partner or associate may be tricky. Aquarius dealing with the general public are unlikely to have an easygoing day. No matter how hard your try to please others, it may seem to be impossible, at least until midafternoon. After that time the Moon's energies become more supportive and you can make some progress. A long walk or a refreshing swim could wash away the early stresses of the day. Make an appointment for a massage to ease tired muscles and help restore you to good humor. Don't stay out too late tonight if you must leave the house.

**27. SATURDAY. Variable.** A slow beginning to the day is likely, but this should be a tranquil period. Focus on necessary chores, discussions, or meetings during the morning hours when the Moon is quiet and helpful. Later in the day financial concerns could arise concerning joint assets, and this might not be a pleasant time. If you cannot work out certain problems, seek mediation rather than paying large amounts of money to lawyers, especially if you are involved in a protracted custody battle or divorce settlement. A family member who has been dipping into funds put aside for specific expenses could be the reason for a verbal battle this evening.

**28. SUNDAY. Strained.** Financial disagreements are likely to continue this morning, increasing tension and disharmony at home. This is not the best day to venture to department stores with your mate or partner to look for a special purchase. Reaching an agreement on price and quality may be difficult if not impossible. If saving for a large-ticket item, leave credit cards at home when venturing out to socialize because a practical approach when it comes to money may be missing in action. Go to bed early rather than staying up to prepare for tomorrow. If you try to study for an exam late tonight you are unlikely to retain information no matter how much you cram.

**29. MONDAY. Disruptive.** Planetary influences are mainly obstructive rather than constructive. If you have a special assignment to complete, an examination to take, or a paper to present, expect some upsets. A female relative could cause angst this morning, but only if you allow this to happen. An ongoing legal matter is unlikely to be resolved in your favor. This also isn't the best day to implement new legal proceedings or make any threats to sue. Expect delays with a passport or visa application. Long-distance travelers could encounter a few hurdles. Guard your luggage carefully. Before setting off on a journey, label personal possessions clearly and securely.

**30. TUESDAY. Fine.** Today should be much better than yesterday. A pleasant surprise that may have a monetary flavor could make the day especially enjoyable. Students can expect to receive superior results with a homework project or other assignment. If taking an exam you should be pleased with a successful effort. It would not be wise to borrow money from relatives right now. Although your request may be granted, you might hear about their generosity for a long time even after the money has been repaid. Friends could be the source of good luck. If you are seeking new employment, follow up on information or a recommendation provided by one of your former coworkers or bosses.

# JULY

**1. WEDNESDAY. Pleasant.** Celestial influences are good for Aquarius folk. Your coruler Uranus goes retrograde in Pisces to welcome the first day of the new month. The Sun remains in Cancer, accentuating conditions relating to your health and work. Focusing on health, lifestyle, and balancing the mind and body should provide positive results. Romantic activities promise delights thanks to the universe being in the mood to assist efforts to make this a time to remember. If you take off your rose-colored glasses and refrain from putting anyone on a pedestal, a new relationship could begin to develop and blossom nicely. Be careful when it comes to making promises that you might have difficulty honoring.

**2. THURSDAY. Unpredictable.** Fluctuations and unexpected situations make this a challenging and exciting day. Finances stand to improve, and a windfall could come your way through a promotion, prize, or unexpected legacy. Make sure any increase in cash flow is invested wisely and is not wasted on a spending spree, no matter how tempting this may be. You might be confused regarding what jobs to handle right away and what can be left for another day. Don't expect anything to go exactly as planned. Prepare to take a step back if necessary and revamp your plans. After contact with an ex-lover, you might seriously consider renewing the relationship.

**3. FRIDAY. Suspenseful.** This is another day when a bevy of cosmic action increases life's pace. Anxiety regarding career activities could occur, particularly if you feel that your professional life or your desire for higher status is not moving as fast as you would like. Aquarius who are part of a team or need to work in unison with other people should have no trouble getting along in a group situation, leading to a profitable result this morning. You can successfully take on a leadership role. Mercury visits the sign of Cancer and your health and employment house, further increasing the focus on these areas of your life. Those of you struggling with a chronic illness should seek helpful new information by researching the Internet for pertinent medical articles.

**4. SATURDAY. Stormy.** Although you may be in a holiday mood, the universe isn't sending fun trends today. Talkative Mercury and intense Pluto are in dispute, making it difficult to be happy and outgoing. You may feel tired, out of sorts, or physically ill. It would be advisable to watch what you eat and drink throughout the day. Seriously consider seeking advice to help ease a chronic condition or a stressed nervous system. In any discussion be careful when someone talks down to you or becomes overly patronizing, which will be hard to tolerate. Your inclination to show displeasure may be strong, and an argument could easily and quickly erupt.

**5. SUNDAY. Active.** If social invitations are arriving thick and fast via e-mail, phone, or verbally, thank sociable Venus as she arrives in your Gemini house of fun and good times. Be prepared to dress to impress. Join in with other people to celebrate a special function and generally have a great time over the next few weeks. Spending time with a group of friends at a meeting or a club that specializes in a hobby or sport that you thoroughly enjoy could be a wonderful way to pass the day. Socializing should appeal until a few hours after dark, when the allure of bed and an early night could become overwhelming as you contemplate the work week ahead.

**6. MONDAY. Misleading.** This is not a very auspicious day to begin the new working week. Planetary trends are extremely tricky, and deception rules. Be wary of any financial action that needs to be conducted in secret or behind the scenes. You might not be told the full story or understand what your role would be. The old adage that if it looks too good to be true, it is, holds more than an ounce of truth now. Steer clear of a glib salesperson, someone who comes calling door-to-door, or a suave business type bearing supposed gifts. Love and romance may encounter hit a rocky patch. Your mate or partner may be prone to a sulky attitude or may exhibit possessive or jealous behavior.

**7. TUESDAY. Revealing.** Planetary trends are mildly better than yesterday. You could feel that life appears to be an uphill battle with little reward, and some of you may experience a range of difficulties. The eclipsed Full Moon in Capricorn spotlights your sector of all that is secret and hidden, possibly bringing to the surface a matter that needs to be resolved and ended once and for all. A longtime ailment or health issue could return, requiring renewed attention. If you are looking for a new residence or commercial building to purchase or lease, you could unexpectedly find just what you are seeking and at a price that fits your budget.

**8. WEDNESDAY. Problematic.** If your agenda includes finishing up a number of outstanding chores, act on these first thing. Morning aspects are more suitable for completing ongoing tasks rather than beginning anything new. Informative Mercury is not happy with excessive Jupiter or foggy Neptune, sending confusing messages and increasing an inclination for Aquarius to exaggerate. Business, sales, and staff meetings are unlikely to be successful. If you are in charge, it would be wise to postpone a get-together for a few days to avoid wasted time and energy. Deception is something you again need to be aware of, especially with coworkers or employees.

**9. THURSDAY. Stable.** Good vibes today can help you close a favorable deal or cement a long-term endeavor. The Sun and your co-ruler Saturn, happily link together, increasing effectiveness and organizational skills. Strategizing or meeting with senior people or important clients should produced the desired outcome. Aquarius who are experiencing some type of problem or issue that requires input from outsiders should find that a professional counselor is able to provide necessary guidance. Exercise your nurturing side not only toward other people but also for yourself. Treat yourself to something to make life flow more smoothly.

**10. FRIDAY. Insightful.** Trends continue to improve as the weekend approaches. Creativity reaches a climax with the merger of abundant Jupiter and inspirational Neptune. You should have little difficulty forging ahead in your field of expertise. Note that this isn't the right time to make any major decisions or to contemplate future goals because an overly optimistic and unrealistic approach is too likely now. Take extra care to guard against grandiose plans and schemes. Apply moderation. Spiritual activities could appeal. Travelers visiting sacred sites and religious temples should be delighted by the experience as well as gaining more insight and understanding.

**11. SATURDAY. Positive.** Optimistic trends continue as the Moon sails through your own sign of Aquarius. Your power to bring change into your life remains strong. This is the time to consider how you want other people to view you. Updating your appearance and grooming can be a morale booster if you haven't kept up with the latest trends. Active Mars zooms into Gemini, your zone of romance, creative expression, and children. So you can expect some arguments and conflict in these areas over the next few weeks. A favorite pastime or sporting pursuit can benefit from your increased energy, producing dynamic results.

**12. SUNDAY. Mixed.** Cosmic forces are obstructive until midday, when life should begin to improve. Finances are to the fore, and you may be eager to spend money on recreational interests. If a new creative or leisure pursuit appeals, it might be wise to rent or borrow needed equipment rather than purchase it outright, at least until you have tested how passionate you really are about the new interest. Solo Aquarius should have more energy to put into romance. Love could come calling, but proceed slowly. The relationship might be more about lust and desire than love and affection. Enjoy the intimacy without rushing into any long-term commitment.

**13. MONDAY. Good.** Money is again to the fore. This is a favorable period to look at ways to increase your income or to reduce expenditures. Feeling that you are not being paid what you are worth could cause some stress and upset. Before talking to your boss about a raise, or threatening to quit, write down your strengths and weaknesses to ascertain if there are areas where improvements can be made. If going on a job interview you should do very well providing you answer all questions succinctly. Display a confident but modest manner. Aquarius parents should be prepared for an adult child who has left the nest to ask about coming back home to live, at least for a short while.

**14. TUESDAY. Uneasy.** Frustration and confusion are a recurring theme of the day. Although emotional outbursts could be irritating, you might have to live with them, especially if you share your living quarters. A family member or neighbor could be annoyed either with you or with someone you love. Either way, they may insist on talking to you about their troubles and woes, forcing you to make some concessions. Finishing everything on your schedule might be impossible, but try not to stress over it. Do what you can, and leave the rest for tomorrow. If duties have to be completed before you head for home, don't be shy about asking for assistance; many hands make light work.

**15. WEDNESDAY. Uncertain.** Expressing yourself either verbally or in written form may be more difficult than usual over the next few days. Confusion and forgetfulness will increase and you are likely to struggle to find the right words or the best way to put everything into context. Be very clear when giving instructions to other people. And if you don't understand what is being said, ask again rather than performing tasks incorrectly. You can expand yourself socially through better communication providing you first are clear about what you want to say. Aquarius who are giving a public address or presenting a lecture should take along written notes to help stay on subject while addressing the audience.

**16. THURSDAY. Comforting.** A positive atmosphere prevails along with the potential to work hard, but keeping your mind on the job might require extra effort. Mischievous Mercury continues to run rampant in your solar horoscope. Today the influences suggest wandering off and beginning more than one job at a time, or doing your own thing rather than settling into a planned activity schedule. Do all that you can to reduce anxiety and stress. Enjoy a light, nutritious dinner this evening with family members or good friends. Eat leisurely, savoring the tastes and textures of the meal. Include soothing dinnertime music that can enhance enjoyment as well as digestion.

**17. FRIDAY. Diverse.** This will more than likely be a busy day. There may be some serious work ahead before you reach a desired outcome with an employment issue. Reduce the potential number of future arguments and battles by refraining from important decision making today. Although your optimism is heightened, taking on new opportunities or adopting an unrealistic approach could derail some of your plans. Take care to look at all the pluses and minuses. Mercury moves into your Leo partnership house, increasing verbal exchanges with the other people you see on a daily basis. The tempo of life is likely to increase, with more fun and drama to keep you on your toes.

**18. SATURDAY. Pleasurable.** Be sure to eat well and maintain your vitamin intake. This is another busy day that will keep you on the hop. Running errands, finishing chores, or socializing will demand a lot of your energy. You may also be participating in outdoor activities or a sports event; this is a favorable day for Aquarius with talent in the athletic department. Creativity flows and can be utilized in a project that could bring you public attention and admiration. A speculative venture could be of interest, but be discerning with money matters and avoid impulsive action that could jeopardize your financial stability. Avoid loaning or borrowing anything of value.

**19. SUNDAY. Sensitive.** A mildly gloomy atmosphere could prevail unless you make a concerted effort to remain cheerful. There may be an issue between you and your mate, partner, or a child concerning finances. You are apt to be aware of the necessity to conserve financial resources but not be getting much cooperation from others in the household. If this is the case, it might be time to let them know how far the budget needs to stretch to cover household expenses. This evening put aside any disagreements that you may have with a friend or an acquaintance and concentrate on having a good time sharing companionship. Be prepared for socializing to cost more than anticipated but not more than you can afford.

**20. MONDAY. Expressive.** You should be sharp and alert. Tasks that require attention to detail can be performed without effort as your concentration improves. However, watch your tongue. It will be very easy to speak without thinking, and your remarks could be taken the wrong way even if this wasn't your intention. Progress on the job should be swift. Go with your instincts to rely on your own talents and not on the skills of other people. Aquarius who have a speaking engagement can both charm and inform the audience.

Your verbal expertise is exceptional, allowing you to convey new ideas and possibly spiraling your inspired plans to those high up the corporate ladder.

**21. TUESDAY. Variable.** Contrasting influences are in force. A fresh cycle begins with the culmination of an eclipsed New Moon in the sign of canny Cancer, accentuating employment and health conditions. Whatever you start now regarding your health or work should proceed to a successful outcome. Love and romance are not as well starred, however, as Lady Venus challenges your traditional ruler Saturn. This increases the likelihood of disagreements with your mate or partner or of problems with a legacy. This isn't the time to approach the boss about a pay raise or to apply for a loan. An investment scheme that a family member is involved in could be the cause of some concern.

**22. WEDNESDAY. Major.** With the Moon gliding through your Leo house of partnerships, today's energy focuses on business and romantic connections. If an intimate or professional partnership is not working out as planned, it might be time to take some action. If you desire a change, deciding how to make this happen could be problematical. Further emphasis is on all forms of partnerships as the Sun now enters your Leo house of your relationships with others. Personal attachments, sports teams, and business associations are also to the fore, and you can expect movement in these areas over the next four weeks.

**23. THURSDAY. Slow.** Although this should be a slow day, it probably won't be without a number of obstacles and problems. Try to find contentment in your daily routine by varying activities and duties in a simple manner. Tackle jobs in a different order, or set off in another direction in order to perform tasks. Equipment malfunction or faulty products could create frustration. Take extra precautions if handling items that could cause an injury. If continual discord regarding lack of money is creating problems in your one-on-one relationship, get a grip on income, routine expenses, and what you owe, then work out as good a budget as you can.

**24. FRIDAY. Chancy.** This is another day when money and your mate or partner are in the frame. This isn't the time for serious discussions with a personal or professional partner because conflict is likely to quickly arise. If you need to renew your vehicle insurance, obtain a few price quotes before deciding on a carrier; you could find one that is comparable and cheaper than what you have had in the past. Aquarius employed in debt collection need to be tactful in order to reclaim a large amount of money. Be prepared for arguments or stories to explain why repayments cannot be made. On a personal basis, you may have to write off a loan to a friend or else write off the friendship.

**25. SATURDAY. Edgy.** Today's jittery cosmic trends will test your resolve. Try to relax as much as you can. Worry will just hinder your progress, and you won't have time to come up with solutions to problems. A social challenge could force you to follow your good Aquarius judgment, not blindly act according to outdated hard-and-fast rules. Abiding by your guiding principles should serve you well. A business or personal partner may be hiding a secret, so be alert and take care. Make sure you are aware of your financial position. The long-term future with your mate or business partner could be a little shaky, and you might discover that information is being deliberately withheld from you.

**26. SUNDAY. Fortunate.** This can be a very lucky day for you. Even though physical energy could be in short supply, the promise of abundance and good fortune should be enough to cheer you up. If you have been working to strengthen a shaky relationship, you could find that your effort is beginning to pay dividends, with loving bonds coming back into the frame. You and your mate or partner can share a happy rapport and experience the power and joy of shared love. Just be sure to watch the tendency to overindulge in the good things of life. If you buy a lottery ticket or a raffle chance, current stars make coming up a winner very likely.

**27. MONDAY. Expansive.** The good times continue to roll for those born under the zodiac sign of Aquarius. First-time authors could receive good news about an article or novel, and journalists may have a front-page byline. Philosophical beliefs can be examined. Learning more about different religious or world leaders could be a topic of interest. Legal action instigated now is under auspicious vibes, and you could win a protracted court case. Becoming involved with a local youth club should be an enjoyable experience. Going to bed early that you escape from any friction at home.

**28. TUESDAY. Tricky.** Romantic trends are to the fore, but this doesn't mean that love will be light and easygoing. In fact, you may experience rough times as unexpected situations and events occur that could rock the love boat. Singles meeting a new romantic interest should play it cool because a long-enduring affair has little chance under current disruptive trends. Whatever comes your way, know that you will be richer for having had the experience. Speculation, rash investment, or gambling could make a large dent in your bank balance, so think twice before parting with your hard-earned cash. Property could be a long-term moneymaker.

**29. WEDNESDAY. Trying.** This isn't the best day in terms of employment or career matters. Lunar trends do not support implementing major changes or doing anything out of the ordinary except for those who work the night shift. Misunderstandings and work pressures are likely, pulling you in a number of different directions. Be wary when it comes to romance. Someone could pull at your heart strings, increasing excitement but also adding a dash of impulsiveness and erratic behavior. An unexpected romantic encounter is promised, but the energy and passion might not last beyond the next few days. You will need to take what is real and promising while discarding any fantasy.

**30. THURSDAY. Tough.** A rocky road is in the frame right now as talkative Mercury opposes anything and everything put forward by jolly Jupiter. Clarity and vision can be severely impacted by this planetary influence, warning that this isn't the best time to make important decisions because your judgment is likely to be impaired. Dreaming and visualizing can be a good way to bring into your life whatever you think you require. However, this needs to be done in a realistic fashion, not based on grandiose ideas and plans. Disagreements could develop with a personal or professional partner and might spiral into heated arguments unless emotions are kept under control.

**31. FRIDAY. Varied.** This is another day when planet Mercury makes life difficult for you. Confusion, misunderstandings, and erratic behavior can create chaos and discord with your significant other, associate, or special client. You need to watch what you say and how you say it. Venus, the goddess of love and money, brightens up Cancer, your solar house of work and health. Venus here adds a touch of magic and harmony to the employment environment. An office romance could be in the cards for currently single Aquarius. You can expect to socialize more with your coworkers or employees. A new diet, exercise program, beauty treatment, dental work, or cosmetic surgery is favored.

# AUGUST

**1. SATURDAY. Edgy.** Restlessness could create problems, so consider taking a trip to a new locale or doing something different just for a change. You might not know what to do first as scattered energies hinder your ability to complete tasks. Step back and clarify what is urgent and what can wait for a little while longer. On the romantic front, the influences are sending passionate emotional trends for those who are in love. Be careful, however. Jealousy, possessiveness, and emotional blackmail are also characteristics of current planetary vibes. If these get out of control, problems could undermine your relationship.

**2. SUNDAY. Somber.** An antisocial mood could be on display as the Moon slips through your Capricorn house of rest and solitude. If possible, set aside time to take care of personal tasks. A committed relationship could be in for change. Be prepared for possible erratic behavior or tendencies by your significant other. Messenger Mercury moves into the Virgo, your zone of other people's money. Mercury here over the next three weeks will have you thinking how you can make the most of your shared assets and liabilities. This is the time to do review your financial resources and look at credit card and mortgage interest rates.

**3. MONDAY. Improving.** This is another day to seek peace and quiet and, if found, to value every moment of it. Demonstrate tolerance with your significant other, especially when it comes to personal finances. Any discussions in this regard need to be conducted on an adult level, avoiding a tendency toward know-it-all behavior. This is a good time to settle down to a specific project that has been on the back burner for quite a while. Projects that require dedicated research skills should result in a positive outcome. Your quick wit and verbal ability will help you achieve the results that you are seeking.

**4. TUESDAY. Productive.** Pace yourself throughout the day, especially if health has been an issue recently. Keep to yourself as much as possible, varying your activities. You may be pleasantly surprised by how much you are able to accomplish by the end of the day. If you haven't had a chance to study, write, or engage in special research, today offers the time to do so providing you make the effort.

If focus is applied with a special assignment, company advertising program, or a sales strategy, good progress can be made. Aquarius with something important to impart to other people should have little difficulty doing so, as others are likely to cling to every word.

**5. WEDNESDAY. Emotional.** For the next two weeks postpone plans to move forward with any project that involves a partner or where cooperation is needed, especially from the public at large. Tonight a Full Moon in your sign of Aquarius favors ending or finalizing matters rather than beginning anything new. Focus on issues relating to your physical appearance, fitness, or grooming. You may even be considering a makeover or cosmetic surgery. Beware the cranky attitudes of other people, particularly an associate or your significant other. Emotions are highly charged and it will take very little to spark an argument.

**6. THURSDAY. Spirited.** With the Moon sliding through Aquarius, you can come out into the spotlight and shine. Be adventurous, open to the many discoveries surrounding you. Grasp opportunities as soon as they are presented, and don't squander the chances you receive. As an Aquarius you can be persuasive when you put your mind to it. If you have been working long hours, give yourself a break. Make an appointment for a relaxing massage, or soak in the tub to wash away the stress and pressure that accompanies your current heavy workload. It may be wise to forgo social activities if you are having trouble curbing all the intriguing excesses of life.

**7. FRIDAY. Imaginative.** This is a day to extend yourself and speak up if you have specific wants and needs. Be aware that other people may not be in a listening mode. You need to clarify that your desires are worthy and not over the top. A moderate approach is still essential. Even the shy Aquarius should mix and mingle, striking up conversations with people you might not normally talk to. You may meet influential folks who can assist you socially, careerwise, or romantically. Creative juices may be flowing, although expect a few obstacles to pop up in this regard because you may be inclined to take on a larger challenge than you can comfortably handle.

**8. SATURDAY. Volatile.** Expect a few fireworks to erupt. Keeping a low profile is probably the best way to remain under the radar. Your intimate partner might need more space to work out a problem, but don't take this personally. As an Aquarius you are one sign that values independence and time alone. Concentrate on your ability to generate more income. Money fluctuations are likely, indicating this is a good time to balance the budget so you know how much you have to spend, how much to save, and how much to pay bills. Although this sounds simple enough, it might not be unless you are organized and ruthless when it comes to bypassing what you don't need.

**9. SUNDAY. Fair.** The emphasis is on monetary matters as the Moon glides through your Pisces house of finances and personal possessions. If a lack of ready cash is slowing down progress, seek ways to reduce expenditures. Choose entertainment that is free or inexpensive, such as a walk along the shore, a swim, or going for a trip into the country for a picnic. Testing the strength of a love relationship is likely as you may be forced to discard rose-colored glasses and view your lover in the bright light of reality. There is a risk of becoming involved in a controversy or a dishonest sham, so take extra precautions.

**10. MONDAY. Unsettled.** An edgy day begins the new working week. Warrior Mars challenges your traditional ruler Saturn, reducing your supply of energy and enthusiasm. Aquarius in a new or developing personal or professional relationship should be particularly careful with resources. Don't allow anyone to persuade you to hand over your ready cash or to put assets into a scheme or venture. Avoid an inclination to criticize a child who might not be living up to your expectations; doing so could make the issue worse instead of better. Since you want the best for the youngster, seeking outside assistance could be the most useful way to approach the problem.

**11. TUESDAY. Heartening.** A much better day dawns for Aquarius folk. The cosmos is assisting those who need to communicate clearly and concisely. The phone is likely to ring off the hook and e-mails flood in, making this a very busy day. Any upsets with a neighbor or family member can be set right if you make the effort. Charm and the ability to say the right words at the right time are receiving a welcome boost. Clear thinking and an appreciation of what needs to be done combine to produce gains at work, school, or home. Students should make good progress with any form of writing.

**12. WEDNESDAY. Taxing.** Minor aggravations are likely to arise throughout the day. Domestic upsets are accentuated, and an older family member might cause some concern during the morning hours. Be respectful if you are on the receiving end of a lecture; intentions may be in your best interest even if the delivery or the thought is irritating. Because a home or property settlement is unlikely to proceed as envisioned, consider deferring matters if possible relating to personal or joint finances as well as any type of investment. You may be longing to get away from the hassle of daily work and routine, but the opportunities are not to be found right now.

**13. THURSDAY. Lively.** A bright day dawns on the Aquarius horizon. With dynamic Mars mixing it up in a friendly manner with abundant Jupiter, you can expect your love life to receive a big boost of energy and enthusiasm. More can be accomplished in a lot less time since efficiency is also on the rise. Creative interests and recreational pastimes are favored. If seeking a sports scholarship, sponsorship, or selection for an elite team, you could be in luck. Assert yourself. Go after a lucrative future or current contract that can showcase your skills and expertise, possibly setting you up financially for life. Attending a special recreational event should be enjoyable this evening.

**14. FRIDAY. Moderate.** The Sun currently opposes excessive Jupiter, increasing the chance of egos coming to the surface and of contrasting opinions causing dissension and disputes. This is a time when self-control is definitely a bonus, especially while dealing with a partner or the general public. Handling customer complaints might not be easy for you right now, so it would be advisable to hand over this job to other people. Power issues are likely to arise with your father or another male figure, and there may be a battle for domination and supremacy unless one of you is willing to back down. It is essential to realize that you are inclined to make promises that may be difficult to keep, so tone it down or accept the consequences.

**15. SATURDAY. Cautious.** Wait to spend quality time with your lover or a child until early this evening. The Moon is not sending happy vibes until that time, which increases the chance of disputes and disharmony earlier in the day. Socializing should also be put on hold until after dinner. Shoppers are unlikely to find many good bargains. However, splurging won't be of much interest, resulting in some savings if you only purchase essentials. Take extra precautions if participating in a sport or any risky recreational pursuit.

The potential for a minor mishap or injury is slightly higher than normal. Be sure to wear protective gear and follow safety precautions.

**16. SUNDAY. Restful.** A change of plans this morning could set the tone of the entire day. It could be all downhill from midmorning as issues arise and tension pervades the air. If your health or general well-being is not up to your usual level, it would be wise to take it easy and only do what needs to be done. Pushing yourself could result in becoming so weary that you're not able to accomplish very much at all. Be careful to protect the confidences of other people. A slip of the tongue might set off a wave of problems, requiring considerable time and effort to restore peace and harmony in the domestic or employment scene.

**17. MONDAY. Tricky.** A vast array of planetary influences ensures that this will be a tricky day. Be on guard for underhanded deeds; deceptive trends abound. An optimistic approach is an asset to your overall well-being. This is a good time to look for innovative ways to improve your diet and health. Be prepared to get involved in issues relating to the finances of your mate or partner, especially if someone is trying to persuade him or her to get a loan or sell stock for a risky venture. The power of love is heightened, and a positive healing experience could occur if you and your loved one haven't been as compatible as usual lately. Be genuine in expressing emotions.

**18. TUESDAY. Explosive.** A volatile day is likely, so take extra precautions. Current planetary energy warns against risks involving money, love, and leisure pursuits. Postpone any plans to take part in a dangerous exploit. Injuries are more than likely because even the best-laid plans can go astray. The possibility of a power struggle with your mate or partner when it comes to joint finances can lead to stormy eruptions. Aquarius parents can expect tears and tantrums from a child and, depending on their maturity, money could also come into the equation. Don't loan money to a lover, friend, or adult child if you are relying on being repaid any time soon. Also be wary of buying anything sight unseen.

**19. WEDNESDAY. Affectionate.** Love and all personal relationships are to the fore as Venus, Saturn, and Jupiter combine to bring about changes. If you are in a serious commitment, you might decide to advance your romance into a permanent pledge of love.

Aquarius who have been experiencing some marital-type upsets could decide to take a break to see whether living apart is the answer. An older, richer, or more mature lover could appeal to many solo Aquarius. Socializing or catching up with those you haven't seen for a while could take on more importance. Shoppers with a discerning eye could find a number of quality bargains.

**20. THURSDAY. Mixed.** This is a day when you could be a victim of a money scam unless you take good care. Don't promise to hand over cash or sign paperwork relating to resources because the deal might not be what you are led to believe. Communication problems and misunderstandings could also occur, so be specific when issuing instructions, relaying messages, and in general discussions. The New Moon falls in your opposite sign of Leo, illuminating the significant other people in your life. The chances are good for any new venture that you want to get off the ground in the next two weeks as long as your financial security is not put up as collateral.

**21. FRIDAY. Deceptive.** A realistic approach is essential. However, don't make the mistake of believing that life will always be as it is right now. This could cause stagnation and hinder forward movement. You may change your mind regarding what direction you want to take or what you want to work on as the day begins. Before teaming up with anyone in a project, get together and discuss expectations in detail. You may find that they are not on the same wavelength as you. Aquarius who are involved in a new love affair may be upset by a development that takes place and might need to reconsider the next step.

**22. SATURDAY. Surprising.** The lunar goddess is very busy today, so you can also expect to be on the go as well. Aquarius who are in a committed or blossoming relationship may be inclined to overlook the negative behavior of a lover over the ensuing days. However, would be wiser to face up to any blind spot so you can make the best judgment. Otherwise, at some stage, disappointment could arise when the object of your affection falls off the pedestal. Although underlying stresses remain in force, there is also a mixture of unexpected luck on your side. A pay raise, promotion, or large bonus could give you well-deserved rewards for past efforts.

**23. SUNDAY. Influential.** The Sun has now joined Mercury in the sign of Virgo, further highlighting your sex drive, mutual assets, and joint debt. Investments and money shared with others, including the bank, come under scrutiny now. Benefits will arrive from paying close attention to your current financial stability. Ironing out details relating to insurance, tax, and company accounts can proceed as the energy and enthusiasm you are willing to put into this effort receive a boost. Entering into a business or partnership deal is favored as long as you have done the necessary homework. Focus on property and business concerns. Consider writing out a will if you haven't performed this important task.

**24. MONDAY. Compassionate.** Your ability to show interest in other people and to assimilate new ideas and concepts will increase your popularity. A questioning mind could prompt you to begin a research project that may result in financial rewards at a later time. Information you uncover could provide great material for a novel or article, so keep good notes. If it has been some time since your personal possessions and assets, including jewelry, art, and household contents, were valued for insurance purposes, put this on your to-do list. Not having enough insurance coverage could be devastating if a loss occurred, especially if your belongings had increased considerably in value.

**25. TUESDAY. Active.** Guard against a sharp tongue, which could create trouble for you. Coworkers, employees, family members, and neighbors who are on the receiving end of your sarcasm will think less of you, reducing popularity considerably. Good news should arrive, but the anticipated pleasure might be lessened by your current heavy workload. Active Mars and talkative Mercury are both moving into new signs, which may create a sense of uneasiness as change arrives. Your mind should be infused with high ideals and thoughts as Mercury tours your Libra zone of education, knowledge, and travel.

**26. WEDNESDAY. Attentive.** Assertive Mars is now residing in your Cancer sector of employment, health, and domestic conditions. The fiery energy of Mars is dampened while visiting the sign of Cancer, so you can expect some reduction in physical energy until October 16. Over the next week or so Aquarius folk should be more careful when performing daily duties around the house and on the job. You have entered an accident-prone period and need to be more safety conscious to avert the possibility of an injury. Keep away from dangerous areas, drive carefully, and guard against an infection or virus by washing your hands frequently.

**27. THURSDAY. Vital.** Today is all about love, money, children, and leisure. Venus, the lover, is in dispute with passionate Pluto but is reasonably happy with energetic Mars. Venus has also moved on to visit your Leo sector of relationships with all of the other people in your life. For Aquarius who are married or in a happy union, the next few weeks should be happy and exciting, with a good dash of love, romance, and drama. This is also a great period to put passion and drive into a creative project, especially one on the job or designed to assist an employment venture. If you are currently wondering why you are doing a certain something, the realization could come that it is time to make changes.

**28. FRIDAY. Reassuring.** Self-confidence is on the increase. Hurdles stemming from a perceived failure to effectively communicate, or from doubting your own ability, could magically disappear as present thoughts assist all of your endeavors. This is the perfect time to begin a new course of study or spread your wisdom through lecturing, writing, or holding an informative workshop. Legal action may be settled in your favor. Aquarius who are launching a new activity should be happy with the success. Artistic inclinations are soaring, so take advantage and begin creating whatever takes your fancy.

**29. SATURDAY. Helpful.** Focus on detailed, monotonous tasks as early as possible. Energy is likely to flag around nine this morning as the Moon slips into Capricorn. Your mind may then be willing to engage in physical labor, but your body will be weaker. This is the time of the month when the body signals a need to rest and recuperate for a few days in order to recharge and revitalize batteries. If you have a busy social schedule planned for this evening, it might be wise to take an afternoon nap or arrange to have a massage so you are ready to face friends, family members, or possibly the general public.

**30. SUNDAY. Quiet.** The Moon is taking a rest and is sending out signals for you to do the same. Stay in bed and enjoy a good book or the Sunday newspaper before facing the day. Spending that time with your significant other could be a perfect beginning to the day. Otherwise ask a loved one to bring you breakfast in bed for a change. A behind-the-scenes plan that you are anxious to implement might need further tweaking before you move ahead. If you are feeling sorry for someone who is ill or hospitalized, take time to visit if the person will benefit from your company or at least send a get-well card.

**31. MONDAY. Peaceful.** This is another day when working alone could be your preferred option. Recognize that it is easier to swim with the current rather than going against the flow. A slow and steady approach will produce the best results. Tasks that require a practical application should move ahead favorably. A new relationship should be blossoming nicely, and you may be lucky enough to be enjoying romance and happy rapport. If this isn't happening, now is one of the best times of the year to add a dash of spice to your loving union or to find a new love interest.

# SEPTEMBER

**1. TUESDAY. Trying.** With the Moon sailing through your own sign of Aquarius, you should be feeling good as the new month begins. However, you may be a little irritable on occasion throughout the day, and you could be inclined to make mountains out of molehills. September has a number of negative planetary trends, so be prepared for a period that tests your patience, resolve, and dedication. Fortunately there are also highlights off and on during the month that will provide the lift needed to keep motivation and drive high. Personal affairs take center stage, and the answers that you are searching for could come to mind when least expected.

**2. WEDNESDAY. Encouraging.** Your future plans are today's focus of attention. Take advantage of a lighter work schedule, which provides extra time for you to indulge in a number of personal interests. Although you may try hard to fulfill a promise you made, time, energy, or some other force beyond your control could hinder progress. Do your best, but don't allow yourself to feel guilty if you are unable to keep to a timetable set by other people. You are apt to be more competitive around the work environment and may also experience increased sensitivity to any criticism leveled at your ideas or efforts.

**3. THURSDAY. Spirited.** Breaking free from all restrictions is apt to top your agenda. Your mate or partner could attempt to play an emotional game. But you won't be interested in this sort of behavior, which could soon stop when you refuse to take part. There is also a possibility that disagreements could arise in a love affair. The intentions of someone you're interested in romantically may not be genuine. Enjoy the experience without worrying about whether a long-term relationship will be the final result. Your financial situation should remain as optimistic as it now seems providing you keep both feet planted firmly on the ground.

**4. FRIDAY. Emotional.** You may have a tendency to overemphasize your own problems. Someone close to you could suggest the best way to cope with your current finances and needs. Emotions are highly charged as the Moon comes to the full in the sign of Pisces, accentuating your solar house of money and values. Expect major changes to occur, or an ending to a specific concern regarding current income or personal possessions. Be careful about becoming tangled up in duties or obligations that are not rightfully your responsibility. Someone may be trying to take advantage of your good nature.

**5. SATURDAY. Unpredictable.** Sensitive emotions continue, warning Aquarius be gentle care with the feelings of other people. Keep finances simple. If heading to the mall, leave credit cards at home if you are about at your credit limit. Your rational mind might not be as focused as usual, so postpone major decisions and any matters regarding investments or monetary issues. If anxious to get out of the house during the day, meet friends for coffee or a light lunch, and catch up on the latest news and gossip at the same time. A spontaneous plan could be the best source of entertainment this evening.

**6. SUNDAY. Touchy.** Discussions around the house might not be very friendly. Arguments could develop over petty, trivial matters unless you make an effort to keep interactions on an even keel. A social event could become uncomfortable if the topics and opinions being discussed are opposed to your current views and beliefs. Try to be tolerant and patient because making critical comments could upset a host or a valued friend. Aquarius drivers need to obey all rules of the road. Be sure to keep within the speed limit, particularly during the morning hours; otherwise a hefty fine may put an unwelcome strain on the household budget.

**7. MONDAY. Vibrant.** Talking could be nonstop as the Moon slips through Aries, your zone of communication. Issues can be resolved once and for all, putting these in the past and allowing you and the other person to move into the future. A sudden burst of energy as well as clarity will help with present problems, but be sure to plan with precision without resorting to impulsive action. Extra effort to complete a project should be successful as long as you don't take on board the negative opinions expressed by other people. Someone you love may be keeping important information hidden, but at this point in time it would be better to bring everything out into the open.

**8. TUESDAY. Confusing.** Mercury, the planet of communication, is now moving retrograde in Libra, your solar house of higher education and travel. This transit is likely to cause confusion, delays, and frustrations to those who are planning a long journey, to students researching or writing an important thesis or assignment, and also to anyone involved in legal action. You may need to revise your work more than usual. Information required to submit a claim or to support an idea may be harder to source. A minor crisis at home could create a few problems, but everything should fall right into place quickly once you understand the cause of the issue. In romance, extra tact should help keep emotions under control.

**9. WEDNESDAY. Balancing.** Home is your sanctuary today, even if you will be on the job. Emotional support comes from praise received from family members. Be careful about saying too much or going too far. As an Aquarius you are not know for remaining within set boundaries. Conflict could occur if you decide to interfere in issues that are not your concern. Leave your work problems on the job and concentrate on spending quality time with loved ones and also performing household duties to provide comfort and support. A warm, relaxing shower or bath before bed can help you unwind and relax.

**10. THURSDAY. Constructive.** Lunar trends are sending a fairly routine day, but improved situations will help you accomplish a lot more than usual. As an Aquarius you do not want to be fenced in; if you are, you might sense that you are a prisoner of life. However, home and the domestic circle have had a strong pull again today. Make some minor adjustments to improve living conditions and comfort. If you love to cook, spend extra time reading cookbooks. Stretching exercises or a yoga class can be a perfect way to release the tensions of the working day. A new creative pastime may be of interest to the talented Aquarius.

**11. FRIDAY. Restrained.** Upsets in regard to love and romance are likely as goddess Venus opposes Jupiter, planet of excess. Unless you take a moderate approach to every aspect of life over the next few days, repercussions could be experienced for a long time to come. Shoppers should exert extra restraint with credit cards as well as cash reserves, guarding against an urge to spend recklessly. Keeping personal and professional issues separate may be difficult but essential for your overall well-being. Be careful if thinking big. Although doing so can help you devise innovative ideas and plans, a realistic approach might not be part of the current process.

**12. SATURDAY. Uneasy.** Unsettled feelings are more than likely as your traditional ruler Saturn is in friction with idealistic Neptune. Financial security that you thought was stable and solid could be in danger of dissolving. You may be more self-critical than usual, but try to be gentle with yourself and with other people. You may be very busy throughout the day, and others could seek you out in order to take advantage of your many skills and expertise. Your quick wit is a very important attribute. A property settlement or the ending of a business partnership might be delayed, which may just require a little more patience on your part.

**13. SUNDAY. Sensitive.** Your physical resources are likely to be lower and slower than usual, making this an excellent day to stay in bed for an extra hour or two. At this time of the month taking care of your physical condition is important. Don't wait to begin a new health regime or fitness program if you have been slacking off recently. If you have important household tasks to complete, focus on these around midmorning when you will receive a boost of energy. This is a favorable period to assess where you are in your life right now and where you would like to be. If you have strayed off your chosen course, make appropriate adjustments to get back on the right track.

**14. MONDAY. Variable.** You can present yourself in a positive light in regard to career and professional matters. However, business deals and transactions are unlikely to be finalized to your satisfaction for a few more days. If you are enrolled in any type of training or academic course, this isn't the most auspicious time to take an exam or turn in a paper. Aquarius individuals hoping to obtain a driver's license could find the test more challenging than envisioned even though you studied hard for it. A long-distance journey might result in extended delays, so bring along a good book or some good music to keep you amused while waiting for travel connections.

**15. TUESDAY. Stressful.** Another bumpy period arrives for Aquarius folk as your two rulers, somber Saturn and erratic Uranus, oppose each other, creating problems and challenges in the financial area. Loss is indicated unless you are extremely careful. This certainly isn't the time to enter into any business agreement or to apply for a home mortgage or a company overdraft. Confusion is likely with your sense of values. Be very careful about adding more responsibilities and obligations to your already busy agenda. Love and romance may be under a cloud. You may be inclined to put your mate or partner on a pedestal, which is always dangerous.

**16. WEDNESDAY. Diverse.** Variable trends continue, mainly bordering on the negative rather than the positive. However, this doesn't mean you have to wallow in self-pity, doom, and gloom. The tongues of Water Bearers may be sharper than usual, and you may say more than even you intended, so remain alert in discussions. You could express passing comments that you don't consider inflammatory or offensive, but your listeners may have an entirely different reaction. An overly optimistic view of how much household money is available to spend should be guarded against, especially if you are counting income not yet received. Seek legal advice before signing any important paperwork.

**17. THURSDAY. Tricky.** Complex and challenging cosmic forces are being sent to test your patience and resolve. If you have been making changes to who you really are for the sake of a relationship, rethink this. If you decide that this isn't the way you want to live the rest of your life, sit down for a serious discussion with your significant other. You might be a little wary when it comes to financial stability and security. Even if you are upset about money matters, this isn't the time to panic. Instead, be proactive and look for ways to restore a balanced budget and peace of mind. Dig deep and you should discover a practical solution lurking in the back of your mind.

**18. FRIDAY. Refreshing.** The morning hours are not supportive of many of your efforts, but things should begin to look up as the day progresses. Postpone applying for a personal loan, credit card, or business overdraft at least until the afternoon hours or, if possible, wait until tomorrow. A New Moon in the sign of Virgo culminates this evening, signaling a period when you can look forward to an increase in financial support from other people. The next two weeks will be the best period of the year to seek a loan, to get increased insurance coverage, and to put taxes and other debts in manageable shape.

**19. SATURDAY. Social.** Mixing business with pleasure could be very profitable for the business entrepreneur or the career-oriented Aquarius. Put your best foot forward and you should reap deserved rewards. News regarding a legacy or insurance settlement might be received sometime during the next two weeks, providing a welcome boost to an ailing bank account. If you receive a large sum, be sure to put away some of the money for your financial future. Hold off making vacation or business travel arrangements if time is not important; better results are likely if you wait until the end of the month.

**20. SUNDAY. Loving.** Until now this month has probably been more challenging and tricky than any other period of the year so far. All that should ease off a little now, providing time to settle down, relax, and enjoy life more. This is a starred time to explore your romantic desires. Venus, the goddess of all things beautiful, moves into Virgo, your house of sexual desire and fantasy, until October 14. With the Sun, Mercury, Saturn, and Venus in Virgo now, be discreet. It would be wise to curb jealous or overly protective tendencies and thoughts. Let your generous and sensual feelings come to the surface.

**21. MONDAY. Opportune.** Romantic vibes continue to add magic into the atmosphere, although there may be minor discord with your lover. Disagreements can be quickly resolved by looking at both sides of an argument and adopting a flexible approach instead of your usual fixed attitude. With your renewed confidence you could grab a prestigious employment assignment that propels you into the spotlight. Opportunities could also crop up to take on a leadership role. If this occurs, take quick advantage of the chance to prove you have what it takes to lead other people. Shift or evening workers can expect to confront a number of irritating obstacles tonight.

**22. TUESDAY. Profitable.** Thanks to today's practical atmosphere, this is an excellent period to invest in good-quality stocks or bonds. Fortunate vibes encourage self-employed Aquarius and those of you who depend on your powers of intellect to secure lucrative contracts and tenders. The completion of a work project should bring rich rewards. Today the Sun enters Libra, your solar sector of adventure, spirituality, higher education, and long journeys. So over the next four weeks you will jump at the chance to widen your horizons and broaden your knowledge through traveling, reading, and watching relevant films.

**23. WEDNESDAY. Problematical.** Take extra care in most areas of your life. Challenges are likely to confront you at every turn, and the possibility of danger is also very likely. Aquarius travelers should be extremely guarded, refraining from venturing into any area known to endanger personal safety. Heed government travel warnings if visiting unsafe localities. A desire for power can impede relationships. It would be wise to put off visiting or interacting with anyone with whom you have a past unpleasant history. A court case is unlikely to produce the most favorable results for you.

**24. THURSDAY. Complicated.** A complex day dawns as yesterday's planetary influences continue to impact today's activities even though the Moon is not connecting to other planets and is classified as void-of-course for much of the day. Avoid any get-rich-quick schemes. Be careful if traveling through inner-city areas, in crowds, or where pickpockets are known to lurk. A friend or a member of a group might try to get you to reconsider a recent decision. Give the matter more thought, but don't be persuaded by anyone's opinions or whims except your own. This is a good period to research investment opportunities and strategies or to initiate a savings program.

**25. FRIDAY. Upsetting.** Guard against wasting energy and time. Egos are enhanced, and Aquarius are likely to exaggerate and make mountains out of molehills. Travel and education plans are not under favorable stars. Those of you in a lawsuit could find that the cost of legal action continues to rise. Trouble might be brewing in a group that you are a member of or among a circle of friends. If possible, keep your distance and stay out of the fray. Right now you don't need any extra stress and upset in your life. Do yourself a favor and refrain from mixing family and friends in a social context tonight because this could create unforeseen problems.

**26. SATURDAY. Quiet.** This should be a much slower day in the cosmic heavens, and you are likely to be extremely thankful after the stressful past workweek. Working behind the scenes could be a pleasant diversion, giving you a chance to relax and unwind. This is also a great day to work with other people. Any form of teamwork will give you a welcome sense of belonging. You could be pleased and excited by someone's willingness to show you the ins and outs of an activity that you have never tried before. You might even discover that you have a special ability for this type of work or leisure pursuit.

**27. SUNDAY. Charitable.** Spend extra time in bed this morning and strengthen loving ties. Single Aquarius can catch up on reading or beauty sleep. It is that time of the month when the body is asking you to be more gentle and to slow down a little so that your energy reserves can be replenished. A more sensitive and compassionate attitude is likely. You could decide to volunteer your time and services to those in need. A fund-raising event that you have helped organize should run smoothly, and your generosity is likely to win you admiration. Do all that you can to plan ahead for the coming week.

**28. MONDAY. Expressive.** The desire to assert your personality and characteristics that are often hidden from public view becomes more dominant now as the Moon moves through your sign of Aquarius. Although your sign is generally friendly and cheerful, there is also a part of you that remains aloof and distant, which can create problems in a loving relationship. Today you can allow other people into your world and can express love and devotion openly so that family members or your significant other will be aware of your feelings. A few new items for your wardrobe, or an updated hairstyle, could be just what you need to boost self-esteem and confidence.

**29. TUESDAY. Mixed.** Personal aims and goals are likely to stray off course. The main obstacle may be a lack of money or resources to carry out cherished desires. If you combine a realistic outlook along with a positive attitude, good progress can be made. Mercury, the planet of communication, turns direct in Virgo, your house of resources shared with other people. Mercury here can bring an end to possible delays that have made you anxious. If you are confused about a property or divorce settlement, the legalities should start to become clearer. A topical lecture or dinner at a favorite ethnic restaurant could appeal if you want to venture out tonight.

**30. WEDNESDAY. Lively.** A sparkling, outgoing atmosphere continues as the Moon zips through Aquarius. Work tasks should be easier to complete. Aquarius who are employed in the financial service industry should find work moving in a positive direction. Creativity is enhanced this morning, assisting efforts to complete a special project that requires artistic flair. You may prefer being in contact with other people rather than staying alone. Taking part in a group activity will increase your pleasure. As an Aquarius you enjoy being part of a group or association providing you are not locked into a set schedule.

# OCTOBER

**1. THURSDAY. Supportive.** Expect a day of contradictions as the new month gets under way. If personal finances have been difficult recently, this is likely to continue for a while. However, help is on the way as someone close to you, or the bank, could come to your rescue. It would be advisable to get your budget in order now, especially because the upcoming festive period will lead to heavy spending. An innate trait of Aquarius folk is to remain cool and detached even under pressure. Today, however, you enter unfamiliar territory with the Sun bothering cloudy Neptune, creating confusion and a sense of unease.

**2. FRIDAY. Interesting.** Be ready to deal with a disagreement between your business or intimate partner over shared resources, possessions, or general finances. The main cause might be a recent purchase that you didn't consent to, one that is now creating a lack of available cash. Later in the day the Pisces Moon meets up with your coruler Uranus. An unexpected situation could then arise, providing a boost to your cash reserves or giving you a spark of insight regarding how you can easily generate more income. Postpone any purchases designed to enhance grooming and physical appearance because you could buy items or services that don't do the job or are unsuitable for your skin type.

**3. SATURDAY. Cautious.** Difficulty with decision making is likely. You could change your mind a number of times before reaching any conclusions. This isn't the time to rely on input from other people because their emotions, or yours, could cloud logic and reasoning. Aquarius shoppers heading out for retail therapy should watch spending and, more importantly, be wary of indecision followed by impulsiveness. Don't take offhand comments as personal criticism; either ignore them or accept that they could actually be constructive. Social activities might prove disappointing this evening.

**4. SUNDAY. Fair.** A bevy of celestial influences ensures that this day will be interesting, busy, and unpredictable. You are apt to have a lot on your mind as the cosmos turns and twirls. As an Aquarius you are normally reasonably stable, but today's restless energy could have you anxious to be out and about. Avoiding emotional drama might not be easy as a Full Moon culminates in the sign of impulsive Aries, accentuating your solar third house of communication and transportation. Take precautions to ensure that car problems are kept to a minimum if you plan on driving anywhere; check tires and gas before leaving home, and avoid heavy traffic areas.

**5. MONDAY. Disconcerting.** Anger could simmer this morning. Take care to avoid unconsciously making sarcastic remarks that could provoke other people. Think before you speak in order to avoid verbal confrontations. Drivers should consciously aim to be more courteous on the because road rage incidents can rise under current stars. You and a family member or school friend might not get along too well, perhaps leading to a dispute over a project that you are supposed to work on together. Instead of cooperating and working toward a common goal, one of you may be more interested in proving that there is only one right way of continuing.

**6. TUESDAY. Constructive.** Money and home projects are your likely focus for much of the day. Home owners could enjoy drawing up ambitious plans to extend or renovate, while others could decide to add a splash of color to the walls or purchase new furniture to compliment the home's architectural style. If successfully completing a business trip or a course of study is your aim, success should come fairly effortlessly. It may be worth spending the evening relaxing at home with loved ones rather than seeking outside amusement. A home-cooked meal with all the trimmings could appeal if you want to respect the budget.

**7. WEDNESDAY. Positive.** This bright day is another time when your heart and thoughts will focus on home and family matters. Even the daily routine could generate satisfaction as you realize that you are making a difference in your own life and in the lives of loved ones, regardless of how minor this might be. Any concerns that need to be sorted out will benefit from your logical, sensible approach. Plan to venture out this evening, or invite friends to your home if you are one half of a couple. Aquarius powers of attraction move up a notch, providing encouragement for singles to mix and mingle.

**8. THURSDAY. Communicative.** This is an excellent day to network, aiming for solid connections to increase your database of contacts. With support from communicative Mercury and your traditional ruler Saturn, a sensible and logical approach comes easily. Don't waste this energy. Instead, put yourself where you can take advantage of whatever opportunities and situations arise. Other people will listen intently to your words, viewing you as trustworthy and wise. It may be a case of success coming your way at last, as you receive an important offer, a business proposition, or a windfall on the stock market or with real estate.

**9. FRIDAY. Exciting.** This is another day of vast planetary trends creating excitement and unexpected conditions, especially when it comes to love and money. However, this isn't the day to mix the two together because unpredictable trends could cause problems or heartache in this regard. Being with both a special friend and a new lover could create problems as both of them vie for your attention, creating a power struggle. Romantic urges and emotional desire may be running hot, so take advantage and make love, not war. If you are currently single, don't be surprised if an interesting newcomer enters your life. Just move slowly and without expectations, as passion could fizzle out as quickly as it arrives.

**10. SATURDAY. Favorable.** Mixed trends exist. Luck and good fortune smile on you as the Sun combines happily with generous Jupiter. However, talkative Mercury is also challenging powerful Pluto, and your tongue could run out of control. Holding back on pent-up emotions and speech could be very difficult, especially if you have been bottling up your feelings lately. A family member or a neighbor could be the target of your anger unless you make it a point to maintain self-control. The time is ripe to work at making your financial situation more secure. New investment opportunities are favored. Purchase a lottery ticket and you could be smiling all the way to the bank.

**11. SUNDAY. Fine.** This is another day when you might need to button your lip to lessen the chance of getting involved in situations that would be better avoided. There is no need to stress about anything. Good progress can be made. Your enhanced organizational skills ensure that you will tackle tasks easily and will also be well prepared to face unexpected surprises. Even with a busy work schedule or personal agenda, there is much you can do to ensure that duties are performed in a timely manner. Spend leisure periods relaxing so you are prepared to face the working week tomorrow. Couples can share happy rapport, reveling in each other's company.

**12. MONDAY. Optimistic.** Your relationship sector is in the spotlight. There is still opportunity to make improvements in a business partnership even though profits and sales are likely to be on the rise. Important meetings or interviews are under auspicious stars, and you should have the jump on competitors in most areas. Aquarius who are seeking a new job or a move up the ladder could make good progress by sending an updated resume to prospective employers. At midnight Jupiter, the planet of expansion and abundance, turns in direct motion in your own sign of Aquarius. As a result, issues of a personal nature that have been stalled should begin to move ahead.

**13. TUESDAY. Beneficial.** Positive energy shines through as harmonious Venus happily connects to your coruler Saturn and to active Mars. The potential for financial opportunities are high, and you could reap rewards that are beyond your expectations. A number of your deepest desires might be achieved with little effort. Romantic attractions are being blessed by the cosmos, and an engagement announcement or wedding bells could be forthcoming. Working in tandem with a colleague or a group can be therapeutic, especially if each person takes on a duty that they are particularly good at doing.

**14. WEDNESDAY. Helpful.** Focusing on the intimacy within your relationship can be beneficial to ensure that love continues to thrive and grow. Most of the day should go according to plan even though the lunar goddess is sending a few obstructive influences to slow you down. Approaching the boss about a salary increase or requesting more responsibilities can eventually pay dividends. Venus, the planet of the goodies in life, now visits Libra and your solar house of knowledge and wisdom. Falling in a love with someone from another country or culture is possible now. Don't limit yourself in any way.

**15. THURSDAY. Intense.** Relationships and love remain in focus, with trends leaning more toward intensity and passion rather than serenity and comfort. Graceful Venus clashes with powerful Pluto, which could create power struggles in a committed union as well as jealous and manipulative behavior. Solo Aquarius should take care when flirting or seeking a romantic encounter because under these stars the potential for obsessive and compulsive action rises. Before beginning any type of legal action, gather all necessary paperwork. Also be sure that you are not keeping anything from your lawyer; otherwise this information could surface at an inappropriate time.

**16. FRIDAY. Moderate.** The motto for today is not to overextend yourself or to blow anything out of proportion. Otherwise you would only make life harder for yourself and everyone else than it should be. Dynamic Mars enters your opposite sign of Leo, your relationship sector. Mars here warns you to avoid a love triangle. Also be careful if you are involved in any clandestine relationship; you may be found out now. The restrictions of daily obligations could be causing frustration because you may be yearning to expand your horizons and broaden your knowledge. The desire to travel and to experience different cultures could become overwhelming, so consider researching possible destinations that excite your fantasies.

**17. SATURDAY. Hopeful.** A pleasant day is promised by today's stars. There is great energy, so take action in any way that can help you reach your potential. If you are setting off on a long vacation or business trip, you should have a relatively easy time without many delays or obstacles to impede your enjoyment. If you have always fancied becoming a top chef or just wish to improve your skills in the kitchen, enrolling in a cooking course could help you achieve your goal. Try out a few recipes that feature foreign cuisine if you are hosting guests for dinner this evening. Money and in-laws are not a good mix this evening.

**18. SUNDAY. Revealing.** Today's variety of cosmic trends will keep you on your toes. The attitudes of other people could leave a lot to be desired, and trying to ignore bad behavior may be difficult for you. Forgiveness figures largely in the cosmic heavens, and this could relate to your intimate partner. You might be in the position where you need to decide whether to let the past go or to linger in memories. A New Moon forms in Libra, your sector of spirituality, education, and travel. Here come fresh opportunities to increase your level of wisdom and knowledge through travel and higher education.

**19. MONDAY. Uplifting.** Professional, career, and business matters are to the fore. News could be received regarding an employment opportunity, and this may be the beginning of a new direction in your life. Inventing new methods of performing certain repetitive duties could reduce the time needed to handle these tasks. You may have difficulty dealing with criticism because you are apt to be more sensitive than usual. Even if other people are not intentionally critical of your actions, you might perceive that they are. An influx of social invitations might be arriving daily, for now and for the upcoming festive season. Don't wait too long to respond.

**20. TUESDAY. Starred.** Lucky trends surround Aquarius people. An important meeting could be full of pleasant surprises. If you trade with overseas companies, expect lucrative contracts to come your way. The current energy bodes well for Aquarius who are involved in a legal matter, with the expectation of a positive resolution. If you have been involved in any disagreement with your parents, in-laws, or other relatives, today favors finding a way to broker peace. Talking to friends or interacting with a group that shares a common interest can be relaxing this evening. Aquarius who are traveling overseas could meet an interesting love interest.

**21. WEDNESDAY. Misleading.** Keep romantic intentions under wraps if you have your eye on someone new. There is a chance that you are misguided and that your choice of attraction could be disappointing. Aquarius who accept a blind date arranged by friends or a relative could find that the companion doesn't live up to the hype. Follow your instincts to assist a friend whose faith in the outcome of a situation is bordering on the negative while you are able to see the bigger picture. Your mate or partner could assist your progress within a group or club, and you may be asked to take on a committee role or run for elective office.

**22. THURSDAY. Bright.** You should display a sensible, logical approach that makes you popular among work colleagues and associates. Your unique way of handling matters could also catch the eye of someone in authority, so don't be shy; seize any and all opportunities to showcase your skills and talent. Your passion when it comes to humanitarian causes could overwhelm even some of your close friends who are accustomed to your ardent approach. You might need to tone down your enthusiasm just a little or risk undoing some of the good work that you have already performed.

**23. FRIDAY. Opportune.** By the time you wake up this morning, the Moon will have slipped into Capricorn, your twelfth house of solitude. This will slow down your energy and moderate your activities. Almost simultaneously the Sun will have moved into Scorpio, lighting up your tenth sector of fame, honors, and career matters. How far and how quickly you move up the ladder of success depends on the effort you exert now. Grasp the opportunity to shine in career or business endeavors. Throughout the next four weeks you have the best chance of the year to make a name for yourself. Your ability to get along with people increases, and even those that you normally have trouble relating to could be easier to interact with.

**24. SATURDAY. Dynamic.** Powerful influences are at work as the weekend begins. Visiting a New Age fair could lead to a dynamic encounter with an astrologer, clairvoyant, or someone with vision who can make a positive impact. Important information might be revealed that helps you arrive at a decision providing you are open to receive new data. Don't allow other people to get involved in your private affairs. Remain tactful, but at the same time keep your distance. Attendance at a conference or seminar that provides the chance to increase knowledge for future employment or leisure pursuits could appeal and be enjoyable as well.

**25. SUNDAY. Slow.** If you feel lazy this morning, stay in bed a little longer than usual. Postpone strenuous tasks until later in the day because your vim and vitality may be at a low ebb at least until midafternoon. Social activities should also be put on hold until later in the day. You will probably prefer to withdraw into your own world for a short period of time. As the day goes on, the inclination to interact with other people will return and a more positive atmosphere will arrive. Take care with authority figures if you are out and about after dark, and remember to obey rules. Going to bed early lessens the chance of an argument occurring with your mate or significant other.

**26. MONDAY. Useful.** A more social attitude arrives as the Moon slips into your sign of Aquarius. If you rested yesterday, you should have plenty of energy to face the new working week. Even though a restless approach could be evident, you may be happy to delve into normal routine tasks. Pride comes from performing duties to a high standard, especially if you are working in collaboration with other people. There is a negative tone regarding joint finances throughout the day, indicating that it would be wise to defer plans that have a financial theme. A musical concert or a favorite hobby could be an attractive choice for evening entertainment.

**27. TUESDAY. Pleasant.** The day ahead promises to be happy. You are unlikely to encounter many obstacles along the way. Progress with personal aims can be swifter than usual. If you haven't taken the time to review where you are now and where you are going, this is the perfect opportunity to do so. Take time to build up your own strength. You cannot offer assistance to other people if you are struggling with your own vitality. A full-body massage could be therapeutic. Finances may be a struggle unless budgetary constraints are implemented. Living simply now will mean you have more cash available in the future.

**28. WEDNESDAY. Auspicious.** An abundance of planetary influences prevail. Love and good fortune abound. This is an excellent period to purchase a lottery ticket or enter into a competition or raffle. Mercury, the talkative planet, visits the sign of Scorpio and your tenth solar house of career and business prowess. Over the next four weeks you may be asked to speak in front of an audience or to teach other the intricacies of your profession more frequently than usual. Your sense of purpose increases, so you could experience feelings that you know exactly where you are going and how you can make things happen. An influential person may provide business assistance.

**29. THURSDAY. Noteworthy.** Seemingly straightforward discussions could escalate into disputes if care is not taken. Be wary of forcing your opinions on other people, and remember to listen to the views of competitors as well as colleagues. Use current celestial influences in a powerful manner to move ahead in a career or business enterprise. A major transit occurs today with the movement of your traditional ruler Saturn into Libra, your house of higher education, travel, and philosophical opinions. Your worldview is likely to become more stable, and you could decide to take an overseas journey to study, to grow a business, or to be with a mentor or a lover.

**30. FRIDAY. Varied.** The day begins with a focus on money and the acquisition of possessions. By midday you might be more interested in the errands that are waiting for attention, and you could be too busy zipping around to worry about bills that need to be paid. Regardless of how many appointments and meetings you have to attend, try to keep your emotions and stress level on an even keel. Reconciling with a past love could become a more attractive possibility; weigh all of the pros and cons before making a decision. Even though everyone deserves a second chance, taking a step backward is not always successful.

**31. SATURDAY. Edgy.** As an Aquarius you are usually stable and fixed, but today's energy can cause a fidgety demeanor. Include plenty of variety in your day to keep motivation high, especially if you have to mainly handle routine chores. If you have the chance to do your own thing, take a sightseeing trip to places you haven't seen before. A trip to visit relatives or to view the surrounding countryside could provide special pleasure. Parents who are going on a long journey should pack a few games or amusements to keep children quietly entertained. A new plan or interest should prove more successful than you now envision.

# NOVEMBER

**1. SUNDAY. Fair.** Your personality and sense of humor should be sharp as the new month begins. However, over the next few days your tongue could be the same, so guard against uttering biting comments, especially with clients, partners, and work colleagues. Try to be more objective where your behavior is concerned. Avoid a knee-jerk reaction, assess the facts, and don't use pride as a cover for irresponsible words or actions. Take the most positive approach, even if it means compromising. The opportunity to tap into your higher consciousness can help in areas of life that are creating issues or concerns, so use this to your advantage.

**2. MONDAY. Manageable.** Steady as she goes is the motto for today. Today's Full Moon in Taurus is illuminating your solar sector of home and family domestic affairs. Sometime during the next two weeks a certain matter will come to an end, and this may involve your family. A recent event or decision that appears to have gone awry needs to be reassessed because the direction you chose could be the wrong one. Don't be discouraged if other people are not as accepting of your views or are not on the same wavelength as you right now. A disciplined, practical approach is the ideal way to balance the household budget.

**3. TUESDAY. Satisfactory.** The comfort and security of home will still be a strong focus for Aquarius folk. Spending time with family members will provide contentment even if you only have a few hours in the evening to devote to loved ones. Be especially careful if using gas or liquids around the house, and keep all cleaning products up high, out of reach of young children. Tomorrow Neptune, planet of confusion, will turn direct in your sign, ushering in a period when you can begin implementing changes in your personal life that you hope will be long lasting. Don't be worried if good results don't happen right away. Remember, patience is a virtue.

**4. WEDNESDAY. Pleasant.** Aquarius parents should delight in being with youngsters, interacting and watching them learn and grow. Be generous with advice without making decisions if older children want to discuss their problems and concerns. Keen perception and careful planning blending together can help you move forward in areas that are important to you. Avoid becoming bogged down in a serious debate tonight, when cosmic influences are better suited for lighthearted banter and gossip. Creative potential is enhanced, providing you with extra incentive to design and produce a work of art in yarn, thread, or paint.

**5. THURSDAY. Important.** This is a starred day to forge ahead with career and professional affairs. Maintain a businesslike mood. If you are waiting to hear of an employment promotion or salary increase, you could receive good news. Move ahead with anything that will help you get through red tape and deal with officials. Complicated paperwork or a questionnaire can be completed and sent off with very good assurance that errors will be few if any. Resolving a work matter shouldn't be difficult thanks to the cooperation and willingness shown by colleagues or a superior. Expect to stand out in a meeting and to command respect from those in authority.

**6. FRIDAY. Slow.** Attentiveness and alertness might be lower today than yesterday. Your sense of logic and reason could be tested at times throughout the day, but there isn't any reason why you won't come out on top. Providing you are able to keep your emotion in check when dealing with tricky issues, solutions can be readily found. An appointment with a health practitioner, or independently pursuing remedies to aid an ailment or illness, should be successful. Take time for contemplation and meditation; insight and understanding of what your body requires can help reduce stress and strain. If you need some practical guidance, turn to someone you admire who is successful and ask for advice.

**7. SATURDAY. Demanding.** Communication could be a little tricky, so take extra care. Avoid subjects that might cause an argument to flare up quickly. However, not making a decision in hopes that the problem will disappear is living in a fantasy world. Words can wound, but don't assume that other people will always consider your feelings. Sometimes what is bothering you needs to be brought out into the open. Tonight Venus, the planet linked to love and money, will enter Scorpio, your sector of professional connections and career affairs. Be prepared to socialize more with influential or powerful people. Mixing business with pleasure should pay dividends now and in the future.

**8. SUNDAY. Varied.** There are a number of problematical trends surrounding you, but you can still make significant progress by following your instincts. Your good sense of timing should serve you well throughout the day. Complications with a family business might need to be sorted out, and it could take some time to find a satisfactory solution that everyone can live with. Business impulses remain high, assisting the self-employed or the career-minded Aquarius who is on the job today. Being in the public eye is also a possibility. You can make a good impression providing you take a modest approach and curb any urge to preach to other people.

**9. MONDAY. Social.** This promises to be an excellent day to mingle with associates and business contacts, who are bound to admire your magnetic qualities. Take advantage of the current vibes to promote yourself in the best possible light. This is also a favorable period to spend time with people you respect and admire. Romantic desire is enhanced as lover Venus entwines with powerful Pluto. You can share happy times with your significant other. A relationship that forms now, whether professional or romantic, is apt to be deeply intense and passionate. If you need to firm up forthcoming social arrangements, get this task out of the way before it slips your mind.

**10. TUESDAY. Tolerant.** Sometimes it is essential to shut your eyes to the foibles and flaws of other people in your life. Today, as the Moon slips through picky and pedantic Virgo, this could be more difficult than usual. However, if you desire a hassle-free day you need to be flexible and let things go. Egos could be overinflated. If you are on the job, put your best foot forward but remain under the radar. Otherwise you can expect to receive flak from a boss or other higher-up, which won't be very pleasant. Aquarius employers should ensure that any criticism leveled at a staff member is voiced in private.

**11. WEDNESDAY. Problematic.** Movable Mercury is creating varied trends today, being friendly toward your coruler Uranus but disputing with cloudy Neptune. Patience is the key to getting through the day relatively unscathed. Delays and frustrations will be frequent. Even though you might like every hour of the day filled with activity and pleasure, this isn't the way things usually happen. The challenge is to avoid creating drama and chaos just to add excitement to your daily routine. Apply a heaping dose of discipline, and focus on completing one activity at a time. Otherwise your energy will be scattered and you may not finish anything in a timely manner.

**12. THURSDAY. Stimulating.** Jot down original and innovative ideas that pop into mind. These could someday in the future become a moneymaking venture for the enterprising Aquarius. This is another day when making changes to your routine, even in a small way, can increase motivation and stimulation. Multitasking has never looked so good. As an Aquarius you excel at performing more than one job at a time, and this is especially true for members of the female gender. Take control of the day and of your energy to get the many tasks on your schedule completed and ticked off your list. An investigation could reveal important new information that might cause you to change your mind.

**13. FRIDAY. Dreamy.** If you are unsettled in a current relationship, this might be the time to take some form of action. Putting some emotional or real distance between you and a companion will let you put everything into perspective and sort out your priorities. Discuss fears and plans with someone who has your best interests at heart, someone who can view things in an objective light. Flying off to sights unseen could be your dream, but in reality this is unlikely. Instead, consider researching various locations of interest and implementing a savings plan so one day soon your dream trip can come true.

**14. SATURDAY. Unpredictable.** An unexpected promotion or bonus could come your way, but so could a number of unforeseen bills. Aquarius just starting out in a new career or apprenticeship might discover that the cost of equipment or required work clothes is more expensive than anticipated. You might even need to obtain a loan from a family member to cover start-up costs. Other people will appreciate your willingness to take on a project. Although you might not receive actual credit or recognition, appreciation is likely to come as they recognize that they can count on you. Dealings with coworkers or the public may be irritable or emotional but control an urge to talk back.

**15. SUNDAY. Challenging.** Most of today's tasks and activities could appear more difficult than expected as your coruler Saturn challenges the might of powerful Pluto. Also expect to question your beliefs and educational achievements. There may be annoying alterations to travel arrangements. Compelling forces or interests could encourage you to make one or more significant changes. Aquarius involved in a legal matter could experience the full brunt of the authorities. This isn't the time to take the law into your own hands or to break rules because the punishment might exceed the crime. Deceptive trends also exist, so take extra precautions.

**16. MONDAY. Refreshing.** Mercury, the planet connected to the thought processes, is now residing in Sagittarius, your solar sector of friends, groups, and associations. You have an opportunity to set new goals and desires and to follow these through. Your social life is enhanced, and you can expect your popularity to increase accordingly. Today's bright New Moon culminates in Scorpio, your solar sector of career and business interests, and will help you succeed in the outer world. Over the next two weeks you should experience auspicious energy that enables you to bring vocational interests to fruition. A new venture can be set in motion with a significant chance of a successful outcome.

**17. TUESDAY. Opportune.** Apart from professional concerns, you could be making a name for yourself through your involvement in the world of politics or community affairs. A strong interest in government may find you becoming a candidate for a political office or for a prestigious position in a group or club that you are a member of. Your chances of being elected or appointed to a position of power are enhanced, so make your move and aim high. If attending a social function, chatting with folks who are older or more mature than you can be informative as well as pleasant. Find out what fascinates other people, and do more listening than talking.

**18. WEDNESDAY. Uplifting.** Realize that there isn't any point waiting for other people to make specific arrangements when you could do so as well as the next person. Friends are an important part of your life, and today they can help you relax and unwind because they remind you that there's more than one way to look at life. This is also a good period to participate in a group activity or a hobby with other people. You could be mentioned for a leadership role. Even if you were not expecting this confidence booster, seriously consider accepting the challenge and giving it your best shot.

**19. THURSDAY. Comforting.** A large dash of contentment surrounds you. As an Aquarius you appreciate human kindness and generosity, and you are more than willing to give in abundance as well. Today could find you volunteering your services to a needy charitable group or cheering up seniors or hospitalized patients. With all of your recent progress, it might be hard to slow down and return to old or past issues. However, this is a good time to balance what has gone before and what lies in your future. Postpone beginning new projects because current stars are more helpful for completing ventures rather than beginning anything.

**20. FRIDAY. Tranquil.** With the Moon gliding through Capricorn, it is time to move away from the hustle and bustle of life and seek quiet solitude so you can gather your thoughts. Don't offer to take on more than you can comfortably manage. That may mean you must pace yourself both at home and at work. There might be a dispute with your partner or a client during the afternoon if you are not prepared to pay strict attention to their wishes. Refrain from forcing your point of view. Instead, allow other people to choose for themselves; even if this turns out to be the wrong choice, ultimately it was their decision. You are in a forgiving mood, so if someone steps out of line try hard not to become too annoyed.

**21. SATURDAY. Restful.** Relax and tackle minor chores rather than any large-scale tasks. This is a good day to begin contemplating your festive gift list or the jobs that have to be performed before the big day arrives. Look back at the progress you have made with personal goals, an improved image and grooming, and self-confidence. The lunar goddess is now in your sign of Aquarius, so progress has been made keep up the good work. Or you may decide to focus on yourself now. Aquarius who have gone out of their way to cooperate could reap deserved rewards. Attending social functions may be from duty but should still provide enjoyment.

**22. SUNDAY. Lively.** The Sun is now shining in the freedom and party-loving sign of Sagittarius, focusing attention on your solar sector of friends, groups, and cherished desires over the next four weeks. Expect the tempo of your social life to further increase along with the drive and enthusiasm required to strive toward your cherished ambitions and aims. Sharing interests and philosophical ideals with people you admire should prove exciting. Seek out those who think and believe as you do, perhaps by joining a club or political group. Display integrity and your generous nature. A phone call tonight could be just the news you hoped to receive.

**23. MONDAY. Inspiring.** Widening your circle of friends by joining a new group or club may be of interest, especially if you recently moved into a new area. Today's boost of energy needs to be dispersed in a productive way. This can be through physical exercise, or perhaps by cleaning the house from top to bottom in readiness for the upcoming holidays. A special friend could make a suggestion that sparks off an idea worth following through because it might have the potential to increase your income. Moderation is required over the next few days in most areas of life. Give retail therapy a rest so your bank account has a chance to recover.

**24. TUESDAY. Accomplished.** You should be in a determined mood, ready to set plans into motion. Achieving a number of your long-term goals could also be high on your list of priorities. Even if this requires working longer hours, it shouldn't faze you. Efficient and practical are apt descriptions of the current atmosphere. Your natural Aquarius ability to make a good impression on other people will give you an edge in a job interview or any type of competition. If you are considering a vacation with a tour group or with friends, finalize details and arrangements now. An evening at home might be beneficial.

**25. WEDNESDAY. Motivating.** Focus on mental rather than physical tasks. Set your brain in motion and keep it whirring. Those who have a lot to do in a short space of time can move ahead quickly and effectively if extra effort is expended. Over the next few days success should be the result of meetings and negotiations. You can put forward your ideas and views with conviction and clarity. An inclination to rebel when it comes to love and romance is likely. However, if you are part of a couple, this action could be surprisingly instrumental in adding a large dash of spice to your love life. An unexpected financial proposition may be worth a second look.

**26. THURSDAY. Productive.** Your brain should be working very well, particularly when it comes to thinking things through to an end result. A practical, methodical approach can also help in performing tasks that require efficiency with a minimum of fuss. If you have a heavy work schedule that needs to be reduced before the start of next month's festive season, you can make good progress now if you apply effort and energy. A potential adventure of a lifetime is possible for the currently single if rose-colored glasses are removed. Be ready to take part in an exciting but possibly short-term love affair.

**27. FRIDAY. Constructive.** A few stressful moments are likely as this day unfolds, but don't let these unhelpful trends get you down. Fortunately they should be short-lived and not too hard for you to handle. If you are up and about early, steer clear of controversial topics because other people may easily take offense. Continue to juggle responsibilities by completing one project thoroughly before beginning the next one. In this way you should make steady progress throughout the day. Once your chores and duties are finished, plan a relaxing evening with special friends or neighbors, preferably close to your home base.

**28. SATURDAY. Upbeat.** Most of today's cosmic trends are fine, with only a minor hiccup occurring during the afternoon. Whenever the Moon is in the impulsive sign of Aries, there is a propensity to be more argumentative than usual. Try to cool it throughout the day to avoid disagreeing with people who may be in a position to provide you with assistance at a later time. If you want to purchase a car or electronic equipment, you could find what you are looking for during the morning hours; if you are prepared to barter, the price should be right. Put aside more serious matters tonight and plan a fun social gathering with favorite folks.

**29. SUNDAY. Unsteady.** This will be a day of mixed energy. If you are attending or presenting a lecture, seminar, or public address, expect appreciation from the audience. Favorable news received earlier in the week concerning an application for school or work or a lease could now be the focus of your attention. This is a good time to start filling out necessary paperwork so you are ready to submit it ahead of the deadline. Impatience because results you are seeking are slow coming in could cause heightened stress. Don't give up, but realize that Rome wasn't built in a day. Perhaps a change of tactics could promote quicker advancement than the current slow progress.

**30. MONDAY. Demanding.** Mercury, the planet of messages, is challenging your coruler Uranus. So be prepared for an emotional roller-coaster ride today. Take a break from the daily grind if you can, and vary your routine as much as possible. Turning restless energy into a physical pursuit will help you contain unsettled feelings. Reorganizing around the house could be a positive way to utilize your increased vim and vigor. It would not be a smart idea to mix money and friends because such a decision could have unexpected repercussions. Unless you keep the two separate, you may not see either your money or your friend again.

# DECEMBER

**1. TUESDAY. Happy.** The beginning of the last month of 2009 brings situations that could take you or someone close to you by surprise. Generally these developments should lean toward positive because your energy to meet and greet is strong and other people can brighten your mood. Expect a bevy of invitations to arrive. For the solo Aquarius, this could provide the chance to meet more than one eligible romantic potential. Your imagination will be ignited with various artistic possibilities, and a strong desire to explore can be utilized in a favored creative outlet. Those of you attending a meeting can expect a pleasant time but probably not much in the way of productive outcome.

**2. WEDNESDAY. Major.** Uranus, planet of erratic action, and your modern-day ruler, turns direct again after several months retrograde in Pisces, your solar house of personal finances. Delays that have held up receiving a special check, an important repayment, or some other money matter of significance should now begin to move forward. You might discover you have a skill you never recognized, and this has the potential to increase your current income. Venus, planet of love, has joined the Sun and Mercury in Sagittarius, conveying increased social interaction with friends and groups just in time for the upcoming festive season to begin.

**3. THURSDAY. Smooth.** Slipping into your work routine should be easy. Relationships with coworkers will proceed smoothly. If you have a favor to ask of the boss or another superior, take the initiative now. The worse case scenario would be a loud negative to your request. If you have hardly made a dent in your holiday shopping, now is the time to make your move and enjoy looking for just the right items. Head to the shopping mall with your gift list and be one step ahead of the crowds seeking out bargains. If single, you could meet someone who has the potential to become a very special person in your life.

**4. FRIDAY. Loving.** Love and romantic vibes continue to pervade the air as beautiful Venus harmonizes happily with stable Saturn, your traditional ruler. Your attitude to love may be changing. Aquarius singles could seek out a partner who is older or more mature than you. Your ability to make good investment decisions is high, providing the potential to make a lucrative profit. Removing limitations, restrictions, and barriers to your work can be more easily accomplished if your focus is centered on techniques and processes that require improvements. Take extra care with your diet and exercise program. Don't overindulge or stray too far from your normal daily intake of food and drink.

**5. SATURDAY. Productive.** For Aquarius on the job, this is another good day to examine and redefine work methods and procedures. The self-employed might need to consider slowing down a little, or at least not pushing too hard, because energy is limited today. Visiting older family members could cause consternation, forcing you to be at your diplomatic best. Keep your lip buttoned to reduce the chance of family discord occurring. A situation that arises could encourage you to consider changing tactics, but this might not be the wisest course to take. Remain confident about your own ability, and realize that what happens now may be for the best in the long term.

**6. SUNDAY. Encouraging.** Be sensitive to the needs of those close to you, especially your intimate partner. Make full use of your intellectual skills. Utilize conversation to draw other people out of themselves. If an ongoing problem is of concern, seek a solution through confident discussions, bringing any current issues out into the open. Sun and Venus gracing your Sagittarius sector of friends and social activities, you are being encouraged to go out and have fun. If you are keeping an eye out for festive gifts, you are apt to spot a number of wacky, fun type of presents. However, be careful regarding who you give them to.

**7. MONDAY. Insightful.** Although as an Aquarius you are capable of deep thoughts today, you might be shy about sharing what is on your mind or about speaking up. If you have to conduct research, this is a good day to dig deep for hidden information. This is also a good period to consider implementing some of the plans that have been on your mind. However, minimize any tendency toward impulsive action while messenger Mercury is challenging steady Saturn. This is a good time to assess your holiday preparations to ensure cards have been bought, travel plans for the big day are finalized, and a list of presents is being checked.

**8. TUESDAY. Complex.** Complicated tasks can be dealt with more easily today. Keep a smile on your face and interact with positive people, avoiding some inclination to become overly serious during the day. Communications with other people might be difficult, requiring you to think fast on your feet. Playful conversation could quickly shift into a serious confrontation, so endeavor to keep topics light and breezy. Be careful when handling customer complaints or dealing with clients and associates. Thoroughly check what is being said because someone might be inclined to exaggerate or tell lies to further their cause or case. A personal or professional partner is now able to handle the truth.

**9. WEDNESDAY. Upsetting.** This day doesn't provide the most social of influences, and it also doesn't bode well for matters relating to finances. Do your best to assess any difficulties by taking a realistic approach. Avoid coming on too strong or being too pedantic even if you feel that it is warranted. Someone of importance might not be as helpful and supportive as you had hoped, possibly backing down on a promise. Although this is bound to be disappointing, there won't be much you can do about it right now. The urge to relax becomes stronger this evening. Put aside routine chores and share companionship with your nearest and dearest.

**10. THURSDAY. Opportune.** Aquarius folk can come across as know-it-alls, and today this characteristic might be on display but only slightly. Try to remain modest if not humble. Allow other people to share their knowledge and views along with your own. You may be more interested than usual in research and in learning new activities. This openness to increasing your knowledge can be put to good use through writing, reading, and public speaking. Consider participating in further study, especially if this could increase your worth to a current or prospective employer. Be wary of talking too much or too loudly if you go out tonight.

**11. FRIDAY. Cloudy.** Your physical energy might be strong, but clarity of thought and clear mental faculties could be on the low side. Confusion threatens plans and communications. Today does not favor intricate work that requires analysis or focus because concentration could also be lacking. A quick trip around the mall to see what's on sale would be enjoyable. This can also provide a chance to tick off a few items on your long list of gifts and requirements needed for the upcoming holidays. If you are stuck for a gift for a hard-to-buy-for person, a new novel or how-to manual could be just the right choice.

**12. SATURDAY. Lucky.** Unexpected good fortune is indicated through a career pursuit or involvement with education or a trade. Someone higher up the career ladder might attempt to point you in the right direction, so be prepared to listen and learn. New friendships are a good way to widen your social network and gain insight and knowledge. Welcome the chance to meet and mingle with other people, especially if they share a common interest with you. A social function this evening will provide required stimulation. Solo Aquarius might find luck improving as a friendship shifts to romance.

**13. SUNDAY. Busy.** With the upcoming holiday period on your mind, use lists to help handle stress. If going on vacation or to visit for the festive celebrations, review plans and preparations to ensure that everything is ready for your departure. Aquarius who are unhappy in current employment should ask friends and family members to be alert for other jobs that would offer the challenge and satisfaction currently lacking in your present employment. Even though it is close to the holiday period, some employers are looking for reliable and trustworthy workers. Socializing can be relaxing; attending a company party should be special fun.

**14. MONDAY. Surprising.** Expect a day of contrasts as the Sun squares off with your coruler Uranus and happily entwines with Jupiter, the planet linked to abundance. An unexpected happening will produce a very good chance of increasing your bank balance. This bolt out of the blue will create excitement, with the possibility that another development will occur and also take you by surprise. The urge to rebel in some fashion could become almost overwhelming. However, as an Aquarius you live with this kind of energy every day of your life, so you shouldn't have too much trouble containing the urge. Don't neglect the urging of your partner.

**15. TUESDAY. Fortunate.** With luck again on your side, don't waste opportunities to take advantage of fortunate trends. A spiritual atmosphere prevails. This is a starred time to arrange a festive gathering or to take part in a musical performance. Perception, intuition, and insight are heightened. Knowing the best way to counsel a troubled friend should be an automatic response for you. Give guidance and moral support without becoming too deeply entrenched in the problem. Creative imagination is ignited. If you prefer to give handmade gifts to special folk, power ahead now with your baking, sewing, or craft work.

**16. WEDNESDAY. Inspired.** This is another great day for socializing, although by evening you might prefer to go into hibernation for a couple of days. Artistic talents remain enhanced. Aquarius who paint, draw, or design should experience increased productivity. A New Moon culminates in the outgoing sign of Sagittarius, conveying opportunities to increase your friendship circle and also to develop fresh goals and aims. Clarify your cherished desires and aspirations, then over the next two weeks come up with plans to make these happen in your life. Set positive boundaries, make your wish list, and prepare for all that's good to arrive.

**17. THURSDAY. Sentimental.** You need private time, a chance to get away from the hustle and bustle of this hectic season if just for a short while. Reenergize with a brisk walk around the park or anywhere away from crowds. A nostalgic, sentimental mood could come over you and as you are drawn to thinking of someone who is no longer around. Shed a tear if that helps, while remembering at the same time that no one would want you to be sad at this time of year. Taking a well-calculated risk is likely to bring lucrative results. Love is favored as the power of romance and emotional intensity increases.

**18. FRIDAY. Slow.** If you are beginning to feel run-down and exhausted by an increased workload and pressures at home, focus on pacing all of your activities. Write a list of what needs to be completed before the last week of the month so you can see where you are and how much more time and effort will be needed to finish tasks. Healthy eating and an extra dose of vitamins could give you a boost of energy. This is a starred day for drawing closer to people you care about as you are wrapped in the love and warmth that comes from your nearest and dearest. A charitable event to aid a good cause may be the most appealing entertainment this evening.

**19. SATURDAY. Mixed.** A surge of energy arrives today as the Moon slides through your own sign of Aquarius. Money could come between you and your significant other, creating upset feelings. There is a possibility that one of you may object to the amount being spent on the festive season, or feel that certain purchases are not good value for the money. Whichever side you are on, try to see the other point of view. Be wary of making a big deal about something that won't really matter in the long term. Current prevailing energy is excellent for committed lovers as a flash of romantic desire adds more zip to the relationship.

**20. SUNDAY. Serene.** A great start to the day is promised by the prevailing stars. Lover Venus beams at excessive Jupiter, ensuring love and romance will continue to remain at the top of your agenda. Although you are in the mood for fun and games, a cautionary note needs to be added because moderation can fly out the window when these two planets meet up. Currently unattached Aquarius are in for a pleasurable period. Just don't become too overindulgent or too flirtatious. A religious gathering or social event should be particularly enjoyable. Delivering gifts or food to the needy will provide a feeling of emotional gratification along with gratitude for all you have.

**21. MONDAY. Rejuvenating.** An idea could come to mind that has the potential to be a moneymaker. Record the intricacies of this idea so that at some future period you can decide about the possibility of implementation. Today the Sun joins Mercury and Pluto in Capricorn, your house of solitude and private matters, for a four-week stay. Although it might be difficult for you to get off on your own with all of the social activities going on, this could be your preferred option. If this isn't possible, at least pace your activities, seek some privacy, and rest whenever you get the chance. Each year your body needs to become reenergized, and now is your time to do this.

**22. TUESDAY. Quiet.** There isn't a lot happening, which should suit you just fine. If there are bills that need to be paid, get this task out of the way so you don't forget about them later on. Be thoughtful and observant. Refrain from trying to move ahead too quickly because other people could rebel, which will be quite a change since it is usually you that does the rebelling. Revealing your true feelings should lift the clouds from an issue that has been plaguing your love life. Take time to review what has occurred during the past year. Although your confidence could be down a little, be assertive as you consider plans and goals for 2010.

**23. WEDNESDAY. Fine.** Money is the main theme of the day. Aquarius folk who are still looking for gift bargains are in luck. If you are game to battle the crowds, you should find a number of presents and at reduced prices. Knowing your financial limits can help ease the strain on the credit cards, which you will be grateful for when the statements arrive in the New Year. Business negotiations conducted in confidence or behind the scenes should prove beneficial. An end-of-year bonus could be more than you envisioned, or an unexpected promotion might have you smiling broadly. If hosting an upcoming festive celebration, try to complete as much in advance as you can.

**24. THURSDAY. Festive.** Get an early start if you have a large list of chores on your to-do list. You will be able to think clearly even while on the run. Your mood should be upbeat and enthusiastic. Any challenge is likely to appeal, which can include being out among the last-minute Christmas crowds. This should be a social day for many, or you might prefer to settle down and catch up on e-mails, make some long-distance phone calls, or read a good book. Research, or any activity carried out in private, should proceed without a hitch. Spend this evening with loved ones. Attending a religious service and singing songs of the season should appeal.

**25. FRIDAY. Merry Christmas!** This promises to be a pleasant and happy day spent with the special people in your life. Your physical resources might be limited, but by being well organized you shouldn't encounter too many obstacles or at least be able to quickly overcome them. Take extra care if driving. Be sure to obey the rules of the road; otherwise a hefty fine could spoil the pleasure of the day. Venus, the love goddess, moves into the sign of Capricorn, spreading her magic in your twelfth house of spirituality and solitary pursuits. As a result you may opt to withdraw a little from social activities and even from someone close in order to meditate on your own.

**26. SATURDAY. Fair.** Visiting friends or loved ones could be especially pleasant this morning. Or you may want to rush to the stores to return festive gifts or to search for post-Christmas bargains. Postpone sending off important paperwork because Mercury will be retrograde in Capricorn, your twelfth house of secrets and solitary actions, from now until January 15, 2010. Avoid large purchases such as a car or a home. Seek legal advice before signing any contract or lease agreement. This midafternoon and evening favors expressing love to those who share your home. Don't take anyone for granted. Someone you never got to talk to yesterday would appreciate a call or an e-mail.

**27. SUNDAY. Enjoyable.** Your energy resources may be at a low level, but this is unlikely to hold you back from enjoying the day. An extra hour in bed could be an excellent pick-me-up. Indulge yourself and read a novel, peruse the Sunday newspaper to catch up on current affairs, or doze off and dream of what might be. If family members are becoming restless, enjoy an interesting outing away from home. An excursion that includes a historical theme could quell any boredom. For Aquarius singles, even if exciting amusement is absent, fun is out there for those willing to seek it.

**28. MONDAY. Pleasurable.** Your powers of attraction are extremely strong right now, with an ability to look fantastic no matter what you are wearing. Exploring deep fantasies is likely as lover Venus merges with intense Pluto. A renewal or transformation of a love affair can gladden your heart. A mystery lover could take you by surprise, and singles can expect more romantic activity to occur. The stars favor taking up a new hobby or leisure pursuit that allows you to express your creative nature. If you haven't had your fill of festive fare, this is the perfect time to indulge in a romantic outing that includes fine food and wine.

**29. TUESDAY. Variable.** The passion and the intensity that have followed you over the last few days are likely to cool off now. Lovely Venus challenges your traditional ruler, serious Saturn. This planetary aspect could create discord between you and your loved ones. The party atmosphere may disappear because you are unlikely to be in a social mood. Your focus turns to friends rather than spending most of your time with your nearest and dearest. Intensely personal relationships are under a cloud. Any recreational pursuits or activities that have an artistic component has the potential to be enjoyable. Postpone a shopping expedition because receiving satisfaction from purchases is unlikely.

**30. WEDNESDAY. Tricky.** You might not be impressed by the insensitive behavior of someone close to you. A few tactful comments early on may be the best approach, lessening the chance of a full-scale argument later in the day. Give gossip a wide berth, and be on guard for deceptive or sly actions. This isn't the best period to be involved in any type of hidden love affair if you are hoping to keep the relationship under wraps. Aquarius who have been keeping secrets from a significant other should prepare for information to surface that may be embarrassing or upsetting. It might be wise for you to reveal what has been going on before being exposed.

**31. THURSDAY. Happy New Year!** Don't expect too much if celebrating and going out to party. Under today's Cancer Full Moon, socializing could be uneasy as highly emotional charges are sent out into the atmosphere. If you become agitated or stressed, let off steam in a physical manner through dancing, exercising, or chores around the house. Overindulging may lead to upsets, so watch how much alcohol you consume this evening. An intense encounter could spoil the night if you are with people who are quick-tempered. If an effort is made, fun can be shared with those you love the most. Opt for public transportation, even if this means a long wait to go home at the close of celebrations.

# AQUARIUS
# NOVEMBER–DECEMBER 2008

## November 2008

**1. SATURDAY. Comforting.** Your experimental ideas will be well received. Effectively communicating with other people is the key to success in business, home, or your love life. Check your schedule first thing this morning so that you don't overlook an appointment or social activity that you promised to attend. A secret admirer may make their feelings known in a charming manner, and you are unlikely to mind this special attention. However, if you are currently attached, it would be better to downplay your pleasure at the compliment. Socializing should be fun, but make sure you don't burn the candle at both ends. This promises to be a night of delight for those in love.

**2. SUNDAY. Promising.** Aquarius stamina will be at a lower level, with routine weekend chores taking longer than usual and requiring more effort to complete. This is because you have entered the low period of the month when the body signals it is time to rest, relax, and recharge your batteries. Neptune, the planet of inspiration and confusion, has now moved forward in your sign, impacting your personality sector. Personal plans and ambitions that stalled recently should begin to regain fresh energy, ready to once again move forward. At this juncture you may have to adhere to a different set of conditions, but these are likely to be positive. Confidence in your abilities and intuition should be restored.

**3. MONDAY. Constructive.** With the Scorpio Sun continuing to light up your career sector, moving ahead with personal ambitions remains a constant priority. You will soon reap what you sow. A boss or other senior supervisor should remain pleased with your efficiency. What has seemed baffling in the past might suddenly become clearer. If increased responsibilities have created a divide in your romantic relationship due to lack of attention or neglect, arrange a romantic dinner for two or an upcoming weekend retreat to bring the zest back into your love life. For singles, this is not the time to enter into a serious relationship commitment. Long-term investments of any kind might produce disappointing results.

**4. TUESDAY. Positive.** A forthright attitude prevails and there will be no stopping you now. You will also be very persuasive if you lace your arguments with facts and figures. Your personality is a big asset, and you can shine in any situation in which you find yourself. Having been born under one of the idealistic signs, you see the good in all people and you try to live up to your own high standards. Informative Mercury zooms into Scorpio, your career sector, and will boost your ambitions and mental energy. Looking at old problems from a different angle should lead to solutions. Give yourself an opportunity to try something that is out of your comfort zone, such as public speaking.

**5. WEDNESDAY. Outstanding.** Imagination is very active, and you are in touch with your aesthetic sense. If you have been putting off an expensive purchase, this is the time to consider going ahead and adding it to your list of possessions. Just be careful not to overdo the good life as you seek emotional comfort from rich food, fine wine, and upscale surroundings. This is an excellent day to pursue your schemes and dreams as well as helping loved ones realize their hopes. An affair or attraction could form with someone you meet at a group with which you are currently involved. If you are unemployed you might now experience luck with a job placement.

**6. THURSDAY. Motivating.** Energy and enthusiasm are at a peak, and you have ample concentration to focus on tasks at hand. Put special effort into projects that may pay dividends at a later time. For best results, act on one thing at a time. Be prepared to take some chances without doing anything too risky or impulsive. Also be open to whatever opportunities come along now, even if they don't appear to be that great to begin with. If it has been some time since you had a professional manicure or hairstyle, indulge yourself. Contact with influential persons could lead to worthwhile new opportunities just made for your talents.

**7. FRIDAY. Diverse.** You might change your mind about the direction to take as the new day begins. This is a good period to work out the details of an upcoming venture that you recently became involved in. Make sure you look at the whole picture. Otherwise, you might become so tangled up in minor details that you ignore more important ones. As passion and intimacy come to the fore, an exciting and romantic evening is in store for those in a loving union. There may be some financial pressures to deal with, or you could discover that something is now costing too much. Be careful what you wish for because you might just get it.

**8. SATURDAY. Stimulating.** Generally this should be a pleasant day for Aquarius folk. If a financial windfall arrives unexpectedly, try to keep some money in reserve. There is much to be said for implementing a sensible household budget or savings plan. Aim to consolidate earnings and restrict spending. Choose entertainment that is not going to break the bank. Irritation involving matters relating to money could put a damper on socializing later this evening. Someone from your past could return, shaking life up a little. Make sure you don't become your own worst enemy by not understanding the consequences of actions taken now.

**9. SUNDAY. Volatile.** This is another day when counting pennies is important. Shoppers heading out to the mall should keep a tight grip on cash and credit cards. If a certain item isn't worth the money, leave it for someone else. A volatile situation with a friend could brew around lunchtime. It might be advisable to make yourself scarce until an issue blows over or fiery tempers abate. Enlist the support of friends if there is a special project that needs to be completed and you are unable to manage it on your own. Make good use of your inclination to talk and gossip by visiting people with whom you have a lot in common.

**10. MONDAY. Lucky.** This is a very auspicious day, with good fortune smiling your way. Career and business matters will benefit most from the positive linkup of the Sun, Uranus, and Jupiter. Unexpected gifts and favors are likely. On the job you can excel with negotiations, business meetings, and public relations, all moving forward to a successful conclusion. Employment changes are on the horizon, so identify prospective employers and update your resume. A pay raise, promotion, or offer of a new job are possible scenarios. An honor or special award could be bestowed on you. At least put yourself in a position to be a winner by purchasing lottery or raffle tickets.

**11. TUESDAY. Fortunate.** Expect another day of solid advancement in most areas. As the golden light of the Sun meets up with your coruler Saturn, you can now expect to reap the rewards of your hard work and extra effort. Finances are improving. Your mate or partner could receive a promotion or wage increase, helping to nicely boost your joint finances. An inheritance, lottery prize, or some other type of major windfall could come your way. Discussions with other people regarding an ongoing problem can bring a positive resolution in your favor. If possible, defer business or staff meetings until the latter part of the day to get better results.

**12. WEDNESDAY. Pleasing.** The good times continue to roll for you. Today lovely Venus not only mingles with intense Pluto but also swings into Capricorn, your sector of behind-the-scenes activities. Venus in Capricorn until December 7 promises passion and affection from your significant other. Aquarius singles will be seeking warm and loving gestures from a potential love interest. A hint of jealousy also marks the day. You need to resist an attempt by someone close to bend you to their will through emotional blackmail or another manipulative strategy. Creative juices are greatly enhanced, increasing your ability to derive extra income from your natural talents.

**13. THURSDAY. Confusing.** A mixture of influences prevails, with an abundance of luck as well as plenty of confusion. Today's Full Moon in the sensual and stubborn sign of Taurus, your sector of family and home, could be the source of much irritation and agitation. Emotional feelings may be rather strained, leading to bad feelings on the job, especially if actions and sharp words are not kept under control. Because of clouded thinking, errors are more than likely, so important decisions should be deferred for a few days. With Venus in Capricorn, your sector of secrets, a clandestine romance is a possibility.

**14. FRIDAY. Misleading.** Today's energy is similar to yesterday's. Be discreet and tactful when handling business matters. Cooperate fully with clients and colleagues to reduce possible dissension. Guard against overspending when arranging a future outing or social occasion. There is an increased chance that you could be misled in some area, so analyze facts and figures carefully before jumping into action. Be impartial if called upon to mediate a family dispute. Spiritual awareness and devotion to other people are enhanced. Volunteering a few hours of your time at a local nursing home or hospital can be emotionally gratifying and uplifting.

**15. SATURDAY. Manageable.** An unusual opportunity to make extra money could crop up. Before becoming too excited, however, investigate all details thoroughly before proceeding. Aquarius lovers can find comfort spending the day together, exploring shared interests and passions. Problems could arise with someone who is inconsiderate and dominating. Let other people's bad temper wash over you without become upset and stressed, especially if this is a child demanding attention. Younger Aquarius in a social setting may be the target of a jealous friend trying to undermine your popularity. Retain your sense of humor without responding to petty comments.

**16. SUNDAY. Liberating.** To be kind to yourself, begin the day on a healthy note. Enjoy a nutritional breakfast before enjoying a solid workout. With the friendly linkup of intellectual Mercury and your coruler Uranus, natural spontaneity and inventiveness will rule the day. Don't waste time on routine activities and chores. Instead, find something interesting and different to do that provides a mental or physical challenge. As motivating Mars moves into fiery Sagittarius, this is the signal for an all-systems-go approach. Cherished goals and humanitarian activities will benefit from your increased drive and enthusiasm.

**17. MONDAY. Demanding.** Maintaining a regular fitness program is very important because it releases pent-up aggression and stress in a positive, constructive way. There are a number of cosmic patterns in today's skies, with deception being one of the major trends that you need to avoid. Only with a very cautious approach to everything you undertake can you reduce the chance of being hurt by a dishonest person or people. Shoppers should take care with money and be sure to count change received. Memory failure could strike, so write notes to yourself and record all important meetings or discussions. A lover could handle the truth carelessly. If a proposition sounds too good to be true, more than likely it is.

**18. TUESDAY. Low-key**. You would be well advised to keep a low profile and just go about your normal business on this uneven day. Achieving daily objectives may take more effort than usual but can be done. Brush aside feelings that someone is taking you for granted; this is apt to be a figment of your fertile imagination more than anything else. Be alert for opposition from a hidden source. Before deciding to team up with anyone for any reason, discuss all mutual expectations so that there are no mistakes or surprises when it comes to what is required from each party. An open discussion with your mate or partner can lead to a better understanding.

**19. WEDNESDAY. Testing.** Getting what you want will take effort and patience because there are a number of minor aggravations that you must deal with. Considerable resistance could come from a partner or associate, requiring both parties to work toward cooperation and reasonable compromise. Unresolved problems with a legal issue, inattentiveness to business prospects, or client complaints could increase your workload and stress. Take things as they come and proceed at a steady rate. Trying to rush could upset matters further. Some of your plans may need to be shelved for now.

**20. THURSDAY. Tricky.** Don't be too eager to share your secrets. Also take care not to accidentally disclose a secret told to you in confidence. Careful trading could realize a profit for the savvy Aquarius. You are entering a period when past hard work can bring rewards and practical economic dreams can become a reality. Slowly and steadily work toward achieving financial security. Consider long-term investments and review all fiscal arrangements. If it has been some time since your assets were appraised for insurance purposes, look into increasing coverage on your house, car, and personal valuables.

**21. FRIDAY. Reassuring.** To take full advantage of this good period for Aquarius, exercise plenty of patience to gain the upper hand in most situations. Discussion of mutual goals with a personal or professional partner can be helpful if you both stay on the same wavelength. The Sun now visits Sagittarius, your solar sector of friends and associates, and will emphasize the groups and organizations to which you belong. If you recently relocated, you could discover that this is a great time to cultivate new friends. Make the most of opportunities. Go to bed early so you can catch up on sleep in preparation for an exciting weekend ahead.

**22. SATURDAY. Successful.** Focus on a few big ideas and do all you can to exploit these productively. A plan for a pleasure journey can now be made; obtaining a good package deal within your price range is likely. Spend time doing all that you can to improve your body, mind, and spirit. As an Aquarius you have a thirst for knowledge and the truth. This can take you on some fascinating adventures, even if you are just reading a book or watching an exciting documentary. A nomination to chair a committee, social club, or a special interest organization could come as a happy surprise. A social activity with friends should be memorable.

**23. SUNDAY. Varied.** There are a bundle of celestial offerings today, and most could cause agitation and aggravation. Take care of a homework assignment early in the day. If you have been biting your tongue about a problem situation, you may now be ready to speak out. Quick-witted Mercury has taken up residence in Sagittarius, your house of social contacts and groups, joining the Sun, Mars, and Pluto there. This is a heavy emphasis on this area of your solar chart. Throughout the next week spend time thinking about your special hopes and goals for the future. This is also a good time to give your brain more exercise with some intellectual calisthenics.

**24. MONDAY. Favorable.** This is a favorable day to speak or work with a large group of people or to organize a conference. Aquarius in charge of planning a festive social gathering should be able to find a venue and entertainment that will suit different generations and tastes. Enlarge your friendship circle by inviting new and unusual people to be part of your group. Keep your ego in check and aim for moderation. Employment matters could prosper. This is a good time for a job performance review or to go on an interview for a new job. Strike a compromise with a friend this evening rather than butting heads.

**25. TUESDAY. Supportive.** If you are not making enough positive progress on the job, speak to the boss or another supervisor and ask for support or guidance. Your thinking is innovative yet sound. You can charge ahead with set tasks providing you avoid a tendency to procrastinate. Business negotiations and transactions should be successful. You might consider joining a hobby group or other special interest club, but don't let anyone push you into it. Take time to think before coming to a final decision. Spending quality time with close friends will help to recharge intellectual batteries. Don't undervalue the importance of news or information received in confidence.

**26. WEDNESDAY. Vexing.** You may be overwhelmed by the number of duties that need to be completed. However, once you get started, most should fall neatly into place. Aquarius in a position of power should rely more on staff members to prove assistance and advice. Someone could put in a good word for you from behind the scenes. It might be wiser to wait until tomorrow to make a large or important purchase. Difficulty when it comes to making choices could keep you from the shopping mall. Tonight Pluto, planet of transformation, will reenter Capricorn for a long transit here in your twelfth house of self-analysis and personal limitations.

**27. THURSDAY. Revitalizing.** A bevy of cosmic forces makes this an interesting day. A Sagittarius New Moon places further emphasis on your hopes and cherished desires. This may mean finally having enough money to pay for an overseas vacation or for a special academic or training course. Income from business activities or career advancement should help boost the bank account. Even the most hardworking Aquarius needs a hobby. If you don't have a stimulating personal interest, find something new to put your energy into on your days off. Uranus, planet of the unexpected, has now moved forward in Pisces, your personal money house, bringing positive changes to your cash flow.

**28. FRIDAY. Accomplished.** The next two weeks will be an excellent period to examine your dreams and goals and determine what you have accomplished so far in 2008. If you feel that you haven't been as successful as you hoped, begin planning specific aims for 2009. Getting together with friends, and possibly making new ones, can send your spirits soaring. This is a positive time to seek new trade connections. Intermingling business with pleasure should introduce a few new future prospects to your client database. An unexpected romantic encounter may cause your heart to skip a beat.

**29. SATURDAY. Interesting.** Love and romance are again in the air. Unfortunately this might not be all good news because your mate or partner's preoccupation with work may be the source of conflict. A blind date could be interesting for singles and might be the start of an enduring love affair. For those getting married or engaged today, the good news is that a long and loyal union together can be expected. With love goddess Venus and disciplined Saturn happily connecting, there should be no problem for shoppers with a keen eye for quality and a bargain. Maximizing your home comforts will make your personal and emotional life more relaxing and stable.

**30. SUNDAY. Revealing.** Be contented with your own company or with close loved ones. If the weather is overcast, this can be the perfect excuse to remain a little longer in bed and catch up on your reading or loving. Heed your good intuition. The day ahead could provide great insight into decisions you need to make regarding future goals. Keep your mind open to new ideas and information. Remind yourself to listen as well as speak. A charitable act will not go unnoticed. Visiting a lonely relative or neighbor could be a wonderful way to spend a few hours of your leisure time.

# December 2008

**1. MONDAY. Fortunate.** What a lovely way to begin the new month and workweek! Venus and Jupiter in conjunction are bestowing the good things in life, and you will be in the mood for some fun and games. Good progress can be made with just about any venture you tackle. Forgiveness features strongly now. So if a relationship has been fractured lately, consider holding out the olive branch. Even if you feel like spending some time alone, mix and mingle at least for a little while. This is an excellent time to entertain other people or to be entertained. The more people you are around, the merrier it will be. An invitation to a glamorous occasion could bring a thrill of anticipation.

**2. TUESDAY. Expressive.** The day favors working behind the scenes on projects that require detail and precision, at least through the morning. Take a giant step toward achieving a goal. Artistic talents are supported, and creativity should be high as the Moon shifts into your sign of Aquarius, increasing your inspiration and imagination. You should have more clarity, with a solid understanding of the direction in which you wish to move. You are feeling good about yourself, so use spare time to focus on personal improvement and grooming. Singles can enjoy a romantic escapade, and partnered Aquarius can strengthen loving bonds.

**3. WEDNESDAY. Satisfying.** Energy and enthusiasm continue to remain upbeat. To help let go of stress, remember that more can be accomplished by being yourself right now. Networking is the key to getting a project off the ground. Use conversation to draw other people out of their shell. Take a friendly approach and ask the right questions so they relax in your presence. Handle any personal details that you have overlooked. A sense of support and harmony surrounds you. Talk over your personal problems with someone older or more experienced who may be able to provide guidance and point you in the right direction.

**4. THURSDAY. Pleasant.** Another enjoyable day is in store. A major task needs to be completed, so get an early start that will push you into action. With three planets in Sagittarius, your sector of friends and social activities, you are encouraged to get out and socialize. If you have to work, plan to meet up with special companions after hours to catch up with all the news. Just be sure to resist the temptation of extravagance if you cannot afford to splurge. As an Aquarius you are known as a communicative and detached air sign. Right now you have the ability to know when to mind your own business and when to pry.

**5. FRIDAY. Stimulating.** Be flexible and adjust to the flow of influences as they come along. Mixed trends increase both your vitality and restlessness. A harmonious angle between the Sun and Mars strongly suggests that action applied to achieving a special goal can be successful. This is also a time to take extra precautions. Mercury, the thinking planet, merges with your coruler Uranus, which is all the encouragement needed for Aquarius to behave in a rash, erratic, or impulsive manner. You may be full of ideas, but you won't know if these are brilliant or brainless for a few days. Write them down for consideration and evaluation at another time.

**6. SATURDAY. Uneven.** Expect another day of uncertain vibes. Mixed emotions of being both angry and full of relief are likely when a friend or family member who you have been worried about contacts you to share happy news. Unexpected expenses could cause a shortfall in your budget, requiring a quick adjustment to ensure you have ready cash available. Shoppers should guard against being lured into a festive spending spree. It might be a waste of your time to expect a sensible discussion with someone who is not prepared to listen. Don't worry if plans need to be altered or postponed; this is likely to work to your advantage.

**7. SUNDAY. Bright.** Positive influences sent by the universe confirm that it won't be much longer before trends begin to improve. Charming Venus steps into your sign, impacting your first house of self and personality. Venus in Aquarius until early January 2009 accents your magnetism and attracts outside support. This is a favorable period to gather with friends and other kindred spirits, interacting and sharing ideas. Just avoid completely dominating the conversation. The period also favors making changes to your appearance or image. Love and affection are positively highlighted. Singles can expect to encounter a number of romantic potentials, one of whom may soon take on a dominant role.

**8. MONDAY. Heartening.** Expect a busy day with lots of errands to run and people to see. Save time and potential trouble by putting extra effort into your planning and decision making. In a group setting you should have considerable influence over other people, assisting your efforts for reform or improvements. You could be called upon to contribute to a charitable organization either through a financial donation or volunteering time, which can be an emotionally satisfying experience. Try to add more warmth to your immediate environment. Make love, not war, tonight. Even if discussions become heated, as they often do at this time of year, you can keep the peace.

**9. TUESDAY. Vigorous.** You have plenty of vim and vigor to share. Adopt a tactful approach with someone who is overly sensitive, but avoid becoming stressed regarding situations that are out of your immediate control. If a colleague doesn't approve of the way you are handling a project, let that person try to devise a better method. It might be time to get out the holiday decorations, clean the house, and begin organizing what's needed for holiday catering. If you haven't yet decided on entertainment for the festive season, get together with loved ones to make plans that will suit everyone.

**10. WEDNESDAY. Fair.** You could be traveling a bumpy road today if restless trends prove to be more disruptive than usual. Be prepared, remain flexible, and expect the unexpected. Help set the tone for a group that is looking for a new direction. Once you sell an idea to members, others are sure to follow your lead. Rearranging your living space to accommodate unexpected arrivals over the holiday can save time and energy later on. Taking a few hours off for festive shopping can help put you in the spirit of the season. Get with friends to participate in something different tonight.

**11. THURSDAY. Trying.** Boredom remains your worst enemy. You need an innovative approach to avoid succumbing to monotony. Add plenty of variety to your day to help negate restlessness and impatience. A quick wit and creative imagination can help guide you through any rough patches. If that isn't enough, consider a change of scenery for additional variety. Hobbies and special leisure pursuits can be a relaxing form of amusement later on. Keep alert for some surprising opportunities close by. Check to be sure you haven't been neglecting anyone who has supported you in the past. If you have, find a way to make amends without delay.

**12. FRIDAY. Worrisome.** Despite what appears to be relative calm, deep down you may be worried. Postpone taking any action until a situation becomes stabilized and you are able to see the way ahead in a clearer light. A Gemini Full Moon brings emotions to the surface and indicates the time for closure and finalization. There may be unexpected expenses that could disrupt your future goals. Mercury now enters Capricorn, your twelfth house of solitary action, which encourages you to seek more peace and quiet. This begins a period when meditation and creative visualization can help to facilitate emotional and mental healing.

**13. SATURDAY. Low-key.** Introduce a festive feel to reduce the possibility of isolation and lonely feelings brought on by the duel between Sun and Saturn. Finish your holiday shopping, trim the tree, and decorate the house. Items that are out of stock could cause some problems if you have specific gifts to purchase, so you may need to compromise and settle for the next best thing. If celebrating this festive season is not of interest to you, gather with like-minded folks for a casual meal and socializing. You could finally master a creative art that you have been trying to acquire for some time. It won't happen without effort on your part, but the results will be well worthwhile.

**14. SUNDAY. Lively.** A pile of work could await you this morning, so get an early start. Friendly people make for friendly times, and your current social popularity can assist in bringing everyone together. Playing matchmaker to help a single friend recover from a relationship breakup can be successful as long as you handle the matter delicately. Your mind might be working faster than other people in the family, so explain in detail a plan that affects everyone and you should receive needed cooperation. If you are on the job, your problem-solving abilities are sure to be appreciated by coworkers. Stay out of trouble and stay at home after dark.

**15. MONDAY. Bumpy.** With the Moon in your opposite sign of Leo, this is a period when you may not be on top of your game. But even if you do decide to slow down a little, you are unlikely to come to a full stop. You might need to be the chief negotiator in a dispute with business associates. Be prepared to take on this job and not give into unreasonable demands. Bring your strengths to the table and hope that other people will take a similar approach. You might want to contemplate some type of business partnership, but it would be wise to keep all options open at present to avoid conflict in other areas of your life.

**16. TUESDAY. Eventful.** Stop wishing and start thinking on a grander scale. Deserved recognition and appreciation could be forthcoming. On the personal front, yesterday's discord with a partner over neglected obligations can be harmoniously resolved and put to rest. Talks with business promoters can be beneficial. This is an auspicious period to expand your network of friends and associates. Although teamwork is a welcomed alternative to the petty antics that have been on display recently, flattering or insincere words could make you uneasy or suspicious. Remain alert because you might have some cause to worry.

**17. WEDNESDAY. Cheering.** Today's trends are less complicated than yesterday's. Telling or showing affection and support to someone special will help rebuild their self-esteem and confidence. Aquarius employed in selling or buying should experience an increase in profitable leads. Efforts to build a nest egg can progress with a little advance planning and self-discipline. News of a windfall could put a smile on your face. If someone for whom you have romantic feelings has been absent or too busy to call lately, your relationship should begin to return to normal. If you have experienced a relationship breakup, you may feel that you are now emotionally ready to get back into the dating game.

**18. THURSDAY. Demanding.** Tone down criticism of other people, especially if this is just your way of trying to get a point across. Joint financial affairs require attention. Aquarius employed to look after the finances of other people should exercise extra care. Take someone along with you if you are carrying a large amount of cash to the bank or for any other reason. It might be hard to understand a particular person's motives unless you dig deep for the answers. Being overly idealistic can be counterproductive. A friend could be a little offhand with a special request, but don't take it personally; they may have too many other things on their mind at present.

**19. FRIDAY. Difficult.** There isn't an overabundance of festive cheer in today's stars, although that is unlikely to stop you from going out with friends or family members to celebrate this fun season. A misunderstanding with a good friend can be resolved. Long-term intentions need to be clear if you are to be successful. Aquarius students might not be very happy with the outcome of an assignment or special project and may have to redo the work to obtain a higher grade. Steer clear of controversial topics. If you are intending to party this evening, arrange to travel by taxi or public transport so that there is no danger of drinking and driving.

**20. SATURDAY. Varied.** This morning expect delays or changes to your travel schedule. If setting off for the airport, leave early to avoid traffic and security delays. As intellectual Mercury moves closer to your coruler, innovative Uranus, the sparks of new ideas can lead to some type of a breakthrough. The next few days will be a favorable time to purchase a new computer, car, or other electronic equipment. Your persuasive ability is moving into top gear, which will help you in selling or in public speaking. Positive results are likely if you go on a job interview as long as your answers to questions are not too casual or evasive.

244 / AQUARIUS—DECEMBER 2008

**21. SUNDAY. Enlightening.** Cultural activities could be enlightening, or you might prefer to spend the day shopping for last-minute gifts or visiting friends. The role you play in family festivities could change this year. You may be the one hosting the celebration or be pampered as the guest of honor. Today the life-giving Sun enters Capricorn, your house of secrets and solitary activities. The Sun in Capricorn until next January 19 will spotlight various health issues. This is the time to review events of the past twelve months and prepare for the year ahead. Your energy and confidence may slip a little from now until your birthday period, when the Sun makes its entrance into your sign of Aquarius.

**22. MONDAY. Introspective.** Conditions favor reviewing old ideals, old traditions, and old lifestyle patterns. Aquarius who have spiritual leanings can gain greater insight from looking deep within. Private information could assist in furthering your career goals, and a promotion could be an added Christmas bonus. Behind-the-scenes negotiations concerning money or business may be finalized, with a long-overdue promise finally coming to fruition. Your feelings regarding higher-ups might go through a transformation as you realize they are not as insensitive as you thought.

**23. TUESDAY. Active.** Significant discussions could take place with a colleague, bringing forward informative ideas and plans to be dissected, reworked, and then implemented. Make sure credit also comes your way when the accolades are handed out. Check that there is enough food stashed away in the kitchen for upcoming celebrations. If you have any time to spare, you might enjoy cooking and preparing festive foods. During this sociable time of the year you don't want to miss out on the fun, so don't be fazed if you still have a long list of things to do before the actual holiday. Take a deep breath, slow down, and begin delegating employment chores to colleagues and domestic tasks to family members.

**24. WEDNESDAY. Happy.** The way you view the world should be clearer and sharper than ever. As an Aquarius you can be emotionally detached, but at last you might notice that someone is showing you romantic attention. An old friend may reappear unexpectedly, just in time to join in celebrating the holiday. Be careful if you are finishing festive purchases because you are likely to be attracted to stylish, classic, and very expensive gifts. An interest in the mystical and spiritual could find you going with the family to attend a caroling or church service this evening. Try to get to bed at a reasonable hour so you are in good shape tomorrow.

**25. THURSDAY. Merry Christmas!** This promises to be an enjoyable and festive day without too many obstacles to stifle your enjoyment. Although it is a time of overindulgence, good cheer, celebration, and joy, a moderate approach is the best route to take. If you know of a neighbor or someone close by who may be spending the day alone, welcome them to your home to share hospitality and friendship. If you have to travel between homes throughout the day, be sure to take care on the roads. Enlist the help of everyone to clear away festive trappings before going to bed, allowing you to catch a few extra stress-free winks in the morning.

**26. FRIDAY. Harmonious.** A practical and pleasant atmosphere exists. If you haven't heard from a friend recently, give them a ring to say hello. Inviting them to help demolish leftover festive fare could be a good way to make sure that they are doing well. Exchanging unwanted gifts should go off without a hitch, and some bargain shopping might be just what you need to relax even if the crowds are at a peak. If you have some time to spare, write down goals and aims that you hope to accomplish in 2009, giving you a head start on future planning.

**27. SATURDAY. Slow.** This is a favorable day to spend with those who are older or wiser than you. Visit an elderly relative who you were unable to see earlier this week, or spend time with a lonely neighbor. This is a time of reflection and endings, so go with the flow. Instead of trying to make changes, review successes and mistakes and prepare to move forward. Don't worry if you feel tired. It is perfectly normal to experience lower energy now and during the next four weeks leading up to your birthday period. Energy could dip even lower with the entrance of Mars into your Capricorn sector, so you may want to withdraw a little from the social whirl.

**28. SUNDAY. Revealing.** Although you might appreciate peace and quiet and having some time to yourself, that privilege might not be experienced now. Expect a busy time over the next few days as feisty Mars merges with passionate Pluto. You would do well to tap into this aggressive energy. Health could improve, and you could experience a resurgence of vim and vitality. With six planets currently gracing Capricorn, your house of secret plans and solitary action, this is a time of revelation and of discovering something significant. Personal confidences are highlighted. You may be more involved in spiritual activities.

**29. MONDAY. Good.** With the Moon entering your sign of Aquarius this morning, your energy should be at a high level. But you might not want to be at work, especially if you are struggling to keep your thinking in some type of order. Don't allow side issues to add to your confusion. Constantly daydreaming is unlikely to impress the boss but is very good if you are involved in creative work. Imagination can spark a flow of inspiration. Self-employment may not be an option. But the more autonomy you can muster, the happier you will feel. If you will host a New Year's celebration, don't leave everything until the last minute.

**30. TUESDAY. Supportive.** If you are suffering from mental overload and need time alone, find a solitary spot to relax and recharge your batteries. An old boss working in a new company could be the source of luck for those of you looking to move up the career ladder. Ask this person to put in a good word for you, and soon you may be relocating or accepting a new position. The post-Christmas sales could attract you, but go easy with the credit cards if you splurged during the festive period. Encourage other people to talk and open up emotionally if they are troubled. Aim for an early night so you have enough energy to stay up late tomorrow evening.

**31. WEDNESDAY. Promising.** The Moon is in your sign, and there is good cheer in the air. Although there is abundant luck, keep an eye on personal belongings. Otherwise, you may waste a lot of time searching for mislaid valuables. Love and romance are well starred. Aquarius singles should be delighted by the caliber of a romantic partner who shows real interest in you. Those of you in a steady union shouldn't allow a stubborn streak to get in the way of fun or romance when welcoming in 2009. Both your rulers, Saturn and Uranus, are in forward motion to end the year and to begin the new one on a promising note. Happy New Year, Aquarius!

NOW AVAILABLE IN PAPERBACK

#1 *NEW YORK TIMES* BESTSELLING AUTHOR

# SYLVIA BROWNE

WITH LINDSAY HARRISON

# PHENOMENON

Everything You Need to Know

About the Paranormal

NEW AMERICAN LIBRARY

#1 *New York Times* bestselling author
# Sylvia Browne

# *Visits from the Afterlife*

With her sixth sense, coupled with stirring true
encounters, Sylvia Browne describes visitations
with ghosts, in-transition spirits, and other
troubled souls seeking peace and closure.
Through these spiritual visits, Browne explains
the reasons behind many of the world's most
bizarre and mysterious hauntings.

Available wherever books are sold
or at penguin.com